# Introduction

I met Mercy Banda in July 2013, soon afte
to conduct research on the history of domes
Mercy was eighteen years old and lived with l
to Bauleni compound, an informal settlemen
the city. She had recently completed her sec
Kabulonga Girls' High School, with high grac
jects. While at high school, Mercy's family l
her school fees, a common challenge for Lusal
To fund her education, she found a job as a p
nearby wealthy suburb of Woodlands. She four
around at her church and securing work in tl
congregation member. She had a range of amb
When she first left high school, she had hope
education or a vocational training course, but sl
that she could not afford the course fees. She co
domestic service and developed a new goal of c
(small market stall) outside her home.[1]

Mercy's employer was a woman named Pri
Priscilla through the Faith and Encounter C
(FENZA), a Catholic mission and education cen
I was taking Chinyanja lessons at FENZA, anc
viously worked there as a librarian. When we
was fifty-nine years old and retired. She had c
mary and secondary education in Zambia duri
1970s and pursued higher education in Nigeri

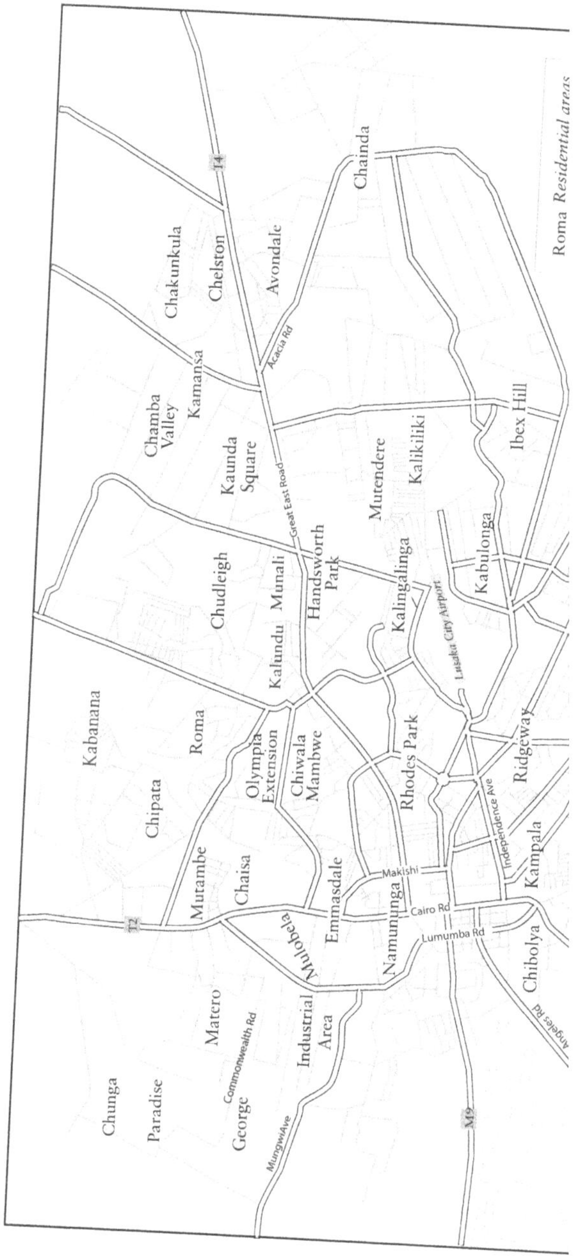




1970s, after which she worked at the National Archives of Zambia (NAZ) and the United Nations Educational, Scientific and Cultural Organisation (UNESCO). She had then spent time living in the United Kingdom (UK) during the early 1990s when her husband's employer transferred him to their London office. Her fortunes had changed by the time we met. Her husband lost his job in 1995 when his employer went out of business, and he then struggled to find permanent employment, instead pursuing numerous small business ventures. He passed away in 2006. When we met, Priscilla received a small income from her pension and from teaching sporadically at FENZA, and she had recently moved into the servants' quarters of her Woodlands property so that she could rent out the main house. Despite her challenging financial situation, she continued to employ two domestic workers. Mercy worked inside her home, cleaning, washing clothes, and helping with cooking, and a gardener came to her property three times per week.[2]

Life stories such as those of Mercy and Priscilla provide key insights into the issue at the heart of this book: the history of domestic service in southern Africa's post-colonial cities. Domestic service expanded across urban southern Africa following decolonisation and the end of apartheid because increasing numbers of individuals and households incorporated it into their livelihood strategies. Domestic labour was, and remains, central to daily and generational reproduction and to capital accumulation, and rising numbers of households have needed help to perform this vital labour. Domestic labour shortages became acute in households in which female members worked beyond the home, because gendered constructions of domesticity assigned to women responsibility for domestic labour in their own homes.[3] Female labour force participation steadily increased over time across southern Africa's post-colonial cities, and most working women faced the 'double burden' of performing domestic labour alongside employment beyond the home. Employers like Priscilla sought to address these competing demands by employing domestic workers in a variety of arrangements. Domestic service was even more important to the livelihood and survival strategies of the workers involved, enabling domestic workers like Mercy to support themselves and their dependants in the city and further afield. In this way, domestic service has acted as a lifeline for both the households who employ and those who are employed.

With a few exceptions, historians and economists have paid scant attention to domestic service and its role in post-colonial African economies and societies. *Home economics* addresses this comparative neglect. It provides an innovative history of domestic service in southern Africa's post-colonial cities by foregrounding labour relations in Black households and the women and girl workers who predominated in these spaces.[4] Drawing on rich oral histories and diverse documentary sources, it develops an original theoretical approach to domestic service which, for the first time, brings waged and kin-based domestic labour and child and adult workers into a single frame of analysis. In so doing, it challenges the narrow focus of existing scholarship and policymaking and breaks new ground in the theorisation of work.[5] Using Zambia's capital city Lusaka as a case study and drawing wider comparisons, it reveals how Black employers and workers reworked domestic service practices as part of broader responses to changing gendered employment patterns, economic decline, and endemic poverty. It also examines the challenges of formalising and organising this largely informal and intimate form of work, and domestic workers' struggles to improve their conditions.

*Home economics* also seeks to do more than simply address the silences and gaps around the history of domestic service in post-colonial Africa. As Mercy's and Priscilla's life stories suggest, this history is about so much more than the maintenance of homes and their residents. It is about the survival strategies of workers and their employers and the approaches that adults and children have taken to support themselves and their dependants in the face of social pressures and economic crises; it is about how gender and age shaped labour relations within the household and broader economy; and it is about the exploitation of labour and the making and maintenance of social hierarchies grounded in class privilege and relative wealth. Drawing comparisons across urban southern Africa, the book provides essential new insights into the nature of gender, work, and urban economies.

## Labour and gender in Lusaka

Lusaka is the ideal focus for examining the history of domestic service, and of labour and gender more broadly, in urban southern

Africa. The changing character of labour relations in the city were in many ways a precursor to what would happen in other southern African urban centres after independence and the end of apartheid. Cities and towns across the region are living through the 'temporal aftermath' of colonialism, and many remain spatially and socio-economically scarred by colonial racial hierarchies and inequalities.[6] There are also important distinctions between the region's towns and cities, including differences in patterns of urbanisation, labour, and gendered employment. These similarities and differences allow for meaningful comparative analysis and highlight trends and particularities in southern Africa's labour and gender histories. In this book, I compare Lusaka primarily with urban centres in Mozambique, South Africa, and Zimbabwe.

Lusaka became the capital city of what was then the British protectorate of Northern Rhodesia in 1935. It had previously been a relatively small railway outpost and was gradually transformed during the 1930s into a colonial garden city. British colonial planners aimed to create an attractive environment for government officials and settlers including through the planning of suburban housing areas for middle-class and wealthy White residents. They also aimed to spatially reinforce the racial basis of colonial rule, placing housing areas for (predominantly male) African workers out of view on the outskirts of the city. These residential areas were and continue to be called compounds, a term used across colonial southern Africa and originating on the South African mines. The racial segregation built into the planning of Lusaka characterised colonial urban policies across southern Africa, and the colonial government expected African workers to work in urban areas only on a temporary basis and to maintain permanent homes in rural areas. However, the government did not legally characterise Africans as aliens in urban areas as in South Africa, nor did it have the capacity to repatriate African men, women, or children from urban to rural areas in significant numbers.[7]

Like many other colonial capitals, Lusaka's economy was based on its functions as an administrative centre, and it was also a significant transport hub. The main areas of waged employment were government work and domestic service, and the city also had a burgeoning informal economy and housing sector, with growing numbers of unplanned and often unauthorised compounds. These

**Figure 0.1** A leafy road in affluent Kabulonga, Lusaka, 2 February 2014.

latter features distinguished Lusaka from the urban centres of the Copperbelt and the Witwatersrand where the economy centred on mining, and employment and housing were largely controlled by mining companies.[8] The centrality of mining to the settler colonial economy of Northern Rhodesia also meant that the Copperbelt towns were far more economically and strategically important than Lusaka right up to independence.

The employment practices and housing which developed in the Copperbelt towns influenced practices elsewhere in the protectorate. This is particularly clear in relation to gender relations. From the 1930s, there was growing acceptance and even encouragement by mining companies for married couples to live together in the Copperbelt towns. This strategy marked a break from the model of temporary and migrant African labour which had characterised urban planning across the region and promoted the stabilisation of African urban residence. The mining companies aimed to encourage male workers to remain in Northern Rhodesia rather than migrate to work on the mines of Katanga, South Africa, or Tanzania; to encourage male workers to complete their contracts; and to capitalise on women and children's labour within and beyond the home. This had important and longstanding implications for gendered and

**Figure 0.2** Block of flats in Kabulonga, Lusaka, 2 February 2014.

generational constructions of labour and for urban employment opportunities, with men constructed as workers and breadwinners, women as housewives, and women and children as dependants of men.[9] These planning practices also became influential in Lusaka, with most planned compounds containing sections of married housing. The growing number of unplanned compounds in Lusaka, which developed mostly at the edges of the city, created even greater opportunities for married couples to live together and for women and children to carve out a place for themselves in town.[10]

Independence in 1964 brought both change and continuity for work and its gendered dynamics in urban Zambia. The country experienced an economic boom into the early 1970s. Like governments across the continent, Zambia's first post-independence government, led by the United National Independence Party (UNIP), pursued economic development and investment which aimed to address the racialised inequalities of the colonial period. The racialised system that had governed access to employment, housing, and migration under colonial rule was abolished. White-collar jobs in government departments were created, and employment within the construction and import-substitution sectors increased. African ownership of commerce also grew, and the government became the majority stakeholder in partnerships with mining companies and a number of foreign-owned enterprises. State involvement in the economy increased further from 1972, when the nation moved from being a multi-party democracy to a one-party system still under the control of UNIP.[11]

Despite these developments, into the 1970s Zambia's economy remained skewed towards the mining industry and dependent on imports, because the manufacturing base remained small and investment in agriculture was limited. Rural farmers faced a challenging situation, which was made worse by the government's failure to properly invest in rural infrastructure and guarantee producer prices. This reflected broader trends across the continent, with most newly independent African governments prioritising modernisation and industrialisation at the expense of the needs of rural communities.[12] Moreover, despite some expansion in employment opportunities for Zambian women, gender inequality in employment remained pronounced, with male workers dominating all areas of the paid labour force.[13] The realities of Zambia's economy in the immediate post-independence years draw our attention to, in Franco Barchiesi's words, the 'uneven, delayed and contested' development of wage labour, and of capitalist relations of production more broadly, in twentieth-century Africa.[14] Despite newly independent Zambia's comparatively high rates of urbanisation and industrialisation, the majority of Black workers did not engage in wage labour, and those who did often faced insecure and precarious employment conditions.[15]

The uneven development of wage labour and the precariousness of employment in Zambia did not decrease over time and in many ways became more pronounced. Like many African countries, Zambia was hit hard by the oil crises of the mid- to late 1970s and subsequent decreases in global commodity prices. Crucially, it depended on copper exports to earn the cash required to buy imported goods. The country also suffered economically in this period from UNIP's support for southern African liberation movements and from embargoes against Zimbabwe which impacted Zambia's access to trade. From the late 1970s, the economy went into decline, resulting in stagnating employment in mining and other sectors and difficulties in accessing waged employment.[16] Reflecting broader trends across urban Africa in this period, the informal economy grew and became an increasingly important part of economic, social, and political life. Poverty and inequality also grew in urban and rural areas, as did the gulf in wealth between urban and rural communities, resulting in increased rural-urban migration.

Migration trends during the 1970s and subsequently had clear gender dynamics, with female migration rates increasing significantly across Zambia and undermining the male dominance of rural-urban migration that was established before independence.[17] Reflecting female migration practices to other southern African cities, many Zambian women and girls left their rural homes to join husbands, relatives, and friends who were already living in urban areas. Some also sought greater autonomy over their lives and labour, hoping to escape gendered and gerontocratic hierarchies in the countryside.[18] Overall, rural-urban migration contributed to the country's continued urbanisation. Lusaka's population grew exponentially, from just over 83,000 in 1969 to over 530,000 by 1980.[19] Demand for employment, housing, and services in the city grew concurrently. Reflecting trends across southern Africa's postcolonial cities, supply of all three failed to meet demand, and the unplanned compounds on the outskirts of the city grew to accommodate new urban residents and jobseekers.[20]

During the 1980s, governments across Africa, under pressure from donors and international financial institutions (IFIs), implemented neoliberal structural adjustment programs (SAPs) so that they could access international loans and development aid. SAPs mandated severe government cutbacks, economic restructuring, and privatisation. In Zambia, the currency was devalued, price controls were removed, and a range of austerity measures were introduced, including the removal of some food subsidies. These processes contributed to wage stagnation and rising inflation, and further exacerbated socio-economic inequalities and increased economic hardship across the nation.[21] In rural areas, earnings from cash crops shrank, and households experienced sharp reductions in their budgets; these problems were intensified by a series of droughts. It became increasingly difficult for rural households to meet their basic needs.[22] Many rural residents hoped that migration to the capital would bring a better life, but urban households were also struggling to survive. Large numbers of formal sector and civil service workers in Lusaka lost their jobs or found that the value of their wages had reduced significantly. The male breadwinner model established under colonialism had become untenable, and many women and children clambered to generate income to support themselves and their households, and to replace the earnings of retrenched family members. In Lusaka, and in cities across the region, urban labour markets became increasingly crowded as newly unemployed residents competed with existing urban jobseekers and recently arrived migrants for a declining number of jobs. Overall rural-urban migration rates in Zambia began to decrease as a result of the shrinking urban job market.[23] In an effort to revive agriculture and cash-cropping, the government suggested that people go 'back to the land'.[24]

Lusaka had a far more diverse economy than other urban centres in Zambia and continued to buck these broader trends by attracting migrants from the countryside and other urban areas, including significant numbers of female migrants.[25] Gendered and generational barriers to accessing urban wage labour endured, however, and most urban working women and children generated income through the informal sector, often by drawing on and commoditising skills they utilised within the home. In Lusaka, as in urban centres across the region, women sold vegetables, cooked food, and baked goods; they brewed beer; and they performed other personal services, including sexual services and hairdressing. Many children worked alongside their mothers and female kin or else took on whatever piecework they could find, including in market trading and vending.[26] Countless women and children also sought employment in domestic service, which, unlike many informal sector activities, required no capital or other start-up materials. Domestic service was a particularly useful source of employment for rural-urban migrants, and women and girls who came to the city to work in the households of urban kin constituted a large proportion of domestic workers. Domestic service became a 'reservoir of employment', not only for women and girls but for male workers too, and was estimated to be the largest sector of Zambia's urban wage labour force by the mid-1980s, employing almost twice as many people as the mining industry.[27] These broad changes in Zambian women and children's employment practices resulted in, in Aili Mari Tripp's words, 'massive reversals in dependencies and reverses in the direction of resource flows'.[28] Crucially, many women and children shifted from being dependants of men and of parents to having their own incomes and being providers themselves. These gendered and generational shifts in dependency appear to reflect broader trends in post-colonial African cities, from Dar es Salaam to Harare.

The impacts of SAPs intensified during the 1990s. In many African countries, including Zambia, this was related to broader processes of democratisation and liberalisation. Zambia's one-party system came to an end in 1991 when multi-party elections were held and UNIP was defeated by the Movement for Multi-Party Democracy (MMD). The MMD inherited a near-bankrupt economy and pursued extensive and aggressive economic liberalisation in an effort to revive it. Public services were slashed further, price controls were removed, and agricultural subsidies were stopped. Though they aimed to revitalise the devastated Zambian economy, these policies led to further losses in industrial and public sector employment and a continued decline in urban and rural living standards.[29] Employment was concentrated in the informal sector and services, and was largely precarious, low-paid, and insecure. Economic liberalisation further exacerbated social and economic inequalities, and the gap widened between better-off households and everyone else. This growing inequality was shaped by gendered and generational dynamics, including unequal access to resources within marriage, families, and households. Women and children responded by continuing to seek ways to support themselves, further intensifying the reversals in dependencies and resource flows.

Overall rates of rural-urban migration in Zambia continued to slow down during the 1990s. As Zambians sought ways to manage sustained urban economic decline, many looked (back) to the countryside for a livelihood, and the distribution of the population shifted away from urban areas.[30] Lusaka once again continued to buck these broader trends and to attract migrants from the countryside and other urban areas.[31] Female in-migration to the city continued to be high and was most pronounced amongst female children and youth and women over the age of forty.[32] This resulted from a combination of factors, including continued high rates of poverty and gender inequality in rural areas, and from high rates of illness, especially HIV/AIDS, tuberculosis, and malaria. Of these factors, the social breakdown and economic hardship that households affected by HIV/AIDS experienced cannot be underestimated. Across southern Africa, the epidemic created many single-headed households – with women increasingly bearing the burden of caring for the sick – and men and women struggled to survive without their partners. It also led to a proliferation of households headed by the elderly or by children who had lost one or both parents.[33] In these contexts of profound and multifaceted hardship, domestic service provided a lifeline to many women and children who were struggling to support themselves and their dependants, offering access to an income and, especially in cases of kin-based employment, housing, and other resources.

During the 2000s, Zambia's economic situation finally began to improve in several key areas. Investments in the mining industry led to a significant increase in output; copper production by major mining companies reached an all-time high and was complemented by additional production from small-scale mines. Agricultural output also increased. These increases coincided with rising international commodity prices, and led to a return to positive GDP rates. However, only a minority of Zambians benefited from these macro-level economic improvements. The majority of urban and rural residents continued to live in poverty and economic inequality remained pronounced. Real incomes were only half what they had been at independence.[34] This combination of economic growth combined with unequal wealth distribution and high poverty characterised economies across the continent during the 2000s, but inequalities were especially high in southern Africa.[35] In Zambia, continued poverty and inequalities stimulated continued in-migration to Lusaka, further contributing to the city's population boom, which exceeded 1.7 million by 2010.[36] Rates of female migration remained particularly high and outnumbered male migration throughout the decade. Many of these migrants continued to seek and find employment in domestic service, with more women and girls employed in the sector than ever before.[37]

## Recognising domestic labour as work

Although there has been wide-ranging analysis of Zambia's postcolonial economy, domestic labour and household economies are not well understood. The existing literature focuses predominantly on issues surrounding formal wage labour and trade unions, and the adult male workers who predominate in these areas.[38] This narrow focus is problematic for many reasons. Most adults and children in Zambia and across southern Africa have never engaged in formal employment or been members of trade unions, and opportunities for wage labour, and forms of worker organising associated with this, have decreased markedly from the late 1970s onwards. By contrast, domestic labour and unpaid work – and the women and children who largely perform such tasks – are generally excluded from historical and economic analyses, despite their centrality to the functioning of household, informal, and formal economies. The narrow focus of the existing literature is underpinned by and perpetuates limited understandings of what constitutes work, who workers are, and how economies have functioned. In southern Africa, and more broadly, understanding domestic labour, in its paid and unpaid forms, is fundamental to grasping the totality of political economy and the intertwined processes of production and reproduction.

Throughout African history, more time has been allocated to performing domestic labour than any other form of labour.[39] Domestic labour involves providing for the household's basic needs, from cleaning the house and washing clothes to preparing meals and caring for household members. Such tasks are labour-intensive and require a combination of physical, mental, and emotional labour.[40] Ideas about who could and should perform this labour have been shaped by gendered constructions of domesticity, with domestic labour often regarded as part of women's 'natural' roles and female children's training for these roles. Women in rural areas, especially those engaged in labour-intensive hoe production of staple crops, have long borne responsibility for the 'triple workload' of housework, childcare, and agricultural production.[41] An unequal gender division of domestic labour has also occurred in Africa's towns and cities, where women have shouldered responsibility for fulfilling their household's basic needs whilst often also engaging in paid work beyond the home.[42] These trends can also be observed in other parts of the Global South, with women and girls in urban and rural areas spending large proportions of their waking hours performing domestic labour.[43]

Domestic labour has consistently been undervalued in historical and economic analysis of Africa and other parts of the world. It has often been characterised as 'reproductive' labour and distinguished from 'productive' labour. This distinction is based on the belief that the production of material goods in recognised workplaces, such as factories and mines, generates 'surplus value' for capital, whereas 'reproductive' labour, such as preparing meals in domestic settings and raising children, does not generate such additional value. Reproductive labour is consequently characterised as being of lesser value and importance than productive labour – a categorisation that cannot be separated from domestic labour's location within the home and its association with 'women's work'.[44] The undervaluing of reproductive labour can be observed in both Marxist and neoclassical economic approaches across the disciplines.[45]

From the 1970s onwards, Marxist-feminist and socialist-feminist scholars problematised these narrow conceptualisations of labour and demonstrated the importance of labour usually performed by women. Such scholars examined women's labour and debated the precise relationship between domestic labour and capitalism. They generally agreed that women's unpaid domestic labour in private households reproduced labour power and was vital to capitalist accumulation and the functioning of capitalist economies.[46] Some studies also suggested that women shared common experiences under patriarchy and capitalism, with the performance of unpaid domestic labour acting as an 'equalizer of all women'.[47] This and subsequent feminist scholarship challenged the male-centred nature of theoretical and historical understandings of labour by illustrating how gender shaped work and how work is central to the construction and contestation of gender identities.

The field of feminist economics has been especially significant in this regard.[48] Feminist economics encompasses plural approaches and disciplines, including both the rejection of neoclassical, or mainstream, economics and the integration of feminist concerns into mainstream economic analysis. As an approach, feminist economics considers unpaid as well as paid work, highlights interdependence and cooperation within society and in the pursuit of livelihoods, emphasises human well-being as the measure of economic success, and is attentive to the intersecting impacts of gender, race, class, and other social categories and identities on economic outcomes and processes.[49] Feminist approaches within development economics have been particularly important in challenging the exclusion of women's labour from understandings and measurements of economies, not only in the developing world but globally.[50]

The assumption that unpaid domestic labour was a shared experience for women under capitalism was challenged from the 1980s by feminists in a range of disciplines who looked at paid domestic labour. Unpaid domestic labour was shown not to be a great 'equalizer', because some women had the means to pay someone else to do this work for them. Studies focused specifically on how White middle-class and wealthy women bought their way out of their gendered responsibilities for domestic and care labour by employing poor women, Black and indigenous women, and immigrant women in various forms of domestic service. This pattern has been highlighted in many contexts, from apartheid South Africa to twentieth-century Bolivia and the United States.[51] Any semblance of gender solidarity between women employers and women domestic workers was argued to be undermined by class privilege and racial difference.

Scholars also examined how domestic service had been gendered as a male occupation in certain contexts, with especially important studies of domestic service in colonial Africa. Karen Tranberg Hansen's work showed that most domestic workers in Northern Rhodesia were African men and boys who were employed primarily in the households of White settlers and colonial officials. A smaller number of African women and girls were also employed in domestic service, though mainly in African households.[52] The male dominance of domestic service was also observed in colonial South Africa, Southern Rhodesia (now Zimbabwe), and Tanganyika (now Tanzania).[53] In each of these colonial contexts, attempts were made to 'feminise' employment in domestic service and free up male workers for employment in other industries. The success of such attempts varied and was determined in part by the availability of female labour and in part by the local nuances of colonial constructions of labour and gender, with African women frequently excluded from employment in colonial households due to racist stereotypes surrounding African women's intelligence and sexuality.

Feminist scholarship on domestic service in the colonised and non-colonised world demonstrated how household labour relations were not only shaped by prevailing race, gender, and class hierarchies, but also revealed the ways in which they reproduced these hierarchies and cemented existing socio-economic inequalities. They showed how domestic workers' labour bolstered the economic and social status of their employers and freed them to accumulate social and cultural capital. There is also ample evidence of states monitoring domestic service practices as part of broader projects to reinforce social hierarchies. This is especially clear in relation to race, with work by Hansen and Ann Laura Stoler, amongst others, showing how states monitored domesticity and relationships between domestic workers and employers as part of efforts to maintain racial boundaries in colonial and other racially divided contexts.[54] In post-colonial societies such as Zambia, domestic service practices continued to shape the expression and regulation of social boundaries, particularly in relation to class, gender, and age, though the state's role and influence often receded.

Alongside these trends and debates were a number of scholars who had predicted that domestic service would decrease over time as societies became more 'developed' and industrialisation and urbanisation increased.[55] However, by the 1980s and 1990s, it had become clear that industrialisation and economic development did not, in fact, lead to a decrease in domestic service. A range of studies showed how domestic service had expanded in the Global North during the late twentieth century. These included studies of women migrating from the Global South to work in middle-class and wealthy urban households in places ranging from Kuwait to Italy to the United States.[56] Other studies examined how domestic service in industrialised nations was transformed during the twentieth century in line with changing local gendered employment patterns, with employment in domestic service shifting from full-time, live-in work for young men and women, to part-time, live-out work dominated by married women.[57]

Another strand of scholarship examined the persistence and expansion of domestic service in the Global South. Studies explored how independence and decolonisation in Africa and Asia led to an exodus of former coloniser employers of domestic workers but not to a decrease in domestic service. After independence, new post-colonial elites continued to employ domestic workers as they had done in the colonial period, and less affluent households also began hiring domestic workers.[58] Studies also showed that domestic service became a less secure and lucrative form of employment over time in many post-colonial states. As illustrated above, in Africa specifically, the combination of economic decline, structural adjustment, and liberalisation created a situation in which waged work and secure employment were in short supply, and workers scrambled to secure whatever paid work they could find, with many gravitating towards domestic service.[59]

Although existing studies provide key insights into many aspects of the history of domestic service in Africa and other contexts, practices in Black and in poor households are not well understood. In the African literature, studies have focused primarily on White middle-class and wealthy households under apartheid and in colonial societies. Given the highly racialised nature of labour relations in such contexts, we must be careful when interpreting the significance of these findings for post-colonial societies in which racialised hierarchies were in many ways superseded by wealth-based hierarchies, and Black households became the most numerous employers. In Lusaka and other southern African cities, new post-colonial elites and less affluent households employed domestic workers. Domestic workers also sometimes employed persons of lesser means to work in their homes and care for their children. *Home economics* builds on and extends the existing scholarship by examining domestic service practices in Black households in post-colonial Lusaka, and by exploring how these practices were shaped by and involved the reworking of both colonial labour relations and African kinship systems. Although primarily focused on Lusaka, broader trends will be revealed through comparative analysis with numerous cities across southern Africa.

The existing literature on Africa and beyond also provides scant analysis of domestic service practices beyond a formal, wage labour model. But in many contexts, domestic service involved high levels of informality. Moreover, in many post-colonial African cities, including Lusaka, waged work in domestic service was undermined by an increased reliance on extended family networks, and especially on young female kin, for help with housework and childcare.[60] This collective approach to managing domestic labour needs built on long-standing practices of circulating female children and youth within kinship networks as a labour-sharing strategy. There is also evidence that such practices were increasingly commodified and became more exploitative following independence, as African economies declined and urban residents manipulated their kinship networks as sources of cheap labour.[61] Few scholars have examined kin-based labour in domestic service, nor have they considered the experiences and perspectives of the women and girls who predominated in these labour relations, both as workers and employers. This has limited understandings not only of domestic service practices, but of how kinship, gender, and age have shaped labour relations within the home and beyond. *Home economics* provides new insights into these issues, examining kin-based and waged domestic service practices alongside each other, considering when and why employers engaged kin to work in their homes and care for their children, and how gender and age together shaped labour relations within the home and broader economy. In doing so, it highlights the relationship and overlaps between household, gift, informal and formal economies.[62]

The lack of attention paid to girl domestic workers in existing studies reflects a broader neglect of child workers in African historiography. The latter has been explained variously as resulting from limited sources, definitional problems surrounding the meanings of 'child' and 'childhood' in Africa, and the ubiquity and accompanying invisibility of African children's labour, especially in domestic and household settings.[63] The neglect of girls' labour also results from uncritical conflations of 'women and children', with children's work often considered as an extension of women's work and not on its own terms, and by scholars' failure to incorporate age and generation into gendered analysis.[64] A growing body of Africanist scholarship has challenged such approaches, highlighting the significance of children and youth as economic actors in a variety of places and periods and demonstrating how young workers shaped their working and living conditions and challenged gerontocratic hierarchies and gender stereotypes.[65] More broadly, historians working in a number of fields have illustrated the temporality of gender and the intersecting nature of constructions and experiences of gender, age, and generation.[66] There is significant scope to expand on these approaches, particularly in relation to girls' experiences of work and mobility, and children's employment in post-colonial Africa, all of which are explored in this book. By analysing these issues, *Home economics* provides new insights into the intersecting impacts of age and gender on domestic service and broader employment practices in southern Africa, and the contributions that girls have made to the region's urban and rural economies in the past and present.

Contemporary policymaking on domestic service suffers from many of the same limitations as the academic literature. The International Labour Organization (ILO), which is comprised of national governments and workers' and employers' organisations from around the world, has been central to policymaking on domestic service at the global and national levels. The ILO's approach to domestic service largely addresses formal employment involving adult workers and risks excluding the full range of workers and employment practices in the sector, in southern Africa and around the world.[67] Specifically, when child domestic workers are considered by the ILO or by policymakers in government or non-governmental organisations (NGOs), it is mostly in relation to anti-child labour campaigns. Although this draws attention to the exploitation that many child domestic workers have experienced, it also risks limiting our understanding of the complexity of working children's lives and working conditions.

Addressing the limitations of existing academic research and policymaking on domestic service and drawing on feminist historical and economic approaches, *Home economics* proposes a new theoretical approach to domestic service. It considers 'domestic service' to include all forms of domestic labour that are performed in a household or for a household in exchange for payments in cash or kind. This includes wage labour and kin-based labour, forced and free employment, by child and adult workers.[68] This approach brings into a single frame of analysis for the first time a range of workers and labour relations, from girls providing domestic labour for senior kin in exchange for room and board, to women employed under formal labour contracts and in receipt of cash wages. The term 'domestic workers' is used as an overarching category for these workers, alongside a number of role-specific terms that are used by domestic workers and employers in Lusaka to describe themselves. The most used such terms are 'maid', 'houseboy', 'garden boy', 'guard', 'madam', and 'boss'. These English-language terms are legacies of the colonial model of domestic service adopted in Northern Rhodesia and other British colonies in the region, though their meanings shifted following independence.

This theoretical approach encompasses the myriad forms of domestic service that were practised in southern African cities following independence and the end of apartheid, as Black employers and workers adapted and reinvented colonial models of domestic service and longstanding African labour relations rooted in the gendered and gerontocratic hierarchies of kinship. Moreover, it brings female workers to the fore and allows us to examine how women and girls pursued the real and perceived opportunities which employment in domestic service could offer and came to dominate both kin-based and waged domestic service in the process. Though grounded in southern Africa's history, this approach will likely prove useful for understanding domestic service practices in other African contexts and in post-colonial societies beyond the continent.

Chapter 1 explores how gender and age shaped domestic service practices in Lusaka, and how these dynamics shifted over time. It outlines how specific gendered and racialised models of domestic service developed under colonial rule in Lusaka and other southern African cities. In African households, domestic service practices were grounded in the gendered and gerontocratic hierarchies of kinship and marriage, and primarily involved African women and girls' labour. In the households of White settlers and colonial officials, by contrast, the majority of domestic workers were African men and boys. The male dominance of domestic service in White households declined over time in some colonial contexts but persisted in Northern Rhodesia. This dominance was eroded following Zambian independence because of growing demand for female domestic workers, specifically from Black employers, and growing supply of women and girls' labour. The chapter reveals how these dual processes led to the feminisation of domestic service in Lusaka, and Zambia more broadly, a process which involved the reorganisation of work along gendered lines, with female workers coming to dominate indoor roles involving cleaning, cooking, and childcare, and male workers moving into outdoor roles as gardeners and guards. The chapter relates the feminisation of domestic service in Lusaka to broader regional developments and shows that across southern Africa, domestic service was unevenly but unmistakably transformed into a predominantly female occupation during the twentieth century.

Chapters 2 and 3 then turn to examine the experiences and perspectives of female employers and female domestic workers, respectively. Chapter 2 explores the struggles that Lusaka's women have faced to fulfil gendered domestic ideals while working beyond the home. It focuses on women's experiences as mothers and their childcare strategies, exploring the types of childcare that were available, women's perspectives on these options, and their relationships with those who cared for their children. Women's testimonies reveal that the most common forms of childcare were reliance on family members and the employment of domestic workers, both of which primarily involved female labour. The chapter explores how Lusakan mothers' childcare strategies were similar to and different from those of urban women elsewhere in southern Africa. The chapter then examines the emotional and practical challenges that women in Lusaka experienced when leaving their children in the care of others, and the complex and sometimes fractious relationships they developed with those who cared for their children.

Chapter 3 explores the life histories of girl domestic workers, exploring how they found their first jobs, their perspectives on their working conditions and pay, their experiences of spatial and social mobility, and their relationships with employers and kin. The chapter reveals how girls used employment in domestic service in Lusaka to support themselves and their dependants in the city and the countryside, and how they made significant contributions to household and local economies in the process. Making comparisons with girls' employment in other southern African cities, the chapter also makes a broader argument about the ways in which gender and age intersected with sexuality and kinship in the making of labour relations in the region. Furthermore, it engages with contemporary discourses on children and employment in Africa. Specifically, it complicates the representation of girl domestic workers through a lens of victimhood by illustrating how girl domestic workers in Lusaka pursued their own goals and aspirations even in the face of significant personal and structural constraints.

Together, Chapters 1 to 3 provide an important corrective to the largely androcentric focus of existing studies of labour in Zambia and the neglect of girl workers across southern African historiography. They illustrate the increased importance over time of women and girl workers across southern Africa's post-colonial cities, and the ways in which male and female adults and children have been differentially incorporated into formal and informal economies. Moreover, they show how gender and age have shaped work within and beyond the home, and how work has shaped gendered identities.

## Struggles to formalise domestic service and organise domestic workers

Feminist scholars and activists have condemned domestic service because of the ways in which it propagated and reinforced gender, race, and class privilege, and involved the exploitation of poor women and women of colour. At the same time, because of enduring inequalities in gender divisions of labour across the world, many women – feminists included – who worked beyond the home have been reliant upon domestic workers. Some feminists have remained silent on or ambivalent about their own employment of domestic workers.[69] Others have sought ways of improving the conditions under which domestic workers laboured, in many cases to relieve their discomfort with employing other women through an institution that bolstered inequality. This involved discussions of and activism around the formalisation of domestic service and efforts to turn it into a job 'like any other' in which domestic workers could claim decent rights and protections.[70] Such activities occurred alongside, and often in collaboration with, longstanding activism and organising by domestic workers themselves.[71]

During the 1990s and 2000s, the ILO and governments around the world, influenced by domestic worker and feminist activism, began developing new initiatives and policies to regulate domestic service and protect the workers involved. The most high-profile result of these discussions was the ILO's passing of Convention 189 and Recommendation 201 in 2011, which introduced the first international labour standards for domestic service and required ILO member states to introduce or extend relevant national legislation to adhere to these standards.[72] Domestic workers were recognised under the law in a number of countries around the world before the passing of Convention 189, including in the southern African nations of Botswana, Namibia, South Africa, and Zimbabwe.[73] But the development and adoption of Convention 189 prompted the strengthening of existing laws and the passing of new protective legislation for domestic workers, including in Zambia. The latter chapters of the book move away from the social history of the household to examine these developments in the public and political arena.

Successive post-independence governments in Zambia had taken a largely hands-off approach to domestic service before 2011. While

It shows that formal domestic workers' organisations in Zambia have consistently failed to secure broad support amongst the labour force or to achieve significant improvements in domestic workers' rights. These failures resulted from a combination of the limited financial and organisational capacity of such organisations, the government's dismissive attitude towards the sector, and the failure of workers' organisations to tailor their interventions to reflect the breadth of domestic service practices. Crucially, in Zambia and beyond, formal domestic workers' organisations were dominated by adults engaged in wage labour, with too few efforts to organise domestic workers in kin-based arrangements or to engage working children. The formal labour movement model was also unsuccessful because domestic workers could pursue alternative solutions to their grievances at work, including individual strategies of resistance and informal relations of solidarity which provided opportunities to share grievances and access tangible sources of material and emotional support.

## Methodology and sources

This book draws extensively on oral history interviews as these provide a rich source for reconstructing the history of domestic service, in Lusaka and more broadly. Between July 2013 and September 2014, I formally interviewed eighty-one female domestic workers, twenty-six male domestic workers, twenty-three female employers, and four male employers. These interviewees had engaged with various forms of domestic service, from wage labour to kin-based labour. Of the domestic workers, most had completed some primary education. A smaller number received some secondary education, and a smaller number still had completed secondary school or obtained further education. Their economic circumstances varied, though many lived close to or below the poverty line, and none could be characterised as coming from a middle-class background. Most were born in Lusaka, but others had migrated to the city from rural areas in Lusaka Province and further afield, largely from rural areas of the Eastern and Northern Provinces, and from the Copperbelt. Of the employers, most were middle-class, but a small number were impoverished domestic workers who employed persons of even lesser means in their homes. Most were Black Zambians, born in Lusaka or migrants from rural and urban areas around the country; three employers had emigrated from India and held Zambian citizenship; and three employers were White British citizens. To gather a broader range of perspectives on domestic service, I also conducted a small number of interviews with relatives of domestic workers, trade union officials, and staff from 'maid centre' employment agencies and relevant intergovernmental organisations (IGOs) and NGOs.[80]

Most interviews were conducted in Lusaka, but I also carried out a small number of interviews in rural areas of Lusaka Province and Eastern Province. All employers were interviewed in their own homes, as were some domestic workers and the relatives of domestic workers. I met with trade union officials and the staff of maid centres, IGOs, and NGOs at their workplaces. Some domestic workers were also interviewed at their workplaces, but only at the interviewee's request and when her employer was not present, in order to protect the interviewee's privacy and avoid potential conflict with her employer. Interviews were conducted in English, Chinyanja, and several other languages spoken in Zambia.[81] I conducted many of the interviews in partnership with Muyembe Kalbowe, who was a community worker in Bauleni and research associate on this project.

Although the book explores the employment of children in domestic service and seeks to understand their perspectives, no interviews were conducted with children themselves. Childhood experiences were instead discussed during oral history interviews with adults. Nineteen female and three male domestic workers had worked in domestic service as children, and ten female and two male domestic workers had done so in their youth. Seven employers had employed female children and youth as domestic workers, and two had employed male children and youth. My approach reflects the historical focus of the project: the book examines children's experiences of and perspectives on domestic work in the past and not the present. It seeks to place childhood experiences of work in a broader temporal context and to highlight the variety of employment and migratory paths that individual children pursued.

More broadly, my approach to studying childhood experiences of domestic service is informed by theoretical insights from critical studies of childhood and youth. Such studies illustrate that the concepts of childhood, youth, and, relatedly, child labour are historically and culturally constructed, and spatially and temporally specific.[82] In Zambia, there are inconsistencies in legal and cultural definitions of childhood status. The amended Constitution adopted in 2016 defines a child as 'a person who has attained, or is below, the age of eighteen years'.[83] Statutory law stipulates minimum ages for marriage of sixteen years with parental consent and twenty-one years without parental consent, while customary law considers puberty as a minimum criterion for girls to marry.[84] Labour laws generally prohibit the employment of children below the age of fifteen years.[85] Taking both these legal inconsistencies and social constructions of age in Zambia into account, the term 'child' is used for those aged fifteen years and below and the term 'youth' for those aged sixteen and above. A fixed upper limit of 'youth' is not employed here, but marriage and parenthood are used as important markers of the transition between youth and adult status. The terms 'girl' and 'boy' are used to refer to both children and youth.[86]

I do not use oral testimonies as literal recollections of history. Like all historical sources, oral testimonies only provide narratives about the past that are subjective and constructed in particular ways for specific audiences, and their meanings need to be analysed and interpreted.[87] I am also aware that my positionality as a young, White, well-educated, British woman likely impacted my interviewees' perceptions of me and my research, and shaped the power dynamics of the interview and the narratives produced.[88] I use oral testimonies to explore what was remembered about domestic service, how those memories were constructed, and what these issues reveal about the interviewee's sense of self and their perceptions of their past and present.[89] During interviews, some domestic workers were reluctant to recognise the importance of their work. This was especially the case with women, many of whom argued that they had limited education and had no choice but to become domestic workers, which they saw as low-status work and a last resort. But women's narratives also emphasised their resilience, their capacity for hard work, and their ability to support themselves and others and contribute to their households and the broader economy. Most employers, by contrast, were fairly self-confident and assured during interviews, displaying a sense of self that was often grounded in achievements in education or work. Employers' narratives rarely addressed issues of exploitation of domestic workers and focused more on the problems they had faced as employers and urban residents. These testimonies must all be examined closely for which aspects of domestic service they highlight and which they silence, gloss over, or even undermine.

Informal observations and a household survey complemented the insights provided by formal oral history interviews. I observed interactions between domestic workers and employers in various settings, including in the private households in which I lived in Lusaka and in the homes of friends and acquaintances.[90] Observing interactions between workers and employers at close hand helped me to understand how both parties negotiated the intimacies and challenges of labour relations within the home.[91] The relationships I witnessed all involved middle- and high-income employers and domestic workers engaged in formal wage labour. In order to develop a picture of domestic service arrangements in poorer households, I also conducted a household survey in Bauleni during July and August 2013. I spoke with twenty-eight Bauleni householders about their past and present housekeeping practices. The findings of this survey are not intended to replicate social scientific survey methods but are instead used alongside other source material to build up a picture of domestic service practices in poorer households.

Written sources on domestic service are scarce for both post-colonial Zambia and southern Africa more broadly. This absence of sources is part of a broader historical pattern. As Antoinette Burton argues in relation to India, the absence of domestic workers from the documentary record is 'the most dramatic and perhaps paradigmatic example of what can never be fully recovered' in the archive.[92] Danielle Taylor Phillips builds on this argument, asserting that the intersecting hierarchies of race, class, and gender which structured domestic workers' opportunities similarly shaped the production and storage of knowledge about their lives in archives. All too often, the only archival traces of domestic workers are sources produced by their employers or government officials, such as household management manuals or labour force statistics.[93] In post-colonial Africa, and more broadly over time and space, these limitations of documentary sources result also from the broader erasure of women's work in government documents such as the census, and the gender and age biases of labour categories.

The relative scarcity and limitations of written sources notwithstanding, such material can still provide useful insights into domestic service. I take inspiration from the path-breaking work of historians of women and of slavery such as Burton and Phillips who have illustrated ways to work with partial and incomplete archives and documents shaped by race, gender, and class privilege.[94] I draw on a range of archival and documentary sources in which domestic service and domestic workers appear, often only in small glimpses. These written sources include labour reports, statistics, and legal documents produced by the Zambian government and governments across southern Africa; grey literature produced by IGOs and NGOs; the records of domestic worker trade unions; prominent southern African newspapers; and new forms of social media. Amongst other insights, these sources are suggestive of the number of persons employed in waged domestic service; public discourses and legal frameworks around domestic service; and the activities of domestic worker's organisations.

Overall, *Home economics* seeks to do more than provide a history of domestic service in one southern African city. The book's findings speak to wider debates about work, gender, and age that are critical to an understanding of southern Africa's post-colonial and post-apartheid history. They challenge normative assumptions of labour history that overlook women's labour, children's labour, and domestic labour. The book also speaks to debates about the changing nature of work and labour movements in southern Africa.[95] Its findings illustrate how traditional modes of regulating and organising labour have excluded a range of workers and practices, with detrimental impacts for working children and those in 'informal' employment arrangements. Moreover, they show how southern Africa's urban working poor have used alternatives to the formal labour movement model to address exploitation at work, economic hardship, and political grievances. These findings are relevant not only to academic research but also to policymaking on work, gender, children, and development.

## Notes

1 Interview with Mercy Banda, Lusaka, 13 July 2013.
2 Interview with Priscilla Njovu, Lusaka, 22 August 2013.

3 For further discussion of constructions of domesticity in Africa, see Karen Tranberg Hansen, 'Introduction: Domesticity in Africa', in Karen Tranberg Hansen (ed.), *African Encounters with Domesticity* (New Brunswick, NJ: Rutgers University Press, 1992), pp. 1–10.

4 I capitalise the terms *Black* and *White* in order to convey the historically and socially constructed nature of racial categories and identities.

5 The book's title and focus diverge from earlier writing on home economics which focused on the scientific management of the household and the veneration of domesticity and women's roles within the home. For further discussion of the history of writing on home economics, see Giandomenica Becchio, *A History of Feminist and Gender Economics* (Abingdon: Routledge, 2019), chapter 2.

6 Garth Andrew Myers, *African Cities: Alternative Visions of Urban Theory and Practice* (London: Zed Books, 2011), p. 30.

7 Karen Tranberg Hansen, *Keeping House in Lusaka* (New York, NY: Columbia University Press, 1997), pp. 23–28. On the development of Lusaka in the colonial period, see also Garth Andrew Myers, *Verandahs of Power: Colonialism and Space in Urban Africa* (Syracuse, NY: Syracuse University Press, 2003).

8 See Miles Larmer, *Living for the City: Social Change and Knowledge Production in the Central African Copperbelt* (Cambridge: Cambridge University Press, 2021), pp. 96–128.

9 George Chauncey Jr, 'The Locus of Reproduction: Women's Labour in the Zambian Copperbelt, 1927–1953', *Journal of Southern African Studies*, 7:2 (1981), 136–138. See also Jane L. Parpart, 'Class and Gender on the Copperbelt: Women in Northern Rhodesian Copper Mining Communities, 1926–1964', in Claire C. Robertson and Iris Berger (eds), *Women and Class in Africa* (New York, NY: Africana Publishing Co., 1986), pp. 141–160.

10 Hansen, *Keeping House in Lusaka*, p. 27.

11 For further discussion of politics in early post-colonial Zambia, see Cherry Gertzel, Carolyn Baylies, and Morris Szeftel (eds), *The Dynamics of the One-Party State in Zambia* (Manchester: Manchester University Press, 1984); Miles Larmer, *Rethinking African Politics: A History of Opposition in Zambia* (Farnham: Ashgate, 2011); William Tordoff (ed.), *Politics in Zambia* (Manchester: Manchester University Press, 1974); William Tordoff (ed.), *Administration in Zambia* (Manchester: Manchester University Press, 1980).

12 Stefano Bellucci and Andreas Eckert, 'The "Labour Question" in Africanist Historiography', in Stefano Bellucci and Andreas Eckert (eds), *General Labour History of Africa: Workers, Employers and Governments, 20th–21st Centuries* (Woodbridge: James Currey, 2019), p. 4.

13 Ilsa Glazer Schuster's work shows that a small number of better-educated women secured new roles, including as secretaries, clerks, typists, and airline stewardesses. Ilsa M. Glazer Schuster, *New Women of Lusaka* (Palo Alto, CA: Mayfield, 1979).
14 Franco Barchiesi, 'Precarious and Informal Labour', in Bellucci and Eckert (eds), *General Labour History of Africa*, p. 46.
15 *Ibid.*, p. 47.
16 Studies of Zambia's economic decline from the 1970s include Robert. H. Bates and Paul Collier, 'The Politics and Economics of Policy Reform in Zambia', in Robert H. Bates and Anne O. Krueger (eds), *Political and Economic Interactions in Economic Policy Reform: Evidence from Eight Countries* (London: Blackwell, 1993), pp. 387–443; James Ferguson, *Expectations of Modernity: Myths and Meanings of Urban Life on the Zambian Copperbelt* (London and Berkeley, CA: University of California Press, 1999).
17 Republic of Zambia, *1980 Census of Population and Housing. Analytical Report Volume 3. Major Findings and Conclusions and Policy Implications* (Lusaka: Central Statistical Office, 1985).
18 There is an extensive literature on female migration and urbanisation in Southern Africa. Studies include Teresa Barnes, *We Women Worked So Hard: Gender, Urbanization and Social Reproduction in Colonial Harare, Zimbabwe, 1930–56* (Portsmouth, NH: Heinemann, 1999); Belinda Bozzoli with the assistance of Mmantho Nkotsoe, *Women of Phokeng: Consciousness, Life Strategy and Migrancy in South Africa, 1900–1983* (Woodbridge: James Currey, 1991); Rebekah Lee, *African Women and Apartheid: Migration and Settlement in Urban South Africa* (London: IB Tauris, 2009); Parpart, 'Class and Gender on the Copperbelt'; Jeanne Marie Penvenne, *Women, Migration and the Cashew Economy in Southern Mozambique: 1945–1975* (Woodbridge: James Currey, 2015); Elizabeth Schmidt, *Peasants, Traders, and Wives: Shona Women in the History of Zimbabwe, 1870–1939* (Portsmouth, NH: Heinemann, 1992).
19 Republic of Zambia, *1969 Census of Population and Housing. Final Report Volume 1. Total Zambia* (Lusaka: Central Statistical Office, 1970); Republic of Zambia, *2000 Census of Population and Housing. Lusaka Province Analytical Report. Volume 5* (Lusaka: Central Statistical Office, 2004).
20 Hansen, *Keeping House in Lusaka*, pp. 27–28, pp. 51–53.
21 The key IFIs were the World Bank and International Monetary Fund, which required countries to undertake SAPs as a requirement of receiving loans and development aid. For further discussion of the Zambian case, see Bates and Collier, 'The Politics and Economics of Policy Reform

in Zambia'; Austin M. Chakaodza, *Structural Adjustment in Zambia and Zimbabwe: Reconstructive or Destructive?* (Harare: Third World Publishing House, 1993); Neo Simutanyi, 'The Politics of Structural Adjustment in Zambia', *Third World Quarterly*, 17:4 (1996), 825–839.

22 Johan Pottier, *Migrants No More: Settlement and Survival in Mambwe Villages, Zambia* (Manchester: Manchester University Press, 1988); Jeremy Gould, *Left Behind: Rural Zambia in the Third Republic* (Lusaka: Lembani Trust, 2010).

23 See Ferguson, *Expectations of Modernity*, chapter 4.

24 Henrietta Moore and Megan Vaughan, *Cutting Down Trees: Gender, Nutrition and Agricultural Change in Zambia* (Portsmouth, NH: Heinemann, 1994), p. 206.

25 Deborah Potts, 'Counter-Urbanisation on the Zambian Copperbelt: Interpretations and Implications', *Urban Studies*, 42:4 (2005), 588, 592.

26 There is a literature on aspects of informal sector employment in post-colonial Zambia, including its gendered aspects. Studies include Karen Tranberg Hansen, *Salaula: The World of Secondhand Clothing and Zambia* (Chicago, IL: University of Chicago Press, 2000); and chapters by Hansen and B. Mwila Kazimbaya-Senkwe in Karen Tranberg Hansen and Mariken Vaa (eds), *Reconsidering Informality: Perspectives from Urban Africa* (Uppsala: Nordiksa Afrikainstitutet, 2004).

27 Karen Tranberg Hansen, *Distant Companions: Servants and Employers in Zambia, 1900–1989* (Ithaca, NY: Cornell University Press, 1989), pp. 221–222.

28 Aili Mari Tripp, *Changing the Rules: The Politics of Liberalization and the Urban Informal Economy in Tanzania* (London: University of California Press, 1997), p. xiii, pp. 106–134.

29 For further discussion of this period, see Miles Larmer, 'Reaction and Resistance to Neoliberalism in Zambia', *Review of African Political Economy*, 32:103 (2005), 30–32; Patience Mususa, '"Getting By": Life on the Copperbelt after the Privatisation of the Zambia Consolidated Copper Mines', *Social Dynamics: A Journal of African Studies*, 36:2 (2010), 380–394; Patience Mususa, 'Topping Up: Life Amidst Hardship and Death on the Copperbelt', *African Studies*, 71:2 (2012), 304–322; Lise Rakner, *Political and Economic Liberalisation in Zambia 1991–2001* (Stockholm: Nordic Africa Institute, 2003).

30 Republic of Zambia, *2000 Census of Population and Housing. Analytical Report Final* (Lusaka: Central Statistical Office, 2003).

31 Potts, 'Counter-Urbanisation on the Zambian Copperbelt', p. 588, p. 592.

32 Republic of Zambia, *2000 Census of Population and Housing. Analytical Report Final.*

33 The literature on HIV/AIDS in Africa is vast, but two particularly relevant studies for the purposes of this book are Emma Guest, *Children of AIDS: Africa's Orphan Crisis* (London: Pluto, 2003); John Iliffe, *The African AIDS Epidemic: A History* (Oxford: James Currey, 2006). On Zambia specifically, see Lorenzo Guarcello, Scott Lyon, and Furio Camillo Rosati, 'Orphanhood and Child Vulnerability: Zambia', Understanding Children's Work Project Working Paper Series (Rome: University of Rome, 2004); Anthony Simpson and Virginia Bond, 'Narratives of Nationhood and HIV/AIDS: Reflections on Multidisciplinary Research on the HIV/AIDS Epidemic in Zambia Over the Last 30 Years', *Journal of Southern African Studies*, 40:5 (2014), 1065–1089; C. Bawa Yamba, 'Loveness and Her Brothers: Trajectories of Life for Children Orphaned by HIV/AIDS in Zambia', *African Journal of AIDS Research*, 4:3 (2005), 205–210.

34 Gould, *Left Behind*, p. 2.

35 United Nations Economic Commission for Africa and United Nations Development Programme, *Economic Growth, Inequality and Poverty in Southern Africa: Issues and Policy Options* (Addis Ababa: Economic Commission for Africa, 2017); United Nations Development Programme, *Income Inequality Trends in Sub-Saharan Africa. Divergence, Determinants and Consequences: Overview* (New York, NY: United Nations Development Programme, 2017).

36 Republic of Zambia, *2010 Census of Population and Housing. National Analytical Report* (Lusaka: Central Statistical Office, 2012).

37 ILO, *Magnitude of Domestic Workers in Zambia: Highlights of Domestic Worker Survey* (Lusaka: ILO, 2014), p. 2.

38 Amongst others, see Robert H. Bates, *Unions, Parties, and Political Development: A Study of Mineworkers in Zambia* (New Haven, CT: Yale University Press, 1971); Elena L. Berger, *Labour, Race, and Colonial Rule: The Copperbelt from 1924 to Independence* (Oxford: Clarendon Press: 1974); M. Burawoy, *The Colour of Class on the Copper Mines: From African Advancement to Zambianisation* (Lusaka: University of Zambia, 1972); Miles Larmer, *Mineworkers in Zambia: Labour and Political Change in Post-Colonial Africa, 1964–1991* (London: I. B. Tauris, 2007); Henry S. Meebelo, *African Proletarians and Colonial Capitalism: The Origins, Growth, and Struggles of the Zambian Labour Movement to 1964* (Lusaka: Kenneth Kaunda Foundation, 1986); Jane L. Parpart, *Labor and Capital on the African Copperbelt* (Philadelphia, PA: Temple University Press, 1983); Ian Phimister, 'Workers in Wonderland? White Miners and the Northern Rhodesian Copperbelt, 1946–1962', *South African Historical Journal*, 63:2 (2011), 183–233; Esther Uzar, 'Contested Labour and Political Leadership:

Three Mineworkers' Unions after the Opposition Victory in Zambia', *Review of African Political Economy*, 44:152 (2017), 292–311.

39 Deborah Fahy Bryceson, 'Domestic Work', in Bellucci and Eckert (eds), *General Labour History of Africa*, p. 301.

40 Domestic labour involved two forms of emotional labour: the labour that householders (largely women) performed to manage the emotions provoked by childcare and housework, and the labour that domestic workers performed to manage their emotions within the workplace. My approach draws on Arlie Russell Hochschild's original definition of emotional labour and later developments in her thinking. Arlie Russell Hochschild, *The Managed Heart: Commercialization of Human Feeling* (Berkeley, CA: University of California Press, 1983); Julie Beck, 'The Concept Creep of "Emotional Labor"', *The Atlantic* (26 November 2018), available at www.theatlantic.com/family/archive/2018/11/arlie-hochschild-housework-isnt-emotional-labor/576637/ (accessed 24 June 2021).

41 Bryceson, 'Domestic Work', p. 301. For further discussion see Deborah Fahy Bryceson (ed.), *Women Wielding the Hoe: Lessons from Rural Africa for Feminist Theory and Development Practice* (Oxford: Berg Publishers, 1995).

42 Alice Evans, 'History Lessons for Gender Equality from the Zambian Copperbelt, 1900–1990', *Gender, Place & Culture: A Journal of Feminist Geography*, 22:3 (2015), 344–362; Karen Tranberg Hansen 'Negotiating Sex and Gender in Urban Zambia', *Journal of Southern African Studies*, 10:2 (1984), 219–238.

43 For further discussion, see Lynne Brydon and Sylvia Chant, *Women in the Third World: Gender Issues in Rural and Urban Areas* (New Brunswick, NJ: Rutgers University Press, 1993); Sylvia Chant, *Women-Headed Households: Diversity and Dynamics in the Developing World* (Basingstoke: Palgrave Macmillan, 1997).

44 Bryceson, 'Domestic Work', p. 301.

45 Elise van Nederveen Meerkerk, Silke Neunsinger, and Dirk Hoerder, 'Domestic Workers of the World: Histories of Domestic Work as Global Labour History', in Dirk Hoerder, Elise van Nederveen Meerkerk, and Silke Neunsinger (eds), *Towards a Global History of Domestic and Caregiving Workers* (Leiden: Brill, 2015), pp. 17–18.

46 Such scholarship included Margaret Benston, 'The Political Economy of Women's Liberation', *Monthly Review*, 21:4 (1969), 13–27; Mariarosa Dalla Costa and Selma James, *The Power of Women and the Subversion of the Community* (Bristol: Falling Wall, 1972); Heidi Hartmann, 'Capitalism, Patriarchy, and Job Segregation by Sex', *Signs*, 1:3 (1976), 137–169; Wally Seccombe, 'The Housewife and Her Labour

under Capitalism', *New Left Review*, 83 (1974), 3–24; Belinda Bozzoli, 'Marxism, Feminism and South African Studies', *Journal of Southern African Studies*, 9:2 (1983), 139–171; Lise Vogel, *Marxism and the Oppression of Women: Toward a Unitary Theory* (New Brunswick, NJ: Rutgers University Press, 1983).

47 Barbara Ehrenriech, 'Maid to Order', in Barbara Ehrenreich and Arlie Russell Hochschild (eds), *Global Woman: Nannies, Maids and Sex Workers in the New Economy* (New York, NY: Henry Holt, 2002), p. 86.

48 Feminist approaches to economics can be traced to the nineteenth century, but the field of feminist economics became particularly visible and influential from the 1990s when the International Association for Feminist Economics (IAFFE) and the journal *Feminist Economics* were founded. For further discussion, see Becchio, *A History of Feminist and Gender Economics*, chapter 3.

49 For an introduction to and survey of feminist economic theories and approaches, see Ebru Kongar and Günseli Berik (eds), *The Routledge Handbook of Feminist Economics* (Abingdon: Routledge, 2021) and Marianne A. Ferber and Julie A. Nelson (eds), *Feminist Economics Today: Beyond Economic Man* (Chicago, IL: University of Chicago Press, 2020).

50 Key studies include Ester Boserup, *Woman's Role in Economic Development* (London: Allen & Unwin, 1970); Lourdes Benería, 'Conceptualising the Labour Force: The Underestimation of Women's Economic Activities', *Journal of Development Studies*, 17:3 (1981), 10–28; Barbara Rogers, *The Domestication of Women: Discrimination in Developing Societies* (London: Kogan Page, 1980).

51 Jacklyn Cock, *Maids and Madams: A Study in the Politics of Exploitation* (Johannesburg: Ravan Press, 1980); Lesley Gill, *Precarious Dependencies: Gender, Class, and Domestic Service in Bolivia* (New York, NY: Columbia University Press, 1994); Judith Rollins, *Between Women: Domestics and their Employers* (Philadelphia, PA: Temple University Press, 1985). Other important studies of domestic service from this period include Elsa M. Chaney and Mary Garcia Castro (eds), *Muchachas No More: Household Workers in Latin America and the Caribbean* (Philadelphia, PA: Temple University Press, 1989); Juliet Filet-Abreu De Souza, 'Paid Domestic Service in Brazil', *Latin American Perspectives*, 7:1 (1980), 35–63; Deborah Gaitskell, Judy Kimble, Moira Maconachie, and Elaine Unterhalter, 'Class, Race and Gender: Domestic Workers in South Africa', *Review of African Political Economy*, 27/28 (1983), 86–108; Evelyn Nakano Glenn, *Issei, Nisei, War Bride: Three Generations of Japanese American Women in*

*Domestic Service* (Philadelphia, PA: Temple University Press, 1986); Hansen, *Distant Companions*; David. M. Katzman, *Seven Days a Week: Women and Domestic Service in Industrializing America* (New York, NY: Oxford University Press, 1978).

52 Hansen, *Distant Companions*; Karen Tranberg Hansen, 'Household Work as a Man's Job: Sex and Gender in Domestic Service in Zambia', *Anthropology Today*, 2:3 (1986), 18–23.

53 Janet Bujra, *Serving Class: Masculinity and the Feminization of Domestic Service in Tanzania* (Edinburgh, Edinburgh University Press, 2000); Elizabeth Schmidt, 'Race, Sex and Domestic Labour: The Question of African Female Servants in Southern Rhodesia, 1900–1939', in Hansen (ed.), *African Encounters with Domesticity*, pp. 221–241; Charles van Onselen, *Studies in the Social and Economic History of the Witwatersrand, 1886–1914*, Vol. 2 (Johannesburg: Ravan Press, 1982), pp. 1–73.

54 Hansen, 'Introduction: Domesticity in Africa', pp. 4–5; Ann Laura Stoler, *Carnal Knowledge and Imperial Power: Race and the Intimate in Colonial Rule* (Berkeley, CA: University of California Press, 2002), pp. 53–55, p. 74, pp. 133–139, p. 173, pp. 188–194, pp. 198–199.

55 Perhaps the most influential such study was economist Ester Boserup's 1970 work on Latin America. See Boserup, *Women's Role in Economic Development*, pp. 103–104.

56 Rhacel Parreñas, *Servants of Globalization: Women, Migration and Domestic Work* (Stanford, CA: Stanford University Press, 2001); Attiya Ahmad, *Everyday Conversions: Islam, Domestic Work, and South Asian Migrant Women in Kuwait* (Durham, NC: Duke University Press, 2017). Other studies of domestic workers and global migration include Jacqueline Andall, *Gender, Migration and Domestic Service: The Politics of Black Women in Italy* (Aldershot: Ashgate, 2000); Rosie Cox, *The Servant Problem: Domestic Employment in a Global Economy* (London: I.B. Tauris, 2006); Janet Henshall Momsen (ed.), *Gender, Migration and Domestic Service* (London: Routledge, 1999).

57 See, for instance, Selina Todd, 'Domestic Service and Class Relations in Britain 1900–1950', *Past and Present*, 203:1 (2009), 181–204.

58 Stoler, *Carnal Knowledge and Imperial Power*, p. 24; John Pape, 'Still Serving the Tea: Domestic Workers in Zimbabwe 1980–90', *Journal of Southern African Studies*, 19:3 (1993), 387–404.

59 Bujra, *Serving Class*, p. 4, p. 177; Hansen, *Distant Companions*, pp. 219–222, pp. 244–247.

60 Bryceson, 'Domestic Work', p. 314.

61 On Zambia, see Omolara Dakore Oyaide, 'Child Domestic Labour in Lusaka: A Gender Perspective' (MA dissertation, University of Zambia,

2000), p. 3, p. 6, p. 55; Virginia Bond, Chipo Chiiya, Mutale Chonta, and Sue Clay with Jean Hunleth, Ligia Kiss, and Cathy Zimmerman, *Sweeping the Bedroom: Children in Domestic Work in Zambia* (Lusaka: UNICEF, 2011), p. 24, p. 34. More broadly, see Human Rights Watch, *Bottom of the Ladder: Exploitation and Abuse of Girl Domestic Workers in Guinea*, 19:8(A), June 2007, available at www.hrw.org/report/2007/06/15/bottom-ladder/exploitation-and-abuse-girl-domestic-workers-guinea (accessed 14 August 2020); Dorte Thorsen, *Child Domestic Workers: Evidence from West and Central Africa* (Dakar: UNICEF, 2012), available at http://sro.sussex.ac.uk/id/eprint/43303/1/Briefing_paper_No_1_-_child_domestic_workers.pdf (accessed 14 August 2020).

62 Here, I draw inspiration from Jeanne Marie Penvenne's arguments about the need to 'interrogate the utility of the gendered and hierarchical distinctions drawn among formal, informal, gift and household economies'; Penvenne, *Women, Migration and the Cashew Economy in Southern Mozambique*, p. 4.

63 Beverly C. Grier, 'Child Labour and Africanist Scholarship: A Critical Overview', *African Studies Review*, 47:2 (2004), 13–15.

64 Beverly C. Grier, *Invisible Hands: Child Labour and the State in Colonial Zimbabwe* (Portsmouth, NH: Heinemann, 2006), 12.

65 Such work includes Wiseman Chijere Chirwa, 'Child and Youth Labour on the Nyasaland Plantations, 1890–1953', *Journal of Southern African Studies*, 19:4 (1993), 662–680; Abosede George, *Making Modern Girls: A History of Girlhood, Labour, and Social Development in Colonial Lagos* (Athens, OH: Ohio University Press, 2014); Grier, *Invisible Hands*; Sacha Hepburn, '"Bringing a Girl from the Village": Gender, Child Migration and Domestic Service in Post-Colonial Zambia', in Elodie Razy and Marie Rodet (eds), *Children on the Move in Africa: Past and Present Experiences of Migration* (Woodbridge: James Currey, 2016), pp. 69–84; Sacha Hepburn and April Jackson, 'Colonial Exceptions: The International Labour Organization and Child Labour in British Africa, c. 1919–1940', *Journal of Contemporary History* (2021). Online first. Jack Lord, 'Child Labour in the Gold Coast: The Economics of Work, Education and the Family in Late-Colonial Africa, c. 1940–57', *Journal of the History of Childhood and Youth*, 4:1 (2011), 88–115; and Sarah Walters, '"Child! Now You Are": Identity Registration, Labour, and the Definition of Childhood in Colonial Tanganyika, 1910–1950', *Journal of the History of Childhood and Youth*, 9:1 (2016), 66–86.

66 Stacey Hynd, '"Uncircumcised Boys" and "Girl Spartans": Youth, Gender and Generation in Colonial Insurgencies and Counterinsurgency, c. 1954–59', *Gender and History*, 33: 2 (2021), 536–556; Rachel Leow,

'Age as a Category of Gender Analysis: Servant Girls, Modern Girls, and Gender in Southeast Asia', *The Journal of Asian Studies*, 71:4 (2012), 975–990.

67 ILO, *Domestic Workers Across the World: Global and Regional Statistics and the Extent of Legal Protection* (Geneva: International Labour Office, 2013), p. 22.

68 This approach is influenced in part by Elise van Nederveen Meerkerk *et al.*'s inclusive definition of domestic work found in van Nederveen Meerkerk *et al.*, 'Domestic Workers of the World', p. 2.

69 Bujra, *Serving Class*, p. 5, pp. 45–46; Chris Johnson, *Women on the Frontline: Voices from Southern Africa* (London: Macmillan, 1992), p. 146; Julia Wrigley, 'Feminists and Domestic Workers', *Feminist Studies*, 17:2 (1991), 326. See also Laura Schwartz, *Feminism and the Servant Problem: Class and Domestic Labour in the Women's Suffrage Movement* (Cambridge: Cambridge University Press, 2019).

70 Shireen Ally, *From Servants to Workers: South African Domestic Workers and the Democratic State* (London: Cornell University Press, 2009), pp. 5–6. For further discussion, see Martha Chen, 'Recognizing Domestic Workers, Regulating Domestic Work: Conceptual, Measurement, and Regulatory Challenges', *Canadian Journal of Women and the Law*, 23:1 (2011), 167–184; Gabrielle Meagher, 'Is It Wrong to Pay for Housework?', *Hypatia*, 17 (2002), 52–66; Premilla Nadasen, 'Citizenship Rights, Domestic Work, and the Fair Labor Standards Act', *The Journal of Policy History*, 24:1 (2012), 74–94; Joan C. Tronto, 'The "Nanny Question" in Feminism', *Hypatia*, 17:2 (2002), 34–51.

71 Eileen Boris and Jennifer N. Fish, 'Decent Work for Domestics: Feminist Organizing, Worker Empowerment, and the ILO', in Hoerder, van Nederveen Meerkerk, and Neunsinger (eds), *Towards a Global History of Domestic and Caregiving Workers*, p. 530. For further discussion, see Jennifer N. Fish, *Domestic Workers of the World Unite!: A Global Movement for Dignity and Human Rights* (New York, NY: New York University Press, 2017).

72 ILO, C189 – Domestic Workers Convention, 2011 (No. 189), available at www.ilo.ch/dyn/normlex/en/f?p=NORMLEXPUB:12100:0::NO::P12100_ILO_CODE:C189 (accessed 9 July 2020). ILO, R201 – Domestic Workers Recommendation, 2011 (No. 201), available at www.ilo.ch/dyn/normlex/en/f?p=NORMLEXPUB:12100:0::NO::P12100_ILO_CODE:R201 (accessed 12 November 2021).

73 Mmaskepe Sejoe and Linda Magula, *Domestic Workers in Botswana: An Action Research Report* (Gaborone: Ditshwanelo, 1996); Ally, *From Servants to Workers*; Dorte Østreng, *Domestic Workers' Daily Lives in Post-Apartheid Namibia*, NEPRU Occasional Paper No.11 (Windhoek:

The Namibian Economic Policy Research Unit, 1997), pp. 67–75; Pape, 'Still Serving the Tea', 389–391.

74 Hansen, 'Introduction: Domesticity in Africa', pp. 4–5.

75 Benería, 'Conceptualising the Labour Force', 10–11; A. Evans, '"Women Can Do What Men Can Do": The Causes and Consequences of Growing Flexibility in Gender Divisions of Labour in Kitwe, Zambia' (PhD dissertation, the London School of Economics and Political Science, 2013), pp. 81–82; Carole Rakodi, 'Urban Agriculture: Research Questions and Zambian Evidence', *The Journal of Modern African Studies*, 26:3 (1988), 497, 501.

76 Republic of Zambia, Statutory Instrument No. 3 of 2011. The Minimum Wages and Conditions of Employment Act (Laws, Vol. 15, Cap. 276). The Minimum Wages and Conditions of Employment (Domestic Workers) Order, 2011 (Lusaka: Government Printer, 2010), available at www.mlss.gov.zm/?wpfb_dl=38 (accessed 31 July 2021).

77 Interview with Kevin Liywalii, Lusaka, 27 August 2014; interview with Martha Kasaro, Lusaka, 27 August 2014.

78 Republic of Zambia, Statutory Instrument No. 45 of 2012. The Minimum Wages and Conditions of Employment Act (Laws, Vol. 15, Cap. 276). The Minimum Wages and Conditions of Employment (Domestic Workers) (Amendment) Order, 2012 (Lusaka: Government Printer, 2012), available at www.mlss.gov.zm/?wpfb_dl=41 (accessed 31 July 2021). Republic of Zambia, Statutory Instrument No. 69 of 2018. The Minimum Wages and Conditions of Employment Act (Laws, Vol. 15, Cap. 276). The Minimum Wages and Conditions of Employment (Domestic Workers) (Amendment) Order, 2018 (Lusaka: Government Printer, 2018), available at www.ilo.org/dyn/natlex/natlex4.detail?p_lang=en&p_isn=108957&p_country=ZMB&p_count=204&p_classification=12.02&p_classcount=13 (accessed 31 July 2021). On the relationship between politics and the law in post-colonial Zambia, see Jeremy Gould, *Postcolonial Legality: Law, Politics, and State Formation in Africa Since the End of the Cold War* (London: Taylor & Francis, 2021).

79 Examples include Ally, *From Servants to Workers*; Robyn Pariser, 'Masculinity and Organized Resistance in Domestic Service in Colonial Dar es Salaam, 1919–1961', *International Labor and Working-Class History*, 88 (2015), 109–129.

80 The names of certain interviewees have been changed at their request in order to protect their anonymity. The locations and dates of interviews have not been changed.

81 I am a native English speaker and became proficient in Chinyanja, the language most spoken in Lusaka. Interviews were also conducted in

other languages spoken in Zambia, including Chibemba and Chitonga, with translation provided by Muyembe Kalobwe.

82 For an overview of such studies, see Grier, *Invisible Hands*, pp. 22–26.

83 Republic of Zambia, Constitution of Zambia (Amendment). Act No. 2 of 2016 (Lusaka: Government Printer, 2016), available at www.parliament.gov.zm/sites/default/files/documents/amendment_act/Constitution%20of%20Zambia%20%20(Amendment),%202016-Act%20No.%202_0.pdf (accessed 31 July 2021).

84 Oliver Mweemba and Gillian Mann, 'Young Marriage, Parenthood and Divorce in Zambia', Young Lives Research Report (Oxford: Young Lives, 2020).

85 Republic of Zambia, Statutory Instrument No. 3 of 2011.

86 The use of 'boys' and 'girls' should not be confused with the demeaning language used by colonial officials and employers to emasculate and infantilise African men and women.

87 Penny Summerfield, *Histories of the Self: Personal Narratives and Historical Practice* (Abingdon: Routledge, 2019), p. 108.

88 For further discussion of the subjective relationship between interviewer and interviewee, see Lynn Abrams, *Oral History Theory* (New York, NY: Routledge, 2010); Sherna Berger Gluck and Daphne Patai (eds), *Women's Words: The Feminist Practice of Oral History* (New York, NY: Routledge, 1991); Joan Sangster, 'Telling Our Stories: Feminist Debates and the Use of Oral History', *Women's History Review*, 3:1 (1994), 5–28; Valerie Yow, 'Ethics and Interpersonal Relationships in Oral History Research', *Oral History Review*, 22:1 (1995), 51–66.

89 The relationship between oral history, subjectivity, and memory is explored in Alessandro Portelli, *The Death of Luigi Trastulli and Other Stories: Form and Meaning in Oral History* (New York, NY: State University of New York Press, 1991); Luisa Passerini, *Fascism in Popular Memory: The Cultural Experience of the Turin Working Class* (Cambridge: Cambridge University Press, 1987); Paul Thompson, *The Voice of the Past: Oral History* (Oxford: Oxford University Press, 1978); Alistair Thomson, *Anzac Memories: Living with the Legend* (Clayton: Monash University Press, 1994).

90 Other scholars have drawn on their observations of living alongside domestic workers and within servant-employing households. These include Bujra, *Serving Class*, pp. 188–190; Hansen, *Distant Companions*, pp. 7–8, pp. 206–211; and Rollins, *Between Women*, pp. 8–9.

91 There are clear ethical dimensions to consider when using such material. To protect the identities of those I observed and to mitigate against the potential negative impact of being included in this study, all names and locations from this material have been anonymised. The key ethical

issues surrounding forms of indirect observation are summarised in H. Russell Bernard, *Research Methods in Anthropology: Qualitative and Quantitative Approaches* (Oxford: AltaMira Press, 2006), pp. 437–444.

92 Antoinette Burton, *Dwelling in the Archive: Women Writing House, Home, and History in Late Colonial India* (Oxford: Oxford University Press, 2003), p. 144.

93 Danielle Taylor Phillips, 'Moving with the Women: Tracing Racialization, Migration, and Domestic Workers in the Archive', *Signs*, 38:2 (2013), 386.

94 *Ibid.*; Burton, *Dwelling in the Archive*. Other key studies include Natalie Zemon Davies, *Women on the Margins: Three Seventeenth Century Lives* (Cambridge, MA: Harvard University Press, 1997); Marisa J. Fuentes, *Dispossessed Lives: Enslaved Women, Violence and the Archive* (Philadelphia, PA: University of Pennsylvania Press, 2016); Jennifer Morgan, *Laboring Women: Gender and Reproduction in New World Slavery* (Philadelphia, PA: University of Pennsylvania Press, 2004); Camilla Townsend, *Malintzin's Choices: An Indian Woman in the Conquest of Mexico* (Albuquerque, NM: University of New Mexico Press, 2006).

95 Relevant studies include Franco Barchiesi, *Precarious Liberation: Workers, the State, and Contested Social Citizenship in Postapartheid South Africa* (New York, NY: State University of New York Press, 2011); Alex Lichtenstein, 'Challenging "Umthetho We Femu" (the Law of the Firm): Gender Relations and Shop-Floor Battles for Union Recognition in Natal's Textile Industry, 1973–85', *Africa*, 8:1 (2017), 100–119; Blair Rutherford, *Farm Labor Struggles in Zimbabwe: The Ground of Politics* (Bloomington, IN: Indiana University Press, 2016); Fiona White, 'Deepening Democracy: A Farm Workers' Movement in the Western Cape', *Journal of Southern African Studies*, 36:3 (2010), 673–691.

# 1

# Feminising domestic service

Elizabeth Bwalya started working as a maid in Lusaka in 1985 when she was fifteen years old. She had recently moved to the city with her father and siblings from Chilalabombwe on the Copperbelt. Her mother had passed away in the early 1980s, and her father had decided to move the family to Lusaka, where his eldest daughter was already living with her husband. Elizabeth had never attended school, and once settled in Lusaka, she decided to find paid work. Her older sister's husband was a domestic worker for a Black household in the affluent suburb of Roma, and he helped Elizabeth to secure a job in his employer's home. In this role, Elizabeth cared for three children, cleaned the house, and helped prepare meals. She stayed in the job for several years, living with her sister and brother-in-law in the servants' quarters on the property (an example of which can be seen in Figure 1.1).[1] Across the city, Edwin Banda was a domestic worker at a Catholic seminary in Woodlands. Edwin was twenty-five, married, and had three young children. He lived in Mtendere compound in the east of the city and left his home at dawn each day to walk to work, a tiring commute necessitated by inadequate public transport options. Edwin's job involved general cleaning duties and washing clothes. Over the next few years, he held a range of other jobs at the seminary, including as a gardener, a kitchen assistant, and a cook. He stopped working at the seminary in 2012 because his contract was not renewed. By the time he left, all of the indoor domestic service roles at the seminary were held by women.[2]

These snapshots of Elizabeth and Edwin's experiences of working in domestic service provide insights into the focus of this chapter:

**Figure 1.1** Servants' quarters, Kabulonga, Lusaka, 28 January 2014.

how gender and age shaped domestic service practices in southern Africa's urban centres, and how these dynamics shifted over time. Elizabeth's life history was by no means unique, with domestic service providing an important source of urban employment for girls and women, and especially for migrants newly arrived in towns and cities. Edwin's life history is similarly illustrative of broader trends, suggesting how employment opportunities for male domestic workers changed and narrowed over time, not least because of increased competition for domestic service jobs from women and girls.

The chapter shows how the gender and age dynamics of domestic service in Lusaka and other southern African cities were shaped by a combination of historical developments and contemporary pressures. Historically, racialised and gendered colonial models of domestic service had been promoted and adopted in colonial households across the region. In Northern Rhodesia specifically, colonial officials and White settlers promoted a model of domesticity grounded in a gendered separation of spheres and dependent upon the labour of male African domestic workers. A large, waged domestic service sector emerged, which was dominated by African men and boys. Labour relations in African households were influenced by this colonial model of domesticity but also drew on longstanding gendered and gerontocratic hierarchies of kinship and marriage within African societies, and primarily involved the labour of women and children.

Following independence, Lusaka's householders reworked these existing models of domestic service in response to political and social change and the challenges of economic decline. This led to several important shifts in the gender and age dynamics of domestic service. Increasing numbers of women and girls sought and secured employment in waged domestic service. Additionally, kinship-based domestic service practices, and the female labour which underpinned these, came to displace waged forms of domestic service, as employers sought out the cheapest forms of labour available, and women and girls used their kinship networks as sources of employment and a means to migrate to the city. As a result of the increased supply of and demand for women and girls in waged and kin-based employment, male domestic workers like Edwin found their dominant position within domestic service gradually eroded. Overall, this resulted in the feminisation of domestic service in post-colonial Lusaka, and Zambia more broadly – a process which both mirrored and differed from broader gendered transitions in domestic service across twentieth-century southern Africa. In Lusaka, feminisation involved not only an increase in the number and proportion of female workers in domestic service, but the reorganisation of work along gendered lines. Specifically, female workers like Elizabeth became dominant in indoor roles involving cleaning, cooking, and childcare, while male workers like Edwin moved into outdoor roles as gardeners and guards.

The shifting gender and age dynamics of domestic service provide insights into important social, cultural, and structural factors which shape work and labour force participation. Specifically, they allow us to examine how gendered labour market segregation in Zambian and other southern African societies has changed over time; how this was shaped by and influenced social norms surrounding gender and age; and how children, women, and men have been both differentially incorporated into the labour market and reliant upon domestic service as a source of livelihood.

## Models of domestic service in colonial southern Africa

In colonial southern Africa, ideas about who could and should perform domestic labour were grounded in intersecting hierarchies of race, gender, age, and class. In British colonial territories such as Northern Rhodesia, Southern Rhodesia, and South Africa, government officials, missionaries, and settlers promoted and aspired to emulate a model of domesticity which drew on the nineteenth-century domestic ideals of the British middle classes. As Leonore Davidoff and Catherine Hall's pioneering work explored, an ideology of middle-class domesticity developed in Britain over the course of the nineteenth century which emphasised a gendered separation of spheres and differential responsibilities between men and women vis-à-vis domestic and family labour. These ideas associated women with housework, the rearing of children, and the maintenance of domestic harmony.[3] In Britain's African colonies, a model of domestic service was adopted that drew on such ideas, blended them with theories of racial and imperial hierarchy, and posited White women as the managers and guardians of colonial domestic space. White women also bore the main responsibility for the management of domestic workers, who were mostly recruited from colonised African populations.

African domestic workers played a crucial role in helping White women to fulfil their gendered responsibility to maintain clean and 'modern' homes and raise healthy children. These workers performed most physical household labour, including cleaning, washing clothes, ironing, cooking, gardening, and household repairs. The importance of African domestic workers to colonial household management, and colonial economies more broadly, is demonstrated by employment figures. In Northern Rhodesia specifically, the colonial government estimated that around 12,470 African men were employed as domestic workers by 1930, increasing to 20,000 by 1945. This made domestic service the second largest source of urban employment after mining, a situation which persisted into the late 1950s.[4] By the early 1960s, domestic service had become the largest source of urban employment in the protectorate, employing an estimated 27,948 people by 1962.[5]

During the early years of colonial settlement in southern Africa, a preference was established amongst colonial employers for male

African domestic workers. This grew out of the longer history of porterage and personal service in the region. African men secured employment in both sectors from the early years of colonial exploration and settlement in South Africa, and these gendered constructions of labour spread into the rest of the region as British colonialism expanded northwards from the late nineteenth century.[6] Domestic service also developed as a male-dominated occupation under Portuguese colonial rule in Mozambique.[7]

Available employment data, although limited and patchy, clearly illustrates these gender dynamics. In Northern Rhodesia, an estimated 30,000 male and 250 female workers were thought to be employed in domestic service by 1951.[8] By 1957, these figures had increased to an estimated 33,000 male and 800 female domestic workers.[9] On the eve of independence in 1963, male workers remained dominant in domestic service, though overall employment levels in the sector had slightly declined.[10] Male workers' dominance of domestic service declined over time in some parts of colonial southern Africa, particularly where male workers were recruited for employment in the region's expanding mining industries. In South Africa, large numbers of African men and boys left domestic service for work on the mines of the Witwatersrand and domestic service was largely feminised by the interwar period. In Lourenço Marques (now Maputo), high rates of male migration to South Africa's mines during the Second World War similarly contributed to the increased employment of African women in domestic service.[11]

The employment of African men as domestic workers contradicted the ideal gender and generational divisions of labour present in European and in African societies, according to which the performance of domestic labour was predominantly the preserve of women and children. It seems, however, that both colonial employers and male African domestic workers held inconsistent views about gender and domestic labour. Quite simply, domestic labour was perceived to be, in Janet Bujra's words, 'unmanly in the home, but manly if it generates a wage packet'.[12] In the colonial period, the commodification of domestic labour was vital to its valorisation for African men, as was the space in which it occurred, i.e. the European rather than African home. It was also valued because it provided a steady income and, at that time, was an occupation associated with status and respectability for the male domestic workers involved.

The predominance of African men in domestic service in the early colonial period, and later in places including Northern Rhodesia, also resulted from colonial interventions into African gender relations. There were important gendered distinctions in pre-colonial southern African societies, but these were more political than economic. As Elizabeth Schmidt describes, 'men were generally responsible for public governance and lineage and community matters, women had primary responsibility for food preparation and child-rearing. However, both women and men were actively engaged in productive activities outside the household which were crucial to its survival.'[13] Colonial projects across southern Africa sought to restructure these economic relations by designating men as the sole breadwinners and women as responsible for reproductive labour. Crucially, women's unpaid labour reproduced the male labour force and underpinned colonial capitalism and economic power. Missionaries and the wives of colonial civil servants led the charge in reshaping African gender relations along these lines, running mission schools and after-school clubs for male and female children and domestic science training for women and girls. The employment of African women as domestic workers would have undermined these efforts at reshaping African gender relations, because it would have reduced women's ability to perform reproductive labour in their own homes.

Colonial views on race and sexuality also shaped European employers' preferences. From Northern Rhodesia to Mozambique, there were anxieties around the sexuality of African women, with many European women reluctant to employ African women in their homes because they feared that they might engage in sexual relationships with their husbands and other male household members. These fears were rooted partly in racist stereotypes about African women's sexuality, and partly in colonial scandals surrounding European men engaging in sexual relationships and, in some cases, cohabiting with African women. The latter was most common in the early decades of colonial rule and declined from the interwar period when increasing numbers of European women accompanied their husbands to African colonies.[14] These sexual anxieties centring on African women continued to shape European employers' preferences throughout the colonial period and, as will be explored later, also influenced Black employers' preferences in independent

Zambia and Zimbabwe. In South Africa, anxieties around the sexuality of African men were more prominent. Specifically, fears around 'Black peril', i.e. African men sexually assaulting European women, contributed to the gradual replacement of African men by African women in domestic service early in the twentieth century.[15] 'Black peril' hysteria also occurred in Southern Rhodesia during the early twentieth century and through the 1930s, and this contributed to the increased employment of African women in domestic service despite the prevalence of anxieties around female sexuality.[16] While fears around African men's sexuality were not uncommon in Northern Rhodesia, far more anxiety was generated by the sexuality of African women. This likely resulted in large part from demographics: European settlement was lower in Northern Rhodesia than in other colonies in the region, and far fewer European women were present and in need of 'protection' from African male domestic workers. Similarly, in Mozambique, anxieties around African women's sexuality contributed to the low rate of employment of women domestic workers throughout the colonial period. The only female-dominated part of the domestic service sector was laundry work, and it is notable that this work was done outside the home and so involved less close contact with employers.[17]

The predominance of African men in domestic service in Northern Rhodesia and elsewhere was not only the result of colonial inclinations. The differential availability of African men and women for employment outside their own household played a significant role in shaping who entered the labour market. As suggested above, African rural households were based on a complementary gender division of labour, with women bearing the main responsibility for domestic and care labour and food crop production, supported by their own children and dependants. The migrant labour system established in southern Africa under colonial rule further increased pressures on African women. As Deborah Bryceson suggests, 'African rural women were left with a staggering share of housework, basic needs provisioning and childcare, while European urban women, with hired male domestic labour support at their disposal and children often away at boarding school, were often entirely free from household drudgery.'[18] Because of their myriad, and often increasing, responsibilities, African women were thus largely unavailable for employment in domestic service or other sectors. Many also likely rejected the idea of leaving their own house and family to care for someone else's, especially under the strict supervision of a colonial housewife.

African women and their families also appear to have viewed domestic service as an unsuitable employment option for women because of the dangers posed by living away from their families, particularly in urban areas. Existing studies of Northern Rhodesia, Southern Rhodesia, and South Africa reveal how African fathers and male guardians, and some younger men, feared that their female relatives might engage in sexual activity and other immoral activities if employed as domestic workers in urban areas, and ruin their prospects for marriage, motherhood, and respectability. African men also worried, with justification, that their female relatives would be vulnerable to sexual assault while working in domestic service.[19] In Northern Rhodesia, the challenges of recruiting African women for domestic service came to the fore in the African Womanpower campaign of the late 1940s, when colonial officials tried to get urban women to enter domestic service to free up male domestic workers for employment elsewhere, especially for farming. The campaign met with little success and was scrapped by the late 1950s, when Northern Rhodesia's economy entered a slump and male unemployment increased.[20]

Labour relations in African households were influenced by colonial constructions of domesticity and gender, and by longstanding gendered and gerontocratic hierarchies of marriage and kinship. Most African households relied primarily on the labour of wives and children, with many also utilising the labour of extended family members. In extended family systems in southern Africa, children have often been seen as the responsibility of the whole family rather than the natal family alone. As such, care of children, and the labour children can provide, has often been shared between households. Moreover, children and other junior members within the kinship structure, such as unmarried women, have often been obliged to provide labour services to seniors, including in the form of domestic labour. Bryceson insightfully categorises such kin-based domestic labour practices as 'voluntary kin labour exchange', drawing attention to the voluntary nature of such relationships and their roots in kinship networks.[21] Across colonial southern Africa, increasing numbers of women and girls migrated to urban centres following the Second World War, and many secured a place for themselves in towns and cities by engaging in kin-based domestic labour practices.[22] Children also provided labour within and outside formal kinship networks as part of fostering arrangements. Such practices involved an explicit, though not permanent, exchange of parental rights and duties, and were initiated by the biological parents or guardians of the child concerned or by a prospective foster parent. In such arrangements, foster parents were responsible for providing for the child with a home, food, and security, and took on certain parental rights, such as the right to command the child's labour.

A minority of African households also employed waged domestic workers. These practices often involved children. Godfrey Wilson observed that African mineworkers employed migrant children as domestic workers in Broken Hill (Kabwe) during the late 1930s. Some of these children lived with their families in the town and sold domestic labour to help support the family economy, while others came to town without their parents, often accompanying a young male member of their extended family network and finding employment as domestic workers once they arrived.[23] Hansen's research similarly suggests that the employment of child domestic workers in Northern Rhodesia was common in urban African households and amongst single male migrant workers.[24] Similar practices emerged in the mine compounds of Southern Rhodesia, where male children were employed by African and European mineworkers and there were also efforts to recruit female children into domestic service in mining areas.[25]

Women also played an important role in providing domestic labour to African urban households. George Chauncey showed how women performed sexual and domestic labour in mining compounds on the Copperbelt.[26] Chauncey's findings are echoed in Luise White's study of sexual labour in colonial Nairobi, which examined the overlap between the sexual and domestic services that African women provided to African men, and highlighted how prostitutes' many labours reproduced the urban labour force.[27] While Wilson observed that women in Broken Hill exchanged domestic and sexual labour for access to cash and resources and varying degrees of security and companionship, he did not characterise this as productive labour and arguably underestimated the importance of the services that these women provided within the urban economy.[28]

Colonial government records from Northern Rhodesia have little to say about domestic service practices in African households, but colonial officials knew that Africans employed domestic workers. This is demonstrated by several brief but revealing comments found in archival documents. In Labour Department documents from early 1950, for instance, labour officers discussed African employment of domestic workers in relation to the introduction of legislation to regulate the employment of women and young persons, noting that 'very large numbers of Africans themselves employ youngsters as domestic workers'.[29] Despite such knowledge, labour officers in Northern Rhodesia did not collect data on domestic service arrangements in African households, nor did they count such arrangements as part of official employment figures. The exclusion of African domestic service practices from official labour statistics likely resulted from several factors. Because domestic service arrangements in African households often involved children and kin, they were arguably more difficult to recognise and record than was wage labour in European households. It is also possible that colonial labour officials, whose work focused on recording and regulating relations between coloniser and colonised, did not consider labour relations between African employers and African domestic workers to be important enough to be worth counting.

Regardless of the lack of official data, the occasional insights into domestic service practices in African households that are provided by colonial government documents, ethnography, and existing secondary literature illustrate the importance of women and children's labour and of kin-based labour relations. These findings not only provide a window onto African urban housekeeping practices and labour relations, they also challenge the focus on adult male domestic workers and wage labour that dominates the existing scholarship on domestic service in colonial southern Africa. Domestic service may have been a 'man's job' in European households, but this was not the case in African households. As has been shown, African householders engaged in a broad spectrum of kin-based and waged domestic service arrangements which largely involved women and children's labour. These findings also provide insights into the gradual reconfiguration and commodification of kinship-based labour relations, as single male migrant workers and other urban householders sourced labour via kinship networks and increasingly paid for these services in cash and in kind. This commodification of kin-based domestic labour accelerated after independence.

## The feminisation of domestic service in post-colonial Lusaka

Following decolonisation and the end of apartheid, southern Africans were faced with new political realities and changing social and economic pressures. The gender and age dynamics of domestic service gradually shifted as workers and employers responded to these changing circumstances and sought ways to secure employment and maintain their households. In Lusaka, a diverse range of domestic service practices were pursued, and these provided more employment opportunities for women and girls than in the colonial period. The models of domestic service which existed in the colonial period persisted but were reworked in response to economic decline and changing gender relations. Increasing numbers of female workers sought and secured waged domestic employment, and kinship-based domestic service practices, which had long predominantly involved women and children's labour, increased in prevalence, as employers sought out the cheapest sources of labour and workers looked for the support and patronage of senior kin. Combined, these drove the feminisation of domestic service in Lusaka and across Zambia's urban centres.

### *Gender, age, and the search for employment*

During the early years of independence in Zambia, waged domestic service continued to be male-dominated, but the number of women and girls employed in the sector increased. Official labour statistics estimated that there were 26,800 male domestic workers and 700 female domestic workers by the time of independence in 1964. The number of women and girls in waged domestic service increased by 113 per cent by 1966, and a further 17 per cent by 1968. By comparison, the number of male workers employed in waged domestic service increased at the lower rates of 16 per cent by 1966 and a further 16 per cent by 1968.[30] Caution is needed when interpreting these figures, because they only provided estimations of persons employed in the sector and excluded those aged below fifteen years.

Nonetheless, these figures clearly suggest that increasing numbers of women and girls were entering waged domestic service in the 1960s, and at a higher rate than were men and boys. Moreover, they suggest that domestic service became an increasingly important source of waged employment for female workers. Indeed, by 1966, more women and girls were estimated to be employed in domestic service than in any other occupation.[31] These shifts reflected broader regional trends, with domestic service becoming the most important source of waged employment for women in many places. This trend was starkest in South Africa, where domestic service had become an overwhelmingly female occupation by 1970, when approximately 89 per cent of domestic workers were female.[32]

The gender and age dynamics of domestic service during the 1960s mirrored broader employment patterns in Zambia. Although Zambia's post-independence boom had fostered the creation of new opportunities for education and employment, enduring gendered and generational inequalities ensured that these were primarily open to men and boys. Just over 56 per cent of all African men and boys aged fifteen and over were recorded as working in the 1969 census. This was much higher in urban areas such as Lusaka, where nearly three-quarters of male urban residents were recorded as working.[33] For comparison, just over 12 per cent of African women and girls aged fifteen and over were classified as working, with only slight disparities between rural and urban areas.[34] Just as the employment statistics for domestic service need to be treated with caution, so too does overall employment data. In this case, early Zambian census data was based on narrow conceptualisations of economic activity which excluded much of the labour done by women and girls, including domestic and care labour. This resulted in a skewed perception of male and female participation in the labour force, and an underestimation of female economic activity.[35]

During the 1970s, the number of women and girls recorded as working in Zambia increased further. Over 37 per cent of women and girls aged twelve and older were considered 'economically active' in the 1980 census.[36] Although this figure was based on a wider age cohort than was used in the 1969 census, this change alone does not explain the increase, and it is more likely that there had been a marked rise in the number of women and girls in the labour force. As during the 1960s, female labour force participation remained slightly higher in rural areas, compared with urban areas.[37] For comparison, the number of men and boys recorded as working had increased to over 72 per cent, and had reached near parity in urban and rural areas.[38] These figures suggest that while there were continued gendered disparities in employment during the 1970s, significant numbers of women and girls had entered the labour force in this period, and the gap between male and female employment levels had slightly narrowed since independence.

Frustratingly, it is difficult to trace with any certainty how these changing gendered and generational employment patterns related to domestic service. Official statistics for domestic service in Zambia are limited beyond 1970 because the government stopped including the sector in its labour reports and published employment statistics. Some insight into the numbers of people employed in domestic service in the 1970s is available from the Zambia National Provident Fund (ZNPF), a national insurance scheme for Zambian workers. A total of 36,115 domestic workers were registered with the scheme in 1979, increasing to 49,286 in 1985, and to 55,486 in 1990.[39] These figures were the result of both the voluntary submission of records by employers of domestic workers and a registration campaign that was carried out by ZNPF and students from the University of Zambia in 1984 and 1986. These figures provide some insights into the size and demographic composition of the sector in the 1970s and 1980s, but they do not provide a breakdown by sex or age. They also do not capture those workers who were not registered for ZNPF coverage, and, given the prevalence of kin-based domestic service practices in many Black households, it is likely that only a minority of employers registered their workers.

Oral histories allow us to go beyond these limited statistics and gain insights into female domestic workers' experiences of securing employment in domestic service during the early post-independence years. Mariana Banda was born in Kitwe on the Copperbelt in 1944, and she migrated to Lusaka with her husband and children in 1964. During an interview in 2013, she explained that she and her husband had hoped that independence would bring great opportunities, and that this had prompted their move to the capital. Once they arrived in Lusaka, however, they had struggled to make ends meet. The family settled in Bauleni and initially made a living by collecting and selling firewood. In 1969, she decided to look for better-paid work, and she found a job as maid in a Black household in the nearby suburb of Woodlands. She stayed in this job for the next eighteen years, commuting daily from her family home in Bauleni and using her wages to support her husband and children. She also continued to collect firewood for extra income.[40] Justina Banda was born in 1940 in Chipata in Zambia's Eastern Province. She migrated with her husband to Ndola on the Copperbelt in 1958, before moving again to Lusaka in 1960. She described being a housewife and mother from the time of her marriage until 1975, when she sought work in domestic service. Like Mariana, Justina explained during our interview that she had become a domestic worker in order to support her family. She worked in a series of waged domestic service jobs for the next ten years, commuting to work by bicycle from her home in Bauleni.[41]

During the 1980s, women and girls across southern Africa responded to the region's growing economic crisis by entering the labour force in unprecedented numbers. Many sought and secured work in domestic service. According to Hansen's research, there were at least 100,000 domestic workers in Zambia during the mid-1980s, and around 25 per cent of those workers were female.[42] These figures suggest that although domestic service in Zambia continued to be male-dominated during the 1980s, there had been a significant increase in the number and proportion of female workers in the sector since independence. The increase in female domestic workers was even more rapid elsewhere in southern Africa. In Mozambique, war and economic disaster meant that there were few opportunities for expanding waged employment. Increasing numbers of female jobseekers gravitated towards domestic service and came to dominate the sector as men pursued alternative employment and a new class of Mozambican employers emerged and sought female domestic workers, though men and boys continued to be employed in significant numbers.[43] In Zimbabwe too, women and girls came to outnumber men in all forms of domestic service during the 1980s.[44] It is highly likely that the number of women and girls in domestic service in Zambia during the 1980s was higher than Hansen suggested, and more in line with developments in Zimbabwe. Hansen herself described her figures as 'conservative'.[45] Crucially, her research focused on waged domestic service practices in middle- and high-income households and excluded poor households and arrangements which involved children and young people providing labour in exchange for their place in the household. These exclusions likely resulted in an underestimation of both the number and proportion of women and children of both sexes employed in domestic service in Zambia in the 1980s.

Oral histories provide invaluable insights into women and girls' experiences of finding employment in waged and kin-based domestic service during the 1980s. We have already seen how Elizabeth Bwalya found a job as a domestic worker in Lusaka in 1985 when she was fifteen years old, using her family connections to find and secure employment and housing. Like Elizabeth, Dorothy Phiri also became a waged domestic worker as a girl during the 1980s. She was born and raised in Lusaka and completed primary education and some secondary schooling in the city. She sought employment as a domestic worker after finishing school and spending several years helping her mother with her vending business. Dorothy found work as a maid in the home of a White Zambian couple, and she stayed in this role for several years.[46] Esther Banda became a maid in 1981 when she was eleven years old. Unlike Elizabeth and Dorothy, she was recruited into domestic service through her kinship network. She was born and raised in Chipata and was asked by a female relative to leave her parents' home and move to Lusaka to live with a senior kinswoman. In this arrangement, Esther cared for her kinswoman's children and did some household labour, in exchange for which she received accommodation, meals, clothes, and a small cash wage which was sent to her parents. She stayed in this role for four years, before returning to her parents' home in 1985.[47]

The increase in female employment in waged and kin-based domestic service during the 1980s mirrored broader trends in employment patterns and gender dynamics within the labour force. The total number of employed persons in Zambia almost doubled during the 1980s, and this had striking gender dynamics. The female employed population increased by 155 per cent between 1980 and 1990, while the male employed population increased at the lower rate of 64 per cent.[48] This disparity resulted partly from the fact that more men and boys were already employed. It also reflected better enumeration of female economic activities, with census officials more sensitive than in earlier periods to the labour in which women and girls engaged and more open to including this in their calculations. Perhaps most significant, though, was that women and girls were seeking employment in unprecedented numbers because the full impacts of Zambia's economic decline began to be felt during the 1980s. Growing numbers of women and children sought ways to earn money as the economy contracted and many men lost their jobs and were unable to fulfil their gendered economic roles as breadwinners. These challenges also explain the continued high rate of male employment in waged domestic service during the 1980s. As Hansen has observed, as male workers faced declining employment opportunities, many men and boys tried to hold onto domestic service jobs for as long as possible.[49] A similar phenomenon has been observed in post-colonial Tanzania, where Bujra found that men were reliant on domestic service in the face of limited and declining alternative sources of employment.[50]

The number and proportion of women and girls in the labour force in Zambia continued to increase during the 1990s, as structural adjustment hit the economy and the social breakdown caused by the HIV/AIDS pandemic intensified. The female employed population grew by a further 53 per cent during the decade. This increase was higher in rural areas than urban areas, not least because of increased migration to rural areas in response to sustained urban economic decline.[51] By comparison, the male employed population increased at a slower pace, in both rural and urban areas.[52] These trends continued during the 2000s, and the gender employment gap narrowed further. By 2010, 46 per cent of women and girls were recorded as working, compared with 65 per cent of men and boys. Female employment remained higher in rural compared with urban areas, while male employment remained fairly balanced.[53] These figures reflected the continued high labour burden facing rural women and girls, who shouldered responsibility for both agricultural and domestic labour.

As for the 1970s, it is difficult to trace with any precision how the broad shifts in gendered employment patterns during the 1990s and 2000s impacted domestic service, because of limited available data. But oral histories provide useful insights into the varied experiences of female domestic workers during this time. Like many women and girls before her, Imelda Kalobwe migrated from the countryside to Lusaka to become a domestic worker. She was born in Chimusanya village in Lusaka Province in 1978 and moved to

Lusaka in 1996 to take up a job as a live-in maid for a Black household in the middle-class suburb of Avondale. She secured this job through a friend who was already working as a maid in the city.[54] Grace Mwale was born in Lusaka and grew up in Bauleni. She started working as a maid in 1997, when she was fifteen years old, a decision she described as being prompted by her family's poverty. After a series of live-in domestic service jobs in different neighbourhoods in Lusaka, she found work as a live-out maid in the suburb of Chilenje. During our interview, she explained that she preferred living out because it meant that she could continue living with her family in Bauleni.[55]

A marked increase in the number and proportion of women and girls employed in domestic service in Zambia occurred by the 2010s. This is illustrated by data collected by the ILO, which conducted two surveys in 2013 to develop an understanding of the demographic profile of domestic workers and employers in Zambia.[56] These surveys suggested that an estimated 97,652 people were employed in domestic service, of whom 56 per cent were female workers and 44 per cent were male workers. The surveys also highlighted the prevalence of young workers in domestic service, with 15 per cent of female domestic workers and 11 per cent of male domestic workers surveyed aged between ten and nineteen years.[57] By considering both adults and children, these surveys provided useful insights into the full spectrum of persons employed in domestic service in Zambia during the 2010s. It is difficult to gather data on child domestic workers and kin-based domestic service practices, in part because these practices are often not considered to be 'work' by those involved. Therefore, although these surveys clearly suggested that domestic service had become female-dominated in Zambia by the 2010s, they still likely underestimated the total number of women and girls, and overall persons, employed in the sector.

The gradual feminisation of domestic service in post-colonial Zambia reflected broader trends across the African continent, with domestic service transformed into a female-dominated occupation during the twentieth century. This shift occurred unevenly over time and space, but women and girls comprised approximately 70 per cent of Africa's domestic workers by the 2010s. The feminisation of domestic service was even higher in certain cases. In South Africa, over three-quarters of domestic workers were female, and domestic service was the third largest employer of women. In Mozambique, over 85 per cent of domestic workers were women.[58] And in Ethiopia, 91 per cent of domestic workers were female, and domestic service was the fourth largest employer of women.[59] The feminisation of domestic service was clear amongst children, with girls comprising nine out of ten child domestic workers in Africa by the 2010s.[60] Alongside the broader trend of feminisation, there were also distinctions between cases. In Zambia specifically, men continued to hold onto domestic service jobs into the 2010s at a much higher proportion than in most other African countries, largely because of limited employment alternatives. Overall, though, Zambia's male domestic workers clearly struggled in the face of increased competition from women and girls, and found their opportunities in the sector narrowing over time.

## *Employers and the demand for domestic workers*

The changing gender and age composition of domestic service in Lusaka resulted also from shifting race and class dynamics within the sector and wider society. Between the 1960s and 1980s, Black households overtook White households as the most numerous employers of domestic workers.[61] Throughout this period, domestic workers were employed in a growing number of Black households across class groups, with wealthy and less affluent households employing others to perform domestic labour and childcare in their homes. The expansion in the number of Black households employing domestic workers mirrored broader developments across post-colonial Africa's urban centres. For instance, the number and range of Black urban households employing domestic workers increased in Zimbabwe during the 1980s and in Namibia during the 1990s.[62] In East Africa, too, domestic service expanded in Black households in Tanzania following independence, despite the government's professed commitment to egalitarianism and socialism.[63] Though each of these cases has its own specific history, domestic service was in each case part of broader class projects, with elite, middle-class and even poor Africans using their relative wealth to buy their way out of performing domestic labour and to exploit the labour power of those of lesser means.

The types of domestic service which were practised in Lusaka's Black households varied across the socio-economic spectrum. Unsurprisingly, a household's financial situation significantly determined the types of domestic service which were accessible. Waged domestic service practices were generally more expensive than kin-based labour, and were most common amongst middle-class and wealthy Black households. As explored above, waged domestic service was dominated by men during the early post-independence years, but increasing numbers of women and children secured employment in the sector over time, in part because women and child domestic workers generally received lower wages than adult men and so were more affordable to employ. Despite this shift, poverty prevented most households in Lusaka from hiring waged domestic workers in any form. This became the reality for a widening spectrum of urban residents from the late 1970s as the economy declined and increasing numbers of households struggled to make ends meet. The unaffordability of waged domestic service did not limit demand for domestic workers, however, in large part because of the time-consuming and labour-intensive nature of domestic labour. This resulted from a combination of poor living conditions for the majority, including limited access to running water and electricity, and the widespread absence or unaffordability of labour-saving devices.

Kin-based domestic service was the most affordable and accessible option for Black households in Lusaka, and enabled many households to fulfil their labour needs. These practices built on the longstanding practices of sourcing labour from within the extended family system described above, and continued to be shaped by gendered and gerontocratic hierarchies. The typical practice amongst Lusaka's residents was to bring a girl from their family's home area to live with them in the city to help with domestic labour and childcare. This pattern was replicated across the region and Africa more broadly, from Harare to Windhoek, Abidjan to Accra. As Catherine Coquery-Vidrovitch notes, 'everywhere that segregation did not prevent it, urban families … became the place little sisters and other poor female relatives went in the hope of a basic education in the city'.[64] Coquery-Vidrovitch's comments highlight the prevalence of women and girls in kin-based domestic service, and the enduring power of gendered constructions of labour which linked femininity with the performance of such labour.

Kin-based domestic service practices did not remain static over time. In cities across post-colonial Africa, urban residents reworked kin-based labour relations as part of broader responses to economic decline and changing social and gender relations. Crucially, the commodification of kinship-based domestic labour practices accelerated, as certain employers exploited their kinship networks as sources of cheap and vulnerable workers. Women and children were certainly vulnerable to exploitation. As Bryceson describes,

> in some cases, the nature of child and female domestic service has reverted to the earlier reviled pattern of master–slave relations. With the intervention of domestic labour recruiters or the subversion of traditional kin labour exchange obligations, labour forms have arisen to facilitate and cheapen the costs of domestic workers for the expanding urban middle class.[65]

In other cases, kin-based labour relations continued to involve a mutually beneficial exchange, with employers finding affordable and reliable sources of labour from within their own families, and workers securing the support of their seniors and access to much-needed resources. My own findings suggest that kin-based domestic service practices often fell between these two positions, with domestic workers often securing some support from senior kin whilst simultaneously enduring forms of exploitation.[66]

As the above discussion suggests, employers' demands for domestic workers were clearly gendered. As in the colonial period, domestic service practices after independence were shaped by unequal gender and generational divisions of labour within households and kinship networks, and inequitable labour burdens facing African women. In Zambia specifically, enduring social norms present across ethnic groups associated women with the performance of domestic labour and childcare in their own homes. Christian social norms, promoted under colonial rule and post-independence, also linked femininity with motherhood, marriage, and domesticity.[67] These gendered norms put great pressure on women and girls to fulfil gender-defined social and cultural roles, and to perform domestic and care labour in their own homes and for senior kin. The developmental cycle of the household also impacted women and girls' roles and responsibilities. Infants and sick relatives required care, and older children were generally expected to help their mothers with domestic chores and caring for others. These generational dynamics also shaped women and girls' ability to engage in paid work beyond the home. Younger women were more likely to have young children, be less able to engage in the labour force unless they had childcare, and therefore be more economically dependent upon men. By comparison, many older women were less dependent upon men and had more options to earn their own money.

Despite enduring social norms and the heavy domestic labour burden facing women and girls, as shown above, female labour force participation did increase steadily following independence. Working women and girls had restricted time to perform domestic and care labour, but this labour had to be done. To help them manage their often increasing labour burdens, many working women recruited domestic workers. Female labour was at the centre of women's housekeeping and childcare strategies, reflecting not only the increased availability and relative cheapness of women and girls' labour, but also women employers' preferences for engaging the labour of female kin. Shifting preferences amongst Zambian employers appear to mirror broader trends within the region. In Mozambique, for example, by 2010 around three-quarters of employers preferred to hire female domestic workers, a significant shift from employer preferences during the 1980s.[68]

Employers' preferences were also shaped by their understandings of and prejudices around sexuality. Hansen observed high levels of sexual anxiety in interviews with Black female employers in Lusaka during the early 1980s, with many women fearful that sexual relationships might occur between female domestic workers and male household members. Some of Hansen's interviewees chose to employ male domestic workers because of such anxieties.[69] Pape observed a similar phenomenon amongst Black female employers in Harare in the 1980s.[70] Sexual anxieties were also a prominent theme in my interviews with Black employers, with several interviewees recounting stories of sexual relationships occurring between female domestic workers and male employers. For instance, Chombe Nachula described how her mother had once discovered a young female maid sprinkling a 'love potion' into Chombe's father's meals to 'entice him' into a relationship. Chombe stated that the maid in question had denied the accusation, but that her mother was sure of her guilt and had dismissed her on the spot. Chombe's mother subsequently only employed women over the age of fifty as domestic workers because she thought that older women would pose less of a threat to her marriage. Chombe explained that she was influenced by her mother's experiences, and also only employed older women as domestic workers.[71]

Chombe's testimony is suggestive of the ways in which sexual anxieties shaped employers' preferences post-independence in ways similar to and distinct from the colonial period. On the one hand, Chombe's and her mother's approach to female domestic workers seems to show the enduring power of colonial discourses on African women's sexuality discussed above. But on the other hand, their approaches also resulted from gendered tensions within Zambian society, with many women unable to command their partners' fidelity and anxious about the social and economic ramifications of broken marriages and relationships.[72] They also show how gender and age dynamics within domestic service shifted over time. In the colonial period, sexual anxieties prevented many European women from employing female African domestic workers in their homes. After independence, Black female employers, including Chombe and her mother, employed female domestic workers in spite of such anxieties. For many female employers, this was out of necessity, with women and girls the only domestic workers they could afford to employ. Some women, like Chombe and her mother, hired older women who they perceived to no longer pose a sexual threat. Others hired pre-pubescent girls for similar reasons, in those cases because they perceived girls' sexual immaturity to make them safer to employ and more likely to be innocent and pliable employees.[73]

## The gendered reorganisation of domestic service

The feminisation of domestic service also involved the reorganisation of work along gendered lines. As has been shown, men and boys continued to be employed in domestic service in significant numbers into the 2010s. But they became concentrated in outdoor domestic service roles as gardeners and guards, while women and girls came to dominate indoor roles involving cleaning, cooking, and childcare. This reorganisation of work impacted domestic workers in complex and contradictory ways and presented male and female workers with both opportunities and challenges.

For female domestic workers in indoor roles, close proximity to their employers could lead to the development of intimate and positive relationships. These could bring concrete material benefits such as preferential access to food and in-kind payments. For instance, Imelda described the positive relationship she had with her first employers and how they had invited her to share meals with them.[74] Mary Chirwa, who started working in domestic service in the late 1990s when she was in her late twenties, had a similar experience with several of her employers. She also noted that employers often only provided food for their maids and not for their gardeners and guards.[75] Such hierarchies of access to food and other in-kind payments amongst domestic workers built on longer precedents of occupational prestige within domestic service. During the colonial period, it was common for domestic service positions to be hierarchically organised, with cooks at the top of the hierarchy and gardeners at the bottom. This had a clear spatial dimension, with the kitchen the most prestigious area of employment, followed by other areas inside the house, and finally by the outside spaces.[76] Gendered transitions in domestic service following independence involved a reworking of these older hierarchies and seem to have had a more negative impact on men and boys, who were pushed out of the house and into outdoor roles.

Proximity to employers could also present female domestic workers with challenges. It meant that their work and activities could be subject to close inspection and control by their employers. Elizabeth described how the children of her first employer had followed her around while she worked, closely watching her. She explained how this had made her feel uncomfortable because she constantly worried that the children would tell her employer that she had done something wrong. In Elizabeth's next job, her employers had strict rules about which areas of the house she could access and which facilities she could use. For instance, she was not allowed to use her employers' indoor bathroom, and she had to use a plastic plate for her meals rather than her employers' china. When asked why she thought her employers treated her this way, she sighed and stated, 'they don't consider you to be a human being, so they treat you how they like'.[77] Elizabeth's comments must be interpreted against the background of economic inequality that worsened in Lusaka in the decades following independence, with middle-class and wealthy Zambians increasingly socially and economically distanced from poor urban residents such as domestic workers, and seemingly keen to maintain such divides.

Some female domestic workers also experienced abuse within the confines of their employers' homes. Verbal abuse was common, including employers' use of disrespectful language towards their employees, shouting, and making verbal threats. Imelda described being verbally abused by her employer's teenage son: 'he was very naughty … he liked shouting at me, shouting instructions'.[78] Physical abuse was less commonly described by my interviewees, though several women described being slapped by female employers. Some female domestic workers also described experiencing sexual harassment from male employers and household members. Veronica Banda described the challenges she faced while working as maid during the early 1990s in a house inhabited by six young men. The young men would regularly 'propose love' to her, to which she would respond, 'I am here for work'. She described having to be 'on guard' while at work, though she was never physically threatened.[79] At the time of our interview in 2014, Elizabeth feared that her boss was trying to start a sexual relationship with her. She described how he would approach her when his wife was out of the house and how she tried to avoid meeting or talking with him. These issues had caused problems for Elizabeth at work and at home. Elizabeth's husband disliked that she felt unsafe at work and that another man was harassing his wife, but Elizabeth refused to quit because she worried about losing the income.[80] The vulnerability of female domestic workers to forms of abuse has been observed across the continent, from Guinea to Kenya to Zimbabwe.[81] In those contexts, as in Zambia, female domestic workers' vulnerability resulted from a combination of their proximity to employers, unequal power relations, and the private nature of the spaces in which they worked. These incidents often also resulted from endemic gender inequality and high levels of gender-based violence across post-colonial southern Africa and the broader continent.[82]

Although men and boys experienced a gradual narrowing of employment opportunities in domestic service over time, some found new opportunities in outdoor roles. The clearest expansion of employment occurred in the private security industry. From the 1980s, growing fears of violent crime and robberies amongst Zambian's urban population led to a rapid expansion in the employment of security guards in private homes and businesses. This reflected broader trends across southern Africa's urban centres, with private security one of the fastest growing industries in the region from the late twentieth century onwards. The industry grew most rapidly in post-apartheid South Africa, where intense anxieties around crime and violence drove urban residents to pursue whatever strategies they could afford to protect their homes, from employing guards to building high perimeter walls and installing electric fences, razor wire, and panic buttons.[83]

As in South Africa's urban centres, private security companies provided new sources of employment for men in Lusaka. Evaristo Mubanga started work as a guard in Lusaka in 1994. He was born and raised in a village in Luapula Province and migrated to the city in 1990. When he first arrived in the city, he found work as a gardener. After several years he sought a better-paid position and found a job with the private security company, G4S, for whom he worked for thirteen years before retiring in 2007.[84] Other men found employment as guards working directly for a household. Andrew Banda's experience is illustrative. He became a guard in 2012. He had previously worked as a teacher at a community school in Central Province, a job which he had enjoyed but for which he received a small salary that was often paid late. He moved to Lusaka in 2012 in search of a better job and moved in with an aunt who worked as a maid. She helped him to secure a job as a security guard in Kabulonga, an affluent suburb in the east of the city. During our interview, Andrew explained that he was still not content with the wages he received, but he liked that he was always paid on time because this allowed him to contribute to his aunt's household bills and to make plans for the future.[85]

Because gardening and security work were based mainly outside the physical confines of the household, they generally involved less close contact with and supervision by employers, and could offer more freedom and privacy than indoor roles. Howard Phiri started working as a gardener in 2008 when he was thirty-three years old. At the time of our interview in 2014, he worked as a gardener in Kabulonga. He explained that he liked that he was not directly supervised by his employer, because he could work at his own pace and take regular breaks.[86] Such freedoms had to be weighed against the drawbacks of outdoor work, however, such as fewer opportunities to develop close relationships with employers and more limited access to in-kind payments. Paul Chipeta, who worked as a guard in Kabulonga when we met in 2014, complained that his employers did not provide him with the same in-kind payments, such as meals, as their maid. He explained that this was a common challenge for guards who were employed by management companies of housing developments, because individual householders were not directly responsible for their guards' wages or well-being.[87]

Outdoor workers also faced significant dangers in the workplace, though of a different kind to indoor workers. Several of the guards that I interviewed feared the violence that might ensue if they had to face burglars or other criminals. Andrew described how this threat significantly increased after dark, with visitors arriving late into the night at the housing development on which he worked. He explained that he was sometimes unsure if visitors were genuine or if they were criminals on the lookout for opportunities to break into one of the houses. When burglaries did occur, guards were questioned by the police and sometimes detained for several days at the police station, where they might face violence from other prisoners.[88] The dangers facing guards received attention in the Zambian press during the 2010s, with some calling for guards to receive more training and to carry weapons so that they could protect themselves.[89] The threat of violence against guards also took forms which were less publicly acknowledged, with some guards facing violence at the hands of their employers. As Teophilous Mufonko explained, 'some clients beat their guards, even for opening the gate late'.[90] This reflected the broader undercurrent of employer-employee violence which was also referred to by my female interviewees.

## Conclusion

The findings presented in this chapter challenge existing scholarship on domestic service in Zambia which asserted that female workers supplemented rather than replaced male workers following independence.[91] They show that employers sought out female domestic workers on their own terms, and that women and girls both pursued employment in domestic service and came to dominate kin-based and waged practices. By contrast, male workers' dominant position in domestic service was gradually eroded by the increased supply of and demand for women and girls' labour. By drawing comparisons between these processes and developments in other southern African contexts, the chapter revealed broader insights into the nature of gendered labour market segregation across the region. Specifically, it showed how the feminisation of domestic service in Zambia mirrored and also differed from broader gendered transitions in domestic service practices across Africa during the twentieth century. Domestic service was transformed into a predominantly female occupation across the region in this period, but this gendered shift occurred at different times in different contexts because of specific, and at times divergent, political, economic, and cultural conditions. These included the level of demand for male workers in industry and in large-scale and commercial farming, and the extent of White settlement and the virulence of racialised constructions of labour and sexuality.

The chapter also highlighted the difficulty of counting domestic workers and of tracing gender and age dynamics within domestic service because of the limitations or absence of available data. This was and remains a problem, not only in Zambia but across the African continent. As Bryceson notes, 'the full count of formally and informally employed domestic workers in Africa, encompassing "house girls", "maids", "houseboys", gardeners and security guards, is impossible to know … It is safe to assume that millions of domestic workers have been excluded from labour surveys given the often-invisible nature of their work.'[92] As my findings suggest, women and girl domestic workers were even more likely than men and boy domestic workers to be excluded from labour surveys and other data because of enduring gender and age biases in labour categories and their prevalence in less visible employment practices, including kin-based domestic service and forms of child employment. The consequences for academic research and policymaking of women and girl domestic workers' relative absence from statistical data are significant. It results in misunderstandings not only of domestic service – one of the largest sectors of urban employment across Africa since the early twentieth century – but of how women and children have participated in and contributed to household and broader economies across the continent.

## Notes

1 Interview with Elizabeth Bwalya, Lusaka, 13 February 2014.
2 Interview with Edwin Banda, Lusaka, 30 January 2014.
3 Leonora Davidoff and Catherine Hall, *Family Fortunes: Men and Women of the English Middle Class, 1780–1850* (Chicago, IL: University of Chicago Press, 1987), pp. 25–27, p. 30.
4 Oxford University Bodleian Library Special Collections (hereafter BL), RHO 756.1 s. 2, Northern Rhodesia, Blue Book for the Year Ended 31 December 1930 (Livingstone: Government Printer, 1931); BL, RHO 756.1 s. 2, Northern Rhodesia, Blue Book for the Year Ended 31 December 1945 (Lusaka: Government Printer, 1946).
5 National Archives of Zambia (hereafter NAZ), MLSS1/23 83, Annual Reports ILO Lusaka, 1959–1968, Annual Labour Report 1962.
6 Hansen, *Distant Companions*, pp. 31–33.
7 Kathleen Sheldon, 'Markets and Gardens: Placing Women in the History of Urban Mozambique', *Canadian Journal of African Studies/Revue Canadienne des Études Africaines*, 37:2/3 (2003), 363–364; Ruth Kélia Castel-Branco, 'Legislating Worker Justice: The Formalisation of Paid Domestic Work in Maputo, Mozambique' (MA thesis, University of KwaZulu-Natal, 2012), pp. 26–27.
8 Annual Report of the Department of Labour 1951, as cited in Hansen, *Distant Companions*, p. 130.
9 Annual Report of the Department of Labour 1957, as cited in Hansen, *Distant Companions*, p. 131.
10 NAZ, MLSS1/23 83, Annual Reports ILO Lusaka, 1959–1968, Annual Labour Report 1963.
11 Catherine Coquery-Vidrovitch, *African Women: A Modern History* (Boulder, CO: Westview Press, 1997), p. 109.
12 Bujra, *Serving Class*, p. 73.
13 Schmidt, 'Race, Sex and Domestic Labour', p. 221.
14 *Ibid.*, pp. 234–236; Hansen, *Distant Companions*, pp. 87–99.
15 Van Onselen, *Studies in the Economic and Social History of the Witwatersrand*, pp. 45–50.
16 Schmidt, 'Race, Sex and Domestic Labour', p. 223.
17 Castel-Branco, 'Legislating Worker Justice', p. 27.
18 Bryceson, 'Domestic Work', p. 311.

19 For further discussion, see Hansen, *Distant Companions*, pp. 120–135; Schmidt, 'Race, Sex and Domestic Labour', p. 224; Van Onselen, *Studies in the Economic and Social History of the Witwatersrand*, p. 17. On women, urban life, and respectability in Zambia, see Jane L. Parpart, '"Where Is Your Mother?": Gender, Urban Marriage, and Colonial Discourse on the Zambian Copperbelt, 1924–1945', *The International Journal of African Historical Studies*, 27:2 (1994), 241–271; and Evans, 'History Lessons', 344–362.
20 Hansen, *Distant Companions*, pp. 120–135.
21 Bryceson provides a useful diagram depicting the relationship between kin-based labour and other forms of domestic labour relations. See Bryceson, 'Domestic Work', p. 306.
22 *Ibid.*, p. 312.
23 Godfrey Wilson, *An Essay on the Economics of Detribalization in Northern Rhodesia, Volume 2* (Livingstone: Rhodes-Livingstone Institute, 1941), p. 19, pp. 75–76.
24 Karen Tranberg Hansen, 'Labor Migration and Urban Child Labor during the Colonial Period in Zambia', in Bruce Fetter (ed.), *Demography from Scanty Evidence: Central Africa in the Colonial Era* (Boulder, CO: Lynne Rienner, 1990), pp. 220–221, p. 223, pp. 226–227.
25 Grier, *Invisible Hands*, pp. 81–83, pp. 85–86, p. 92; Charles van Onselen, *Chibaro: African Mine Labour in Colonial Zimbabwe, 1900–1933* (London: Pluto Press, 1976), pp. 124–125.
26 Chauncey, 'The Locus of Reproduction', 137, 139–140, 115–138.
27 Luise White, *The Comforts of Home: Prostitution in Colonial Nairobi* (Chicago, IL: University of Chicago Press, 1990), pp. 10–12, pp. 55–58, pp. 79–80.
28 Wilson, *An Essay on the Economics of Detribalization*, p. 148.
29 See NAZ, MLSS1/17 12, Employment of Women, Young Persons and Children Ordinance 1949–1959; letter from Senior Labour Officer to all colleagues in the Department of Labour, February 1950.
30 In 1966, there were an estimated 31,231 male workers and 1,498 female workers in domestic service. By 1968, this had increased to 36,491 and 1,758, respectively. NAZ, MLSS1/23 83, Annual Reports ILO Lusaka, 1959–1968, Annual Labour Report 1966; NAZ, MLSS1/23 83, Annual Reports ILO Lusaka, 1959–1968, Annual Labour Report 1968.
31 NAZ, MLSS1/23 83, Annual Reports ILO Lusaka, 1959–1968, Annual Labour Report 1966.
32 Almost 800,000 Black women were employed as domestic workers in South Africa by 1970. Gaitskell *et al.*, 'Class, Race and Gender', 93–95.
33 The number of African men and boys recorded as working was 72.6 per cent for urban areas, and 50.2 per cent for rural areas. Republic of

Zambia, *1969 Census of Population and Housing. Analytical Report* (Lusaka: Central Statistical Office, 1970). The census divided the population into the four racial categories that had been used under colonial rule: African (referring to Black Africans), European, Coloured (referring to people of mixed racial heritage), and Asian. This was the last Zambian census to use such categorisations.

34 Slightly more African women and girls were recorded as working in the countryside (12.7 per cent), compared with urban areas (12.2 per cent). Republic of Zambia, *1969 Census of Population and Housing. Analytical Report.*

35 Benería, 'Conceptualising the Labour Force', 10–11; Rakodi, 'Urban Agriculture', 497, 501.

36 This age range was used to record labour force participation in all subsequent census reports.

37 Female labour force participation was recorded as 39.9 per cent in rural areas and 32.8 per cent in urban areas. Republic of Zambia, *1980 Census of Population and Housing. Analytical Report. Volume 3.*

38 Male labour force participation was recorded as 73.4 per cent in urban areas and 70.4 per cent in rural areas. Republic of Zambia, *1980 Census of Population and Housing. Analytical Report. Volume 3.*

39 Republic of Zambia, *Monthly Digest of Statistics. January–June 1989* (Lusaka: Central Statistical Office, 1989); Republic of Zambia, *Monthly Digest of Statistics. July–October 1991* (Lusaka: Central Statistical Office, 1991).

40 Interview with Mariana Banda, Lusaka, 29 July 2013.

41 Interview with Justina Banda, Lusaka, 5 August 2013.

42 Hansen, *Distant Companions*, p. 221.

43 Castel-Branco, 'Legislating Worker Justice', p. 31, p. 33; Kathleen E. Sheldon, *Pounders of Grain: A History of Women, Work and Politics in Mozambique* (Portsmouth, NH: Heinemann, 2002), pp. 183–184.

44 Official labour statistics for the 1980s did not break down domestic service by sex, but Pape based these estimates on data from the Zimbabwe Domestic and Allied Workers' Union (ZDAWU) and his own observations. Pape, 'Still Serving the Tea', 401.

45 Hansen, *Distant Companions*, p. 221.

46 Interview with Dorothy Phiri, Lusaka, 10 August 2013.

47 Esther's story was told to me by her former employer, Priscilla Njovu. Interview with Priscilla Njovu.

48 Republic of Zambia, *1990 Census of Population, Housing and Agriculture. Volume 10: Zambia Analytical Report* (Lusaka: Central Statistical Office, 1994).

49 Hansen, *Distant Companions*, p. 259.

50 Bujra, *Serving Class*, p. 4.

51 In urban areas, female labour force participation increased from 23.2 per cent in 1990 to 31.6 per cent in 2000. The increase was higher in rural areas, from 37.3 per cent to 52.7 per cent. Republic of Zambia, *2000 Census of Population and Housing. Analytical Report Final.*
52 *Ibid.*
53 The number of women and girls recorded as working remained higher for rural areas (53.9 per cent) than urban areas (35.5 per cent). By comparison, the number of men and boys recorded as working was 67.3 per cent for rural areas and 62.2 for urban areas. Republic of Zambia, *2010 Census of Population and Housing. National Analytical Report.*
54 Interview with Imelda Kalobwe, Lusaka, 13 February 2014.
55 Interview with Grace Mwale, Lusaka, 29 May 2014.
56 The ILO and local partners conducted sample surveys in Lusaka and Kitwe to capture urban domestic service practices and in two rural areas of Lusaka and Copperbelt provinces to capture rural domestic service practices.
57 ILO, *Magnitude of Domestic Workers in Zambia*, p. 2.
58 Castel-Branco, 'Legislating Worker Justice', p. 33.
59 ILO, *Domestic Workers Across the World*, pp. 33–34.
60 Victoria Flavia Namuggala, 'Exploitation or Empowerment? Adolescent Female Domestic Workers in Uganda', *International Journal of Child, Youth and Family Studies*, 6:4 (2015), 562.
61 Hansen, *Distant Companions,* p. 225. Hansen's definition of Black employers included Black Zambians and expatriates from other African states, a definition I adopt in this book.
62 Pape, 'Still Serving the Tea', 394, 398–401; Østreng, *Domestic Workers' Daily Lives in Post-Apartheid Namibia*, pp. 58–60.
63 Bujra, *Serving Class*, p. 5.
64 Coquery-Vidrovitch, *African Women*, p. 115. For further discussion, see Michael Bourdillon, 'Children as Domestic Employees: Problems and Promises', *Journal of Children and Poverty*, 15:1 (2009), 1–18; Mélanie Jacquemin, 'Petites nièces et petites bonnes à Abidjan. Les mutations de la domesticité juvénile', *Travail, genre et sociétés*, 22:2 (2009), 53–74; Pape, 'Still Serving the Tea', 400–401.
65 Bryceson, 'Domestic Work', p. 332.
66 Chapters 2 and 3 explore this in further detail, using oral histories to examine employers' and domestic workers' experiences of and perspectives on kin-based domestic service, respectively.
67 Evans, 'History Lessons', 4–6; Jane L. Parpart, 'Sexuality and Power on the Zambian Copperbelt: 1926–1964', in Sharon B. Stichter and Jane L. Parpart (eds), *Patriarchy and Class: African Women in the Home and the Workforce* (Boulder, CO: Westview Press, 1988), p. 133.
68 Castel-Branco, 'Legislating Worker Justice', p. 31.

69 Hansen, *Distant Companions*, pp. 263–266; Karen Tranberg Hansen, 'Body Politics: Sexuality, Gender and Domestic Service in Zambia', *Journal of Women's History*, 2:1 (1990), 131–135.
70 Pape, 'Still Serving the Tea', 402.
71 Interview with Chombe Nachula, Lusaka, 18 February 2014.
72 On gender asymmetries in post-colonial Zambian society and their impacts on household gender relations, see Hansen, 'Body Politics', 135–137.
73 These issues are explored in detail in Chapter 2.
74 Interview with Imelda Kalobwe.
75 Interview with Mary Chirwa, Lusaka, 4 February 2014.
76 Hansen, *Distant Companions*, pp. 59–60.
77 Interview with Elizabeth Bwalya.
78 Interview with Imelda Kalobwe.
79 Interview with Veronica Banda, Lusaka, 16 February 2014.
80 Interview with Elizabeth Bwalya.
81 Human Rights Watch, *Bottom of the Ladder: Exploitation and Abuse of Girl Domestic Workers in Guinea* (2017); IRIN, 'Domestic Workers Often Do More Than Housework', IRIN Humanitarian News and Analysis, 26 May 2009, available at www.thenewhumanitarian.org/report/84559/kenya-domestic-workers-often-do-more-housework (accessed 24 November 2019); Pape, 'Still Serving the Tea', 402–403.
82 On gender-based violence in post-colonial Zambia, see Roger Y. Klomegah, 'Intimate Partner Violence (IPV) in Zambia: An Examination of Risk Factors and Gender Perceptions', *Journal of Comparative Family Studies*, 39:4 (2008), 557–569; Darlene Rude, 'Reasonable Men and Provocative Women: An Analysis of Gendered Domestic Homicide in Zambia', *Journal of Southern African Studies*, 25:1 (1999), 7–27. Studies of gender-based violence in the broader region include Amy A. Conroy, 'Gender, Power, and Intimate Partner Violence: A Study on Couples From Rural Malawi', *Journal of Interpersonal Violence*, 29:5 (2014), 866–888; Helen Moffett, '"These Women, They Force Us to Rape Them": Rape as Narrative of Social Control in Post-Apartheid South Africa', *Journal of Southern African Studies*, 32:1 (2006), 129–144; Eunice Njovana and Charlotte Watts, 'Gender Violence in Zimbabwe: A Need for Collaborative Action', *Reproductive Health Matters*, 4:7 (1996), 46–55.
83 Studies of privatised security in South Africa include Bruce Baker, 'Living with Non-State Policing in South Africa: The Issues and Dilemmas', *The Journal of Modern African Studies*, 40:1 (2002), 29–53; Jacklyn Cock, '"Guards and Guns": Towards Privatised Militarism in Post-Apartheid South Africa', *Journal of Southern African Studies*, 31:4 (2005),

791–803; Martin J. Murray, *Panic City: Crime and the Fear Industries in Johannesburg* (Stanford, CA: Stanford University Press, 2020); Thabang Sefalafala, 'Precarious Work: A Case Study of Security Guards in Johannesburg' (MA dissertation, University of the Witwatersrand, 2012).

84 Interview with Evaristo Mubanga, Lusaka, 4 February 2014.

85 Interview with Andrew Banda, Lusaka, 12 August 2014.

86 Interview with Howard Phiri, Lusaka, 17 June 2014.

87 Interview with Paul Chipeta, Lusaka, 17 June 2014.

88 Interview with Andrew Banda.

89 Examples of such coverage include 'Letter to the Editor – Stephen Chanda, State Should Intervene in Security Firms', *Zambia Daily Mail*, 16 February 16; Davis Mulenga, 'Professional Training Vital for Guards', *Zambia Daily Mail*, 27 October 2017.

90 Interview with Teophilous Mufonko, Lusaka, 12 August 2014.

91 Hansen, *Distant Companions*, p. 142, pp. 232–234.

92 Bryceson, 'Domestic Labour', p. 324.

# 2

# Working women and childcare challenges

Stella Soko was born in 1951 in Kitwe, where she lived throughout her childhood. She completed her primary and secondary education in local Catholic schools before moving to the UK in 1969 to study radiography. After completing her studies in 1973, she moved to Lusaka and started work at the city's University Teaching Hospital. She had married a Canadian doctor while living in the UK and, in 1977, she fell pregnant with their first child. When we met in 2014, Stella explained to me that she had felt determined to continue working after she became a mother. But she had also known that she would need help with childcare and housework: 'You have to have someone; someone has to be in the house. In my time, I would have someone to clean my house and especially to look after my children. I needed two people.'[1] Stella described how she had turned to female relatives and friends to secure the help she needed, asking her mother to find a girl from their extended family network to care for her baby, and her female friends in Lusaka to help her recruit an adult woman to do general cleaning and cooking.

Stella was of the generation that came of age in the early post-independence years, and she gained access to the new opportunities in education and professional employment that opened up in Zambia at that time. In Chapter 1, I showed how opportunities for higher education and professional employment rapidly declined as Zambia's economy contracted from the late 1970s but that women's participation in the labour force continued to increase over time, most significantly in the informal sector. Whatever work women undertook, they faced significant challenges in balancing employment with the gendered norms of domesticity which required them to manage and perform domestic and care labour in their own homes. Male household members were not absent from the story, but adult men largely left such work to female household members and, to an extent, male children.[2] This gendered and generational disparity was most clear in relation to childcare. As Jeanne Marie Penvenne notes in her study of women workers in Mozambique, 'Men's stories of their work lives seldom mentioned their children. Women's stories of their work lives usually centred around their children.'[3]

In practical terms, the tasks associated with caring for children took up a significant part of women's daily lives during their childbearing years. Such tasks involved a range of labour, including the practical tasks of nursing, cleaning, and food preparation, and the emotional labour of managing guilt and anxiety over leaving children while at work. More than this, motherhood was – and remains – central to the valuation of southern African women's social worth and often to women's sense of self.[4] For these reasons, many working women found delegating care of their children to another person far more difficult than delegating responsibility for taking care of the house.

This chapter explores the struggles that Lusaka's working women have faced to secure the childcare they needed, exploring the types of care that were available, women's experiences of and perspectives on these options, and their relationships with those who cared for their children. Women's testimonies show that childcare in Lusaka was primarily performed by female family members or domestic workers. Most working mothers left their children in the care of close female relatives, including their mothers, sisters, and older children, or extended family members, many of whom were children themselves. Like Stella, some middle-class women could afford to employ waged domestic workers, a practice which often involved women domestic workers diverting their care labour away from their own children and towards the children of wealthier women. Women's descriptions of their childcare strategies highlighted the practical and emotional challenges they faced, from struggles to secure affordable and reliable childcare to anxieties about the standard of care that children received and familial and societal expectations around mothering. In their testimonies, women represented their relationships with those who cared for their children as involving practical and emotional challenges and of generating affection. Women developed especially complex relationships with girl domestic workers engaged in kin-based labour because such arrangements involved women delegating responsibility of their children to these girls whilst simultaneously taking on certain responsibilities for the girls concerned.

As they created their childcare strategies, working women in Lusaka constructed what Margarita Dimova *et al.* have termed 'highly fragile local care chains'.[5] This concept is a reworking of Arlie Russell Hochschild's theory of 'global care chains', which refers to the reliance of women in the Global North on migrant domestic workers from the Global South.[6] The literature on global care chains has provided wide-ranging insights into global distributions of care labour, but it has provided limited insights into localised forms of care and care chains, particularly in the Global South. There is a small existing literature on localised forms of childcare and care chains in Africa, and this chapter seeks to build on and engage with this body of work by revealing how women in Lusaka and other southern African cities constructed local care chains and by examining women's own perspectives on their childcare strategies.[7]

## Working women's childcare options

The childcare strategies available to working women in urban southern Africa were shaped by many factors, including the availability of alternative labour within the home, women's position within kinship networks, their socio-economic status, and the broader economic climate. Lusaka's middle-class women had access to a range of strategies, including both kin-based and wage labour. In terms of kin-based labour, women commonly recruited a young female relative from their extended family network. Priscilla Njovu, for instance, used this form of childcare extensively when her four children were young. She was working at the National Archives in Lusaka when she fell pregnant for the first time in 1981. Priscilla's mother helped her to find a suitable girl from their family's home area in Eastern Province. Priscilla repeated this process several times during the 1980s and 1990s, employing a series of female relatives to care for her children.[8] Jane Kafula, a primary school teacher in her fifties when we met in 2014, also engaged the labour of young female kin when she first became a mother. Jane gave birth to her first child in 1987, while living with her husband in Kitwe. At the time, she and her husband were new to the area and had few familial contacts in the city. Jane described how she had initially tried to find a local girl to employ for childcare but had failed to find someone. She had then turned to her husband's sister for help with finding a girl from their extended family network in Northern Province.[9] These examples of working women relying on girl domestic workers reflect a wider trend across post-colonial Africa's cities, from Abidjan to Nairobi.[10]

Women's reliance on young female kin for childcare is built on longstanding practices of children moving between households within the extended family system as a labour-sharing device. Within the extended family system, it is legitimate for a woman in need of support to request her brother or sister, and in some cases other relatives, to send a daughter to live with her and labour in or for her household.[11] This practice endured in post-colonial Zambia and countries across the region, where it was reworked in response to changing economic and social pressures. The disastrous economic situation of the late 1970s to 2000s amplified relations of reciprocal dependency between urban and rural areas, with urban women across the socio-economic spectrum having to resort to kinship networks for domestic labour because they could not afford to engage waged domestic workers. The pathways for progression and social mobility that opened briefly for Stella's generation sharply contracted as the economy declined and left younger women in urban and rural areas more dependent upon relationships with older relatives in better circumstances. At the same time, there is evidence that the role of the extended family in post-colonial African societies changed as a result of rapid urbanisation and the development of capitalism. Crucially, the responsibility of caring for family members, including children, shifted away from the extended family and towards the nuclear family, and the mother specifically. Many working women in Lusaka and other cities struggled to shoulder this responsibility and sought ways to maintain and mobilise kinship networks as a source of labour.

Women's preferences for employing girls also resulted from gendered constructions of girlhood and labour, including a perception that girls were more passive and pliable workers than adults. Rebecca Keyala emphasised this when describing how she had employed a series of girls to care for her children during the 1970s and 1980s. Rebecca was born in 1950 in Kabwe, where she completed her primary and secondary education and further training in typing and human resource management. She then worked in administration and human resources before being retrenched in 2000. When we met in 2014, she was running a business that hired out catering equipment and chairs. Rebecca had become a mother for the first time in 1977, and by 1988 she had five children. Like Stella, she described being determined to carry on working after becoming a mother, and she turned to her female relatives to help her to find girl domestic workers. Rebecca described how she would train each girl to ensure that they cared for her children and home as she wanted.[12] Whether the girls followed Rebecca's methods in her absence is unknown, but her emphasis on training suggests that she did not want to employ someone with too much experience (such as an adult) or with the confidence to defy her rules. Many of my interviewees also suggested that girls' 'innocence' and 'trustworthiness' made them better domestic workers than adult women, not least because they feared the latter would seek to engage in sexual relations with husbands and other male household members. Although some women also expressed criticism of men's engagement in extra-marital relationships and infidelities, none of my interviewees described this as having occurred in her own household. Such critiques mapped onto broader discourses surrounding marital breakdown and women's fears of the impacts of male infidelity.

Some middle-class women chose to engage the labour of both female relatives and formally employed domestic workers. As we saw above, Stella followed this approach when her children were young during the 1970s and 1980s. Stella explained her decision to employ two people as resulting from several factors. She had wanted to make sure that the girl who cared for her child could focus solely on this work and provide a high level of care. Moreover, she also had the financial resources to employ a second person to do general domestic tasks, some of which, like washing clothes and food preparation, could be very labour-intensive.[13] In the colonial period, it was common for European households to employ multiple persons for domestic work and childcare in this manner. After independence, some middle-class Black employers like Stella had the means and opportunity to engage in similar practices, though in revised form, as they used both kin-based labour and wage labour.

Other middle-class working mothers chose only to employ domestic workers in formal wage labour. This approach was more common amongst women who had become mothers during the 2000s and perhaps reflected a desire to cultivate more distant and marketised labour relations than kin-based arrangements allowed. Chombe Nachula was in her mid-thirties when we met in 2014 and lived in the affluent suburb of Kabulonga. She was born and raised in Lusaka, where she attended primary and secondary schools and university. She worked in the construction industry, doing freelance management for a range of firms. Chombe's childcare choices were also likely shaped by Zambia's recovering economy during the 2000s, with her career presumably benefiting from the construction boom in Lusaka in the late 2000s and early 2010s. She described how she had first employed a domestic worker in 2008, after giving birth to her first child. Chombe employed an older woman named Betty who had once worked in Chombe's parents' home. Chombe explained that she had felt confident leaving her child in Betty's care because she 'knew her well'. She also liked that Betty was older and had a 'great deal of experience' caring for children. Chombe described being disappointed when that arrangement came to an end just one month after it started. Betty was in her early sixties when she took up the position and, according to Chombe, left the job because she found it 'too tiring'. Chombe then turned to her mother for help with finding a replacement. Her mother recommended another domestic worker, in that case a fifty-three-year-old woman whom she knew from church. Chombe employed this woman for over a year, the arrangement ending when the domestic worker remarried and decided to stop working.[14] Like Chombe, Diana Mumba also employed a woman domestic worker in a formal wage labour arrangement when she gave birth to her first child. Diana was in her mid-twenties when we met in 2014, and she had just completed training to become a solicitor. She was a single mother, and she lived with her baby, an aunt, and two cousins in Kabulonga. Diana asked her female relatives for advice about who to employ, and her aunt recommended that she employ a woman named Given, who was in her thirties and had, in Diana's words, 'lots of experience' working as a maid and nanny.[15]

These examples of middle-class Black women employing poorer Black women as domestic workers reflects a broader pattern across the region's post-colonial urban centres. In Swaziland, women's participation in the labour force increased steadily after independence in 1968, and this created further employment opportunities for women, as urban working women sought out female domestic workers to help them with childcare and housework.[16] Just over a decade later in Zimbabwe, independence was followed by an expansion in female labour force participation, and Black working mothers' similarly sought out Black women childminders.[17] There is also evidence of Black women seeking out Black female childcarers under apartheid.[18] Urban women's employment of women domestic workers has only increased since the transition to democracy in South Africa and the expansion of the Black middle class.

Diana, Chombe, and Stella's testimonies show that when middle-class women were looking to employ a domestic worker in a wage labour arrangement, many sought out personal recommendations from friends and relatives. Some middle-class women took a different approach, however, and instead found their domestic workers through formal employment agencies, known locally as maid centres. Maid centres emerged in Lusaka during the 1990s and reflect a specific brand of outsourced labour pooling associated with late twentieth-century capitalism in Africa. The growth of this sector in Zambia can also be connected to the improved economic situation during the 2000s, both in the sense that more households could afford to employ domestic workers via maid centres and also because other forms of domestic labour were no longer as readily available. Maid centres flourished elsewhere in southern Africa too during this period, most notably in South Africa, which has large numbers of employment agencies for domestic workers, including digital platforms such as SweepSouth.[19] As discussed previously, there were parallel developments in the home security industry in this period, with small and large private security companies increasingly operating in Zambia and across southern Africa. Although at the time of research in Lusaka in 2013 and 2014, few of my interviewees had used a maid centre, it was clear that these agencies had increased in number and influence over time and that they were attracting a growing client base of employers and domestic workers in the city.

There were several reasons why employers chose to source childcare through a maid centre. First, maid centres had a ready supply of workers looking for employment. For women in need of childcare at short notice or who needed help with finding a domestic worker, this was very appealing. At the time of our interview, Chombe was employing a female maid whom she had hired through a maid centre in Mtendere. She explained that she had turned to the maid centre after struggling to find an older female domestic worker through personal recommendations from family and friends. This shortage of labour, perceived or actual, may have resulted from Zambia's improved economic situation during the 2000s and the availability of alternative employment options for women, including in the informal sector. Maid centres also provided employers with increased choice as they could specify the characteristics of their ideal domestic worker. Martha Banda, a staff member at Beverly Hills Maid Centre in the middle-class suburb of Chalala, explained

**Figure 2.1** Advertisement for Beverly Hills Maid Centre, 6 February 2014.

**Figure 2.2** Advertisement for Tikwiza Domestic Services, 1 August 2013.

that her clients can specify the gender, age, and level of experience of their ideal domestic worker, and that she then finds someone who fits these specifications.[20] In providing employers with both a ready supply of labour and choice over the characteristics of their workers, maid centres have contributed to the marketisation and formalisation of domestic service.[21] The employment relationship offered by maid centres was, in theory at least, more organised and more distant than that offered by kin-based labour or the employment of strangers directly.

Most maid centres required employers and domestic workers to agree to a formal, written contract of employment that specified pay, working hours, and conditions. This formality offered employers a range of protections and guarantees that informal hiring practices did not. If an employment arrangement ended because the domestic worker did not uphold her side of the contract, for example by failing to produce a medical note after a period of sick leave, the employer could return to the maid centre to find a replacement domestic worker without paying any additional recruitment fees. For working mothers in need of reliable sources of childcare, and quick ways of finding replacement care if an employment arrangement broke down, such protections could be very attractive. Mikala

Mukongolwa explained that she was drawn to using a maid centre because she had several difficult experiences of employing maids directly and wanted more protections as an employer. Mikala was born in Zimbabwe to Zambian parents, and moved to Lusaka in 1975 when she was ten years old. When we met in 2013, she was the headmistress of a primary school in Bauleni. She lived near the school with her husband, two children, and five dependants, all of whom were the children of her and her husband's siblings. She had formally employed women domestic workers to do housework and childcare since she was first married, but she explained that in recent years she had had several 'difficult experiences' with the women she employed. She had suspected several of her domestic workers of stealing from her home, a common complaint amongst employers. She asked her female friends for advice about how to find reliable and trustworthy domestic workers and was advised by a female colleague to visit a maid centre in Lusaka city centre. She explained that the maid centre had promised to help her if she faced 'challenges' with the domestic workers that she employed through them, including by providing her with a new maid who met her specifications if an employment relationship broke down.[22]

Unsurprisingly, poor women had access to a narrower range of childcare strategies than did middle-class women and relied almost exclusively on the labour of family members. June Phiri was born in Mkushi in Zambia's Northern Province in 1964 and moved with her parents and younger sister to Lusaka when she was four years old. Her family settled in Bauleni, where June continued to reside at the time of our interview in 2013. June married in 1984 and became a mother in 1987, giving birth to a daughter. She went on to have four more children, all of whom were boys. When she first became a mother, June relied on her mother-in-law for help with childcare. As June's daughter grew older, she gave her household chores to do, including caring responsibilities for her younger siblings. June described, for example, how from the age of six her daughter began bathing her younger brothers and watching over them. As June's sons got older, she also gave them chores to do and responsibility for their younger siblings.[23] Like June, Jennifer Banda lived in Bauleni when we met in 2013. She was born in Lusaka in 1979 and had alternated between domestic service and market work since leaving school in her teens. At the time of our interview, she lived with her husband and four children. She explained that she could never afford to pay someone to help her with domestic work and childcare, and instead relied on her own children. In 2014, her fifteen-year-old daughter and twelve-year-old son had left school, and both helped with housework and caring for their younger siblings. Jennifer's eight-year-old son also helped with some housework when he was not at school, such as collecting water from the shared pump.[24] Although June and Jennifer were born fifteen years apart, they faced very similar childcare challenges, including unequal gender divisions of labour within the home and limited opportunities for employment.

Poor women also relied on the labour of extended family members. June described how during her own childhood in the 1960s and 1970s, her mother had relied on the labour of young female relatives. She remembered that her family home was frequently full of visiting relatives from rural areas. She described how adults had tended to stay only for short periods of time while they secured work or completed errands in town but that several young people had stayed for longer periods. One example was a female cousin who came to the city from Mpika in modern-day Muchinga Province. The cousin was twelve years old when she arrived in the city, and she lived with June's family until she got married aged eighteen. June explained that her cousin had shared a room with her and her siblings and had attended school as they did. June remembered that her cousin had been treated differently to her and her siblings when it came to housework, however, because June's mother had expected her cousin to do a lot of domestic work outside of school hours and also to care for June and her younger siblings.[25] Although June did not describe this relationship as a form of domestic service, it meets the definition used in this book, as June's cousin clearly exchanged labour for her place in the household and for material and social support from senior kin. Evidence from urban Mozambique similarly shows how poor working women relied on young female kin to help them with domestic labour.[26]

Female kin were a particularly important source of domestic labour for women domestic workers. Dorothy Phiri became a mother for the first time in 1985, and by the end of the 1980s, she had three children. She described how she had consistently struggled to find adequate childcare. She received limited financial or other support from her husband, who was frequently absent from the family home and who gave her little of his income to put towards household expenses. Dorothy's childcare strategies consisted of a combination of free and low-cost childcare arrangements, including relying on her own children and bringing young female relatives to live with her for short and extended periods of time. The most successful of these latter arrangements was with her niece Anna Banda, who lived with Dorothy for a period of five years from the late 1980s. Dorothy explained that she had provided Anna with a place to live and, when she could, money towards school fees. In exchange, Anna helped Dorothy with childcare, cleaning, and cooking. Dorothy made this arrangement directly with her sister, who was Anna's mother and also in a financially precarious position. From Dorothy's perspective, she had secured reliable childcare by taking Anna into her home, she had helped her sister by relieving her of the costs of Anna's upkeep, and she had helped Anna to continue with her education.[27] Such arrangements between female relatives were crucial parts of the survival strategies that Zambian women and girls developed to mediate the worst impacts of economic decline and hardship during the 1980s. Research on 1980s Harare similarly shows how women domestic workers relied on children's labour as part of broader strategies for surviving in the city.[28] This evidence from Lusaka and Harare is suggestive of a broader trend across southern Africa's urban centres.

Not only did poor women have access to a narrower range of childcare strategies than did middle-class women, many also made their living by diverting their own care labour towards the children of wealthier women. Domestic workers like Dorothy and June left their own children in the care of female relatives or their older children while they cared for other women's children. This strategy was pursued by domestic workers across southern Africa, most infamously under apartheid, where racialised residency and mobility laws forced many women to leave their children in the care of relatives in the countryside while they worked in the city.[29] Women's diversion of their care labour towards the children of their employers had several impacts on the children involved. In the case of domestic workers' own children, it is possible that they received lower standards of care than their mothers might have liked. As Dimova *et al.* observed in Nairobi, 'in this segment of the care chain, the child often experiences custodial care – an adult or even a slightly older child keeps an eye on them. There is little expectation of intimacy or performance of emotional labour.'[30] They argue that this entrenched inequalities in Nairobi, because women domestic workers remained trapped in poverty, and their children received 'substandard care' and struggled to access educational opportunities.[31] My findings from Lusaka suggest a more complex picture. It is certainly the case that domestic service perpetuated gender- and class-based inequality in the city. It is also clear that most domestic workers struggled to provide their children with the same levels of education and broader developmental support that the children of their middle-class employers received. However, as will be examined in the following section, many women's testimonies reveal that they felt that their children received higher standards of care from female relatives than from strangers in more formal childcare arrangements. Many interviewees were also passionate about their children's education, and some, including June and Dorothy, paid for their children's school fees from their wages.[32] This was by no means limited to domestic workers in Lusaka, with evidence from other southern African cities of women working in domestic service to support their children's education.[33] By taking poor women's own perspectives of their childcare strategies into account, we see how working mothers did the best they could with the resources available, even as they faced severe inequalities within their employment relationships and wider urban society.

None of my interviewees, regardless of their economic fortunes, described using a nursery or childcare centre. This resulted from such services being both limited in number in Lusaka for much of the period under study and, where they existed, financially out of reach for most women. This also reflects broader trends across the region's urban centres, with reliance on family members and the employment of domestic workers far outweighing the use of nurseries or childcare centres. In Harare, for instance, childcare primarily took place within families or via the employment of a childminder, partly because of limited government investment in childcare provision.[34] Similarly in East Africa, limited government support and expensive private childcare facilities led most working mothers in Kampala and Nairobi to rely on the labour of family members or young 'house girls'.[35] An interesting contrast to these cases is Mozambique, where government-supported childcare facilities were established during the armed liberation struggle and then expanded in cities and rural areas following independence in 1975, before the combined impacts of war and structural adjustment undermined such efforts from the late 1980s. These childcare facilities were introduced by Mozambique's government, led by the socialist Frente de Libertação de Moçambique (Liberation Front of Mozambique, or Frelimo), to further the cause of women's liberation. They were part of a broader package of support available to working women, which included paid maternity leave and time for new mothers to nurse their infants in the workplace.[36] The standard of care that children received in such centres varied, and some working women clearly used the centres only because they had no other options.[37] Overall, these innovations did not challenge the female-centred nature of care labour or reduce underlying gender inequalities. While government-sponsored childcare facilities provided Mozambican working women with additional support, women remained the primary caregivers in the childcare centres and as parents.

## Women's perspectives on their childcare strategies

Many of my interviewees described leaving their children in other people's care to be an emotionally and practically difficult process. Some women worried about the standard of care that their children received. Hope Chanda, a nurse, described how worried she had felt about leaving her children with formally employed domestic workers during the 1990s: 'Say you are breastfeeding, you don't know if that person is keeping that bottle as clean as you would want it to be.'[38] Other interviewees expressed similar fears over how their domestic workers would care for their children. Diana had only recently employed Given when we met in 2014 and worried about leaving her child in her care. Diana explained that she had tried to show Given how she liked to feed and bathe her baby and how she liked his clothes to be washed, but she feared that Given would do things differently when she worked unsupervised.[39] Chombe shared such fears and her decision to employ older female domestic workers was partly because she thought that they were gentler and more patient with children than were younger domestic workers.[40]

At worst, women had feared that their children might be physically or sexually abused by a domestic worker. Several of my interviewees refused to employ male domestic workers for this reason. For instance, Chombe explained that she would not employ a male gardener because she had daughters and worried about the possibility of 'molestation'. Chombe said that this was a personal issue because her childhood friend had been sexually assaulted by a 'garden boy'.[41] Priscilla echoed Chombe's concerns, suggesting that children were much safer with female carers because, in her words, 'the chances of a girl to defile a child they are very slim, while young men have all those funny ideas'.[42] Both women's testimonies reflected broader concerns in public discourse about the safety of children in relation to domestic workers. Such concerns reflected older fears surrounding African men's sexuality, prevalent in colonial southern Africa, when many European women were instructed not to leave African men unattended with young children and European women who relied too much on their male servants were often judged as failing mothers. They also reflected the realities of gender-based and sexual violence, which were and remain endemic in Zambia and across southern Africa.

For many women, leaving their children with female relatives helped to alleviate their anxieties. Stella, for instance, argued that only kin 'care for the baby like their own'.[43] Bridget Kalobwe, a primary school teacher in her thirties, expressed similar views. When Bridget gave birth to her first child in 2009, she asked her fourteen-year-old niece to help her with childcare. The girl came to live with Bridget and received accommodation, meals, and money for school fees in exchange for her labour. This was by far Bridget's most positive experience of delegating care of her children to another. Her niece won a scholarship to a boarding school in 2011, and Bridget then struggled to find replacement childcare from within her extended family network. For the first time, she employed a domestic worker whom she did not know in a wage labour arrangement. She explained that she had never felt comfortable leaving her child in the care of strangers as, in her opinion, they would not care for her child with as much diligence as she required.[44] Dorothy similarly stated that she had been happy to leave her children in Anna's care because she was responsible and reliable, and although she did not mention it explicitly, the fact that Anna was Dorothy's relative was likely a significant factor in generating such trust.[45]

Leaving their children in the care of female relatives also helped working mothers to alleviate other anxieties about their children's upbringing. Several interviewees stated that because female relatives shared their traditions, they could help to raise their children correctly, for instance, by teaching their children the language spoken in their familial home area and forms of specialised knowledge. For Priscilla, such specialised knowledge was also important for creating an atmosphere of hospitality and respectability at home. She explained,

> Because of the extended family system, there are always visitors coming into your home especially for those of us who were married to the only man in the family who was educated. Everybody looked up to my husband so everybody was coming to our home, it was easy for conversing to talk with a maid who speaks the same language … and even the tradition when they come she knows how to greet, how to kneel down … it helps a lot in the house if you speak the same language or are from the same tradition.[46]

From Priscilla's perspective, the girls she engaged for childcare thus helped her to raise her children 'properly' and to create the right atmosphere for visitors. She represented herself and her husband as seniors within their extended family network, and she was clearly self-conscious about appearing to be both a respectable person and a responsible mother.

For women who chose to employ domestic workers in formal arrangements, personal recommendations from friends and relatives could help to alleviate their anxieties. Women who chose to use a maid centre took some comfort from the fact that most centres required the domestic workers on their books to undergo a programme of training. Veronica Tembo, the owner and manager of Aunty Veronica's Maid Centre in Kabulonga, explained that all the domestic workers she worked with had gone through a training programme which addressed childcare, basic cooking skills, household security, first aid, personal hygiene, dress, and manners. Veronica was also keen to inculcate her trainees with 'Christian values'.[47] Patricia Bwalya, manager of a maid centre based at the

Abundant Life Fellowship, a Pentecostal church in Kabulonga, expressed similar sentiments.[48] Such emphasis on 'moral' training might have helped to allay the anxieties that working mothers felt when leaving their children in the care of strangers. For women like Mikala, who had accused several domestic workers of stealing from her home, the emphasis on moral training and Christian teaching held additional appeal.[49]

## The complexities of local care chains

Women's testimonies revealed the complexity of their relationships with those who cared for their children. This came through most strikingly in women's descriptions of their relationships with girl domestic workers, especially girls they employed through the extended family system. The latter often involved women delegating responsibility for their children to these girls while simultaneously becoming responsible for the girls concerned in numerous ways. Various interviewees described how they were expected to provide their young female relatives not only with housing and food, but also with care, protection, and moral guidance. For instance, when describing how she came to employ her first young maid, Stella stated, 'The girl was given to me by my mother. She had to stay in the house. She was part of my family. She ate what I ate, I taught her how to wash, how to be clean ... I will care for that little girl as my own child.'[50] In stating this, Stella was clearly keen to stress the care that she provided and the close bond that she sought to develop with the child. Stella's use of language also provides insights into her perception of the power relations involved in this relationship. She represents herself as the matriarch, instructing the child and passing on knowledge about how to care for oneself. The girl is represented as passive and as someone whose mobility and options were decided by adults. Her comment that she was 'given' the 'little girl' by her mother suggests also how her childcare strategy replicated longstanding practices of women moving children between their households as a labour-sharing strategy. Stella's description of the girl as 'little' only emphasises the child's youth and seeming passivity. The representation of girl domestic workers as passive and at the whim of adults reflects a broader trend in my interviews with employers and is something also seen in scholarly and public discourses on girls in domestic service, particularly in the twenty-first century. As will be examined in the following chapter, this representation fails to consider the many ways in which girls could and have defied adults' expectations, and have shaped their working conditions and life chances.

A number of interviewees described how they had felt a responsibility not only to provide for girl domestic workers' day-to-day needs but also to help them to improve their future. Stella, for instance, took an interest in educating the girls who cared for her children and paid for them to attend school. She explained during our interview that she had hoped education would enable the girls concerned to access a wider range of opportunities and escape early marriage in the village. Stella's actions may well have been rooted in her own experiences as a girl. She had pursued education and used this to travel internationally, secure professional training and employment, and achieve a high standard of living in Lusaka.[51] Patricia Chanda, the executive director of an NGO, similarly encouraged and paid for her young maids to undertake education and training. Like Stella, she completed her primary and secondary education in the 1960s and attended university in the 1970s. When she established her own household in the late 1970s, she employed a series of girl domestic workers, all recruited through her extended family. She described how women in her position had 'helped their maids move forwards in terms of education'. She herself had paid for one of her maids to complete secondary school and teacher training.[52] Poorer women also felt an obligation to support their young kin through education, even though they had more limited means to do so compared with their middle-class counterparts. We have seen, for instance, how Dorothy Phiri helped her niece Anna to complete her secondary education by giving her small cash payments towards her school fees.

Women's sense of responsibility towards the girls who cared for their children was also rooted in a desire for respectability. As Jill Brown suggests in her work on child fostering in contemporary Namibia, 'women wanted to be considered responsible and trustworthy and believed an avenue to achieving this was through caring for others' children'.[53] My interviewees' understandings of their obligations to provide the basics of care also reflect this and intersected with their desire to cultivate or maintain their respectability.

We have seen, for example, how Priscilla placed great emphasis on fulfilling the role of senior kinswoman and displaying politeness. Stella, Patricia and Dorothy's testimonies are also illustrative of this. Each woman's emphasis on the care that she provided to her young maid may well have reflected her genuine desire to protect and care for the girl, but it can also be read as an attempt to display her own good character and her status as a responsible senior kinswoman who provided for her juniors.

Alongside feelings of obligation and a desire for respectability, women's testimonies also contained expressions of affection. As described above, Stella described treating her girl domestic workers like her own children.[54] Rebecca described her relationship in similarly maternal terms: 'I treat my servants like my own children … The relationship is that between mother and daughter. When they leave they always come back. When they want to get married, they go from my house.'[55] Bessie Chanda, a retired trade union official, used similar language. She was born in 1946 in Mufulira on the Copperbelt, where she lived for most of her childhood and completed her primary and secondary education. Bessie became a mother for the first time in 1967 and quickly employed, in her words, a 'small nanny'. The girl in question was a fifteen-year-old girl named Jaqueline, a distant relative. Bessie described their relationship in the following terms: 'she was part of me … I took her as my sister, my young sister'.[56] In scholarly studies of domestic service relationships, the use of familial or affectionate language by employers is seen at best as a misconception and at worst as a tool used deliberately to disguise the exploitation of workers.[57] It is certainly possible that my interviewees were seeking to downplay their exploitation of girls' labour – in many cases, girl domestic workers were exploited by women employers, as will be discussed in the following chapter – or at least to recast these relationships in a more positive light than was the case. At the same time, however, it is worth taking women's perceptions of these relationships seriously. For while they cannot provide literal recollections of the past, they do provide useful insights into women's perceptions of labour relations involving child workers and into the contradictions of subjectivity and memory.

Women's use of familial language certainly contradicted other aspects of their narrative. For instance, while Stella described how she treated the girls she engaged for childcare similarly to her own children, she struggled to remember any of their names, instead referring to them as her 'little girls'.[58] This could, of course, stem from the limits of memory, as Stella was describing events that occurred forty years earlier. But it is also suggestive of the distance that existed between Stella and these girls. Stella did not seem to be aware of such contradictions, nor was she uneasy at what her forgetting might suggest. Although she may have liked to think of herself as treating these children like her own, she was separated from them by distinct hierarchies of age and social status. That she could not remember their names suggests that these girls made less of an impression on her than she would like to believe – they were certainly more forgettable than her own children. Several other women similarly could not remember the names of the girls they had employed. While they remembered certain details about the girls, for example 'she was very pretty' or 'she was a good worker', their names were either lost to memory or were not important enough to remember.

Another contradiction arose between women's use of familial language and their discussion of the transactional nature of these labour relations. Although most interviewees sought to emphasise the kinship basis of labour relations involving girls, they also quite clearly understood that their relationship with these girls was transactional and that they were required to provide certain payments in exchange for the girls' labour. Stella described how she had paid her young maids by providing them with school fees and clothing as well as a home and meals. She also made sporadic cash payments directly to the girls' parents. Dorothy contributed to her niece Anna's school fees. Other women, including Rebecca, paid their maids solely through in-kind payments. My interviewees thus understood that they were 'paying' for the girls' labour, but they still framed these relationships in familial terms.

While women's use of familial language suggests that they understood these labour relations as a continuation of longstanding practices of kin-based labour involving children, their discussion of the transactional nature of such arrangements also illustrates how kinship-based labour relations have been commodified over time – and have arguably become more exploitative in the process – as urban employers used their kinship networks to find the cheapest available labour. Bourdillon observed a similar phenomenon amongst employers of child domestic workers in Zimbabwe, where employers used the gloss of kinship to disguise their employment of children:

> In order to get maximum service for minimum cost, employers may try to fuse the employment of child domestic workers with the idea of children helping out. The child is said to be cared for as a member of the family, with no contract to limit the demands made on the work or to specify remuneration.[59]

Fictive kinship has been shown to be used as a disguise for the exploitation of child domestic workers beyond Africa too, including in Bangladesh and Nepal.[60] In the Lusakan case, my interviewees may also have been attempting to disguise their employment of child domestic workers because it had been outlawed by the Zambian government in 2011 and had received attention and condemnation as part of local and international campaigns against child labour.[61]

Childcare arrangements involving girl domestic workers could become even more complicated during and after girls entered puberty, because this brought about new choices, obligations, and potential dangers.[62] Priscilla described what happened when Mildred, a twelve-year-old girl she employed in the mid-1980s, got her first period: 'when she became of age ... when she started her first menses I had to send her to her mother'. Aware of social pressures around puberty and transitions to adulthood, Priscilla had worried that Mildred's parents might want her to stay in the village and find a marriage partner: 'even when she was going I told her "Mildred you are looking very nice ... I doubt if those people ... the young men in the village will let you [return to the city]."' Priscilla emphasised that she was proved right: 'someone just got her', she said, referring to Mildred's swift engagement to a young man from her parents' village. During our interview, Priscilla lamented Mildred's situation, not least because it had meant the girl had been forced to discontinue her education.[63] Priscilla's testimony mirrored the critique of rural life and early marriage expressed by Stella. Both women were seemingly angered by the limitations faced by girls and young women in rural areas. They, by contrast, had managed to 'escape' from their rural homes because they had completed their education and found work that enabled them to support themselves.

These findings echo Hansen's arguments that girls' employment in domestic service in Zambia has often been short-lived because of the pressures on girls to marry once they began to menstruate.[64]

Mildred was not the first of Priscilla's young maids to leave her job because of challenges relating to sexual maturity. Before Mildred, Priscilla had employed a girl named Esther. One afternoon in 1985, Priscilla had returned home from work to find Esther, then fourteen years old, lying on the bathroom floor covered in blood. Priscilla realised that Esther was having a miscarriage and took her to the hospital:

> I don't know if she took something to take out the pregnancy … it was small … Me and my husband went to the neighbours and they said 'yes, he [their son] knew when you took her to the hospital and he told our gardener'. So, we sat down, we handled it you know because she was like our child. We said, 'you have to compensate her' … they paid. After that incident, I communicated to my sister and the mother said 'she should come back since she has spoiled her chance'.[65]

It seems that Esther's age and gender led Priscilla to feel protective towards her rather than disapproving of her sexual behaviour. We cannot know if this accurately depicts Priscilla's response at the time of these events, but in her testimony she constructed Esther as a victim, an innocent child who had been unaware of the risks of sex and illicit medicines.

Not all interviewees took this view. Some women argued that girls lost their youthful innocence after the onset of puberty and, for those who came from rural areas, time living in town. For instance, Rebecca stated, 'town girls they know about life, they are difficult, that's what I hear. While girls from the village by the time they wake up, your child might be two years old, but when they do wake up you have difficulties. Boys are on them … they will demand more.'[66] By 'wake up' Rebecca seems to be referring to girls becoming aware of their youth and sexuality. Stella was similarly critical of older girls,

> I had one who stayed a long, long time … she went everywhere we went. She grew up and started looking for boyfriends. She started to wash, to look nice. She would sneak out to see boys, to socialise. My children would say 'mum, she wasn't here!' I would question her

> when she came. Of course, she would tell lies. You send them to the village, maybe they disappear. They don't want to go back.[67]

Stella's description of this incident revealed her anger towards the girl concerned and how she punished her by 'sending' her back to her parents' village. As well as fearing that her domestic worker had not properly cared for her children, it is also possible that Stella feared that the girl's suspected activities had the potential to compromise her own respectability. Such concerns likely related to broader debates about women, girls, and respectability in urban spaces and fears about the potentially corrupting influences of urban life on girls and young women.[68] Women did not often refer to such disciplining strategies in interviews, an absence which suggests not a lack of attempts to control or punish girls, but rather interviewees' desire to represent their relationships in a positive light. As we shall see in the next chapter, girl domestic workers were subject to a range of verbal and physical punishments at the hands of their female employers. The absence of such discussion from women's testimonies may also reflect their desire to hide their failure to prevent the girls concerned from breaking their rules and engaging in rebellious behaviour.

Despite the various challenges working mothers described as resulting from employing girls, they continued to seek out girls' labour. My interviewees argued that this search had become more difficult over time, because of a perceived decline in the availability and willingness of girls to engage in such work. For instance, several interviewees complained that it had become increasingly difficult to recruit girls 'from the village'. Jane suggested that parents in rural areas had become unwilling to let their daughters move to urban areas because they feared that their children might be abused by their employers or other urban residents.[69] Priscilla made a different argument, suggesting that girls have become increasingly savvy and difficult to keep hold of:

> They can still be hardworking but they get too excited ... she will leave to get married or she would want to work, maybe my neighbour is a *muzungu* [White person], she would talk with the maid of the *muzungu* who is getting more and maybe she would leave me for someone who would give her more.[70]

Both women's arguments are difficult to quantify. Priscilla's comments seem to reflect a nostalgia for 'how things used to be', with girls in the past seemingly having lower aspirations or options.[71] Jane's arguments bear some merit and likely reflect the increased prevalence of discussions about child labour and child abuse in public discourse in Zambia and across southern Africa during the 1990s and 2000s.[72]

Increased access to education for children was another issue that likely impacted girls' ability and willingness to become domestic workers in Lusaka and other regional cities, with rates of school attendance amongst children increasing steadily over the period. In Zambia, cultural perceptions about girls' education gradually improved over time, and, during the 2000s, the government was in a better fiscal position to expand school education than in the 1980s and 1990s, when the country was highly indebted. Bridget's niece's success in securing a scholarship to a boarding school reflects these changing circumstances. Bryceson describes how, across Africa, the 'drive to enrol children in school lessened children's domestic labour chores. Sons reduced their input into herding the household's small animal stock and scaring birds away from crops, whereas girls had less time to assist their mothers with cooking, cleaning, fetching water and the care of younger siblings.'[73] We could extend the latter point to cover girls assisting kin with domestic labour and childcare. That said, there were also clear disparities regarding access to education, with not all children equally removed from the potential pool of labour. In Zambia, school attendance figures showed a clear gender disparity, with more male students than female students well into the 1990s. School attendance also had a clear urban bias, suggesting that it would be easier to secure children's labour from rural areas compared to the city.[74] Whether the decline in girls' availability was real or just a perception, oral testimonies show that girls remained many working women's first choice for childcare.

## Conclusion

As Stella stated at the opening of the chapter, most women 'have to have someone' to help them to fulfil their multiple roles as workers, mothers, wives, and kinswomen. The testimonies of working women in Lusaka reveal how they turned to other women and girls for the help they needed to balance their myriad responsibilities, resulting in the construction of complex local care chains grounded in female labour. Most women relied on family-based childcare, including the labour of their own children and the labour of female relatives from their extended family. Some middle-class women also employed female domestic workers in formal arrangements, either recruiting them directly or through a maid centre. These different childcare strategies involved multiple forms of care labour. Most obviously, women delegated care of their children to other women and girls, a process which could involve challenges and often provoked anxiety. Many interviewees preferred to leave their children in the care of female relatives rather than strangers to alleviate their worries. Young female kin were particularly sought after, with working mothers across the socio-economic spectrum seeking out girls to care for their children. This often involved bringing girls from rural areas to the city. These findings reveal how the costs of urban social reproduction in Zambia continued to be borne by female rural residents, replicating and reworking patterns of urban-rural dependence established under colonial rule. These gendered configurations of labour and dependency likely occurred across southern Africa's urban centres, given the prevalence of high rates of gender inequality and rural poverty and established rural-urban linkages across the region. These issues will be explored further in the following chapter.

Childcare strategies involving girls' labour entailed additional forms of care labour because women became responsible for the girls concerned in various ways. Women's testimonies reveal that they were expected to provide the girls with a home, meals, care, moral guidance, and protection. Some interviewees also felt responsible for providing education or other training, and some intervened in the resultant situations from girls' sexual relationships and marriage practices. Women characterised their relationships with the girls who cared for their children as being both pleasurable and challenging. Some women developed productive and even affectionate relationships with these girls and felt confident leaving their children in their care. Other women described facing challenging situations, especially as girls transitioned through puberty and began to push social boundaries. Yet despite such challenges, working women clearly continued to seek out girls' labour following independence and up to the present. Overall, working women's demand for the labour of girls and women for childcare significantly contributed to the broader feminisation of domestic service in Lusaka and across the region's urban centres.

## Notes

1 Interview with Stella Soko, Lusaka, 29 May 2014.

2 On the role of men in global caring economies, see Majella Kilkey, 'Men and Domestic Labor: A Missing Link in the Global Care Chain', *Men and Masculinities*, 13:1 (2010), 126–149.

3 Penvenne, *Women, Migration and the Cashew Economy in Southern Mozambique*, p. 36.

4 Studies showing the importance of motherhood in African societies include Jennifer Johnson-Hanks, *Uncertain Honor: Modern Motherhood in an African Crisis* (Chicago, IL: University of Chicago Press, 2006); Kenda Mutongi, *Worries of the Heart: Widows, Family, and Community in Kenya* (Chicago, IL: Chicago University Press, 2007); Suzanne Preston Blier, 'The Path of the Leopard: Motherhood and Majesty in Early Danhomè', *Journal of African History*, 36:3 (1995), 391–417; Rhiannon Stephens, *A History of African Motherhood: The Case of Uganda, 700–1900* (Cambridge: Cambridge University Press, 2013).

5 Margarita Dimova, Carrie Hough, Kerry Kyaa, and Ambreena Manji, 'Intimacy and Inequality: Local Care Chains and Paid Childcare in Kenya', *Feminist Legal Studies*, 23:2 (2015), 169.

6 Arlie Russell Hochschild, 'Global Care Chains and Emotional Surplus Value', in Anthony Giddens and Will Hutton (eds), *On the Edge: Living With Global Capitalism* (London: Jonathan Cape, 2000), pp. 130–146.

7 Such studies include Jill Brown, 'Child Fostering Chains among Ovambo Families in Namibia, Southern Africa', *Journal of Southern African Studies*, 37:1 (2011), 155–176; Jacklyn Cock and Erica Emdon, '"Let Me Make History Please": The Story of Johanna Masilela, Childminder', in Belinda Bozzoli (ed.), *Class, Community and Conflict: South African Perspectives* (Johannesburg: Ravan Press, 1987), pp. 457–477; Dimova *et al.*, 'Intimacy and Inequality'; Laura Griffin, 'When Borders Fail: "Illegal", Invisible Labour Migration and Basotho Domestic Workers in South Africa', in Elspeth Guild and Sandra Mantu (eds), *Constructing and Imagining Labour Migration: Perspectives of Control from Five Continents* (Farnham: Ashgate, 2011), pp. 15–38; Penvenne, *Women, Migration and the Cashew Economy in Southern Mozambique*, chapter 4; Kathleen Sheldon, 'Creches, Titias, and Mothers: Working Women

and Childcare in Mozambique', in Hansen (ed.), *African Encounters with Domesticity*, pp. 290–309.

8 Interview with Priscilla Njovu.

9 Interview with Jane Kafula, Kitwe, 10 February 2014.

10 Girl domestic workers are known by different terms across Africa, including '*petites bonnes*', 'maids', and 'house helps'. For further discussion see Mélanie Jacquemin, 'Children's Domestic Work in Abidjan, Côte d'Ivoire: The Petites Bonnes Have the Floor', *Childhood*, 11:3 (2004), 383–397; Gladys Muasya, 'The Role of House Helps in Work–Family Balance of Women Employed in the Formal Sector in Kenya', in Zitha Mokomane (ed.), *Work–Family Interface in Sub-Saharan Africa* (London: Springer International Publishing, 2014), pp. 149–159.

11 Michael Bourdillon, *Child Domestic Workers in Zimbabwe* (Harare: Weaver Press, 2006), p. 19.

12 Interview with Rebecca Keyala, Lusaka, 5 July 2014.

13 Interview with Stella Soko.

14 Interview with Chombe Nachula.

15 Interview with Diana Mumba, Lusaka, 25 February 2014.

16 Miranda Miles, 'Working in the City: The Case of Migrant Women in Swaziland's Domestic Service Sector', in Momsen (ed.), *Gender, Migration and Domestic Service*, pp. 190–212.

17 Pape, 'Still Serving the Tea'.

18 Cock and Emdon, '"Let Me Make History Please"'.

19 An online search for maid centres in South Africa demonstrates the wide range of employment agencies operating in that context. Further information about SweepSouth is available at https://sweepsouth.com/ (accessed 4 December 2020).

20 Interview with Martha Banda, Lusaka, 6 February 2014.

21 Attempts to formalise domestic service will be examined in further detail in Chapter 4.

22 Interview with Mikala Mukongolwa, Lusaka, 2 August 2013.

23 Interview with June Phiri, Lusaka, 9 August 2013.

24 Interview with Jennifer Banda, Lusaka, 28 July 2013.

25 Interview with June Phiri.

26 Sheldon, *Pounders of Grain*, p. 183.

27 Interview with Dorothy Phiri.

28 Pape, 'Still Serving the Tea', 402.

29 Cock, *Maids and Madams*, p. 6, p. 27, p. 46, pp. 49–54, p. 61; Rebecca Ginsburg, *At Home with Apartheid: The Hidden Landscapes of Domestic Service in Johannesburg* (Charlottesville, VA: University of Virginia Press, 2011), pp. 90–91, pp. 99–106, p. 117, p. 135.

30 Dimova *et al.*, 'Intimacy and Inequality', 175.

31 *Ibid.*, 169, 175–177.
32 Interview with June Phiri; interview with Dorothy Phiri.
33 See for example, Cock, *Maids and Madams*, p. 28, p. 36, p. 38; Ginsburg, *At Home with Apartheid*, p. 91, p. 106.
34 Pape, 'Still Serving the Tea', 399.
35 Dimova *et al.*, 'Intimacy and Inequality', 169–170; Namuggala, 'Exploitation or Empowerment?', 565.
36 Sheldon, 'Creches, Titias, and Mothers', pp. 291–292.
37 Penvenne, *Women, Migration and the Cashew Economy in Southern Mozambique*, pp. 158–159.
38 Interview with Hope Chanda, Lusaka, 16 July 2014.
39 Interview with Diana Mumba.
40 Interview with Chombe Nachula.
41 *Ibid.*
42 Interview with Priscilla Njovu.
43 Interview with Stella Soko.
44 Interview with Bridget Kalobwe, Lusaka, 5 July 2014.
45 Interview with Dorothy Phiri.
46 Interview with Priscilla Njovu.
47 Interview with Veronica Tembo, Lusaka, 6 August 2014. Comparisons might be drawn with similar tendencies within the Homecraft movement during the colonial period. See, for example, Amy Kaler, 'Visions of Domesticity in the African Women's Homecraft Movement in Rhodesia', *Social Science History*, 23:3 (1999), 269–309.
48 Interview with Patricia Bwalya, Lusaka, 18 February 2014.
49 Interview with Mikala Mukongolwa.
50 Interview with Stella Soko.
51 *Ibid.*
52 Interview with Patricia Chanda, Lusaka, 1 August 2013.
53 Brown, 'Child Fostering Chains', 166.
54 Interview with Stella Soko.
55 Interview with Rebecca Keyala.
56 Interview with Bessie Chanda, Lusaka, 7 July 2014.
57 For an extensive discussion of the use of familial language in domestic service, see Ena Jansen, *Like Family: Domestic Workers in South African History and Literature* (Johannesburg: Wits University Press, 2019).
58 Interview with Stella Soko.
59 Bourdillon, *Child Domestic Workers in Zimbabwe*, p. 28.
60 See, for instance, Thérèse Blanchet, *Slavery Revisited: Adopting a Child to Secure a Servant: Palok Meye, Palok Chele* (Dhaka: Save the Children, Sweden and Denmark, 2004); Thérèse Blanchet and Anisa Zalman,

*Slavery Revisited: Child Domestic Servants* (Dhaka: Save the Children, Sweden and Denmark, 2004); Anita Cheria, *Liberation Is Not Enough: The Kamaiya Movement in Nepal* (Kathmandu: ActionAid Nepal, 2005); B. R. Giri, 'The Bonded Labour Practice in Nepal: "The Promise of Education" as a Magnet of Child Bondedness?', *South Asia Research*, 30:2 (2010), 145–164.

61 Republic of Zambia, Statutory Instrument No. 3 of 2011. Examples of such campaigns include ILO, *Emerging Good Practices on Action to Combat Child Domestic Labour in Kenya, Tanzania, Uganda and Zambia* (Geneva: International Labour Office, 2006); ILO, *Ending Child Labour in Domestic Work and Protecting Young Workers from Abusive Working Conditions* (Geneva: International Labour Office, 2013).

62 On the cultural meaning of girls' puberty and related practices in Zambia, see Hansen, *Keeping House in Lusaka*, pp. 111–112, pp. 154–155; Moore and Vaughan, *Cutting Down Trees*, pp. 171–172; Audrey Richards, *Chisungu: A Girl's Initiation Ceremony Among the Bemba of Zambia* (London: Routledge, 1956).

63 Interview with Priscilla Njovu.

64 Hansen, 'Body Politics', 134.

65 Interview with Priscilla Njovu.

66 Interview with Rebecca Keyala.

67 Interview with Stella Soko.

68 Parpart, '"Where Is Your Mother?"', 241–271; Evans, 'History Lessons', 344–362.

69 Interview with Jane Kafula.

70 Interview with Priscilla Njovu.

71 On nostalgia in oral history interviews with Zambians, see also Mususa, '"Getting By"'.

72 This discourse is certainly evident in media coverage, such as J. Banda, 'Zambia Should Save Its Own Children', *Times of Zambia*, 11 July 2003; N. Mulenga, 'The Plight of an Exploited Domestic House Maid', *Times of Zambia*, 25 September 2004; B. Kayaya, 'Tackling Child Labour in Zambia', *Times of Zambia*, 3 June 2008.

73 Bryceson, 'Domestic Work', p. 313.

74 This is shown in sequential census reports. Republic of Zambia, *1990 Census of Population, Housing and Agriculture. Volume 10*; Republic of Zambia, *2000 Census of Population and Housing. Analytical Report Final*; Republic of Zambia, *2010 Census of Population and Housing. National Analytical Report*.

# 3

# Girl domestic workers' aspirations and frustrations

Esnart Lungu's life story provides key insights into the history of girls' employment in domestic service in southern Africa's post-colonial cities. In March 1981, then-eleven-year-old Esnart left her parents' rural home in Sinda, in Zambia's Eastern Province, and set out for Lusaka. She travelled to the city to become a live-in maid for a family she had never met, accompanied by the wife of her former schoolteacher, who had arranged Esnart's employment in the city. Esnart's parents were subsistence farmers and desperately poor. She had become a maid in the hope of helping her family, stating during a 2014 interview that she had thought as a child, 'even if I send everything home, I will still have something to eat, somewhere to sleep'. She stayed in this job for two years, before returning to the Eastern Province to live with her parents.[1] Esnart was one of a large number of female children and youth who have found work in the homes of strangers and kin in Lusaka and other southern African cities, exchanging domestic and care labour for cash wages and various in-kind payments. As this chapter examines, girls like Esnart supported themselves and a range of dependants with their wages, providing the cheap domestic and care labour that was needed to sustain their employers' urban households. Girls found a place for themselves in the spectrum of domestic service practices which sustained urban homes because of the enduring power of gendered constructions of childhood that linked girls with domestic and care labour, the extensive use of girls' labour within household economies, and the relative cheapness of their labour compared with adults.

African girl domestic workers, like child workers more broadly, have been largely overlooked and undervalued in existing African labour history. They have received the most attention in international development circles and, since the 2000s, from policymakers as part of broader campaigning around children's rights and child labour.[2] The approaches taken by many IGOs and NGOs working in this field have become increasingly sophisticated over time, but the tendency to perceive complex labour practices in often universalising and essentially Western terms remains a problematic feature of their work. Influenced by these initiatives, contemporary public discourses on girl domestic workers, and working children more broadly, in southern Africa have largely centred on victimhood, with girls thought to be exceptionally vulnerable to exploitation and abuse.[3] As will be shown in this chapter, such perceptions of children's employment draw attention to the exploitation that many young workers have experienced, but they also limit our understanding of the complexity of working children's lives and often overlook children's capacity to shape their working and living conditions.

Drawing extensively on oral histories, this chapter places girl domestic workers' experiences and perspectives at the centre of analysis. It examines how and why girls found employment in domestic service in Lusaka, their experiences of mobility, their working and living conditions, and their relationships with employers and relatives. It demonstrates that girls used employment in domestic service to support themselves and their dependants in the city and the countryside, and that they made significant contributions to household, informal, and formal economies in the process. In doing so, it seeks to complicate understandings of girls' employment in domestic service, illustrating how girls could exercise a certain amount of agency and autonomy even in the face of significant personal and structural challenges. It situates these findings within the broader southern African context by using existing grey literature and academic studies to explore the employment of girls in domestic service in other regional urban centres. Building on the previous chapters, these findings provide key insights into the intersecting nature of gender, age, sexuality, and kinship in the making of domestic labour relations in southern Africa's post-colonial cities. Notably, they show how gendered and sexual expectations shaped girls' access to and experiences of work and their relationships with adults, with puberty often serving as an endpoint for employment because of concerns surrounding girls' sexuality.

## Girls' aspirations and frustrations

Zambian girls entered domestic service for numerous reasons. Most needed to support themselves and their dependants as a result of household poverty or the loss of household members; others responded to the requests of senior kin; and some sought a way to fund their education and to pursue a better life. Each of these causes needs to be understood in relation to the broader social and economic challenges facing Zambians in the post-colonial period, with the impacts of economic decline and structural adjustment causing profound hardship in rural and urban households, and enduring

**Figure 3.1** Girl domestic worker and laundry in Bauleni, Lusaka, 19 July 2013.

gender and generational inequalities putting pressure on girls and women.

Oral histories illustrate how financial pressures shaped girls' entry into domestic service. Evelyn Banda was born in a village near Chipata in the Eastern Province in the late 1950s. She completed several years of primary education and left school around the age of fourteen. Her parents had little money and had sometimes struggled to find enough food to feed the family. In the early 1970s, Evelyn's maternal aunt contacted Evelyn's mother to ask if Evelyn would like to come to Lusaka to find paid employment. Evelyn migrated to Lusaka to live with her aunt who was employed as a maid in the city. After three months in Lusaka, Evelyn secured a position as a live-in maid in Kabulonga. During an interview in 2014, she explained that she thought as a girl that she had been offered a good job because it provided her with a cash wage, accommodation, and meals.[4] Esnart faced similar challenging circumstances as a child in the early 1980s. Her parents struggled to support themselves through subsistence agriculture, a situation which was exacerbated by her father's heavy drinking. She was forced to leave school because her parents could not afford the fees. She had been out of school for a year when she was offered the job in domestic service in Lusaka. The proposition came from the wife of her former schoolteacher, who was seeking a girl to work in the household of her Lusaka-based sister-in-law, who was a teacher and new mother. Although Esnart did not actively seek work as a maid, she suggested during our interview in 2014 that she had wanted to take the job so that she could earn money and help her mother. This she did, saving her small cash wage each week and sending regular remittances to her mother.[5]

Existing studies have similarly shown how financial pressures pushed Zambia's children into domestic service. Omolara Dakore Oyaide found that parental poverty was the main reason why children were working in domestic service in Lusaka in 2000. The link between children's employment and Zambia's broader economic fortunes was clear. Many of her interviewees stated that their parents were unemployed, with several having been retrenched from government parastatals and companies during the 1990s.[6] More broadly, household poverty has been observed as driving children's employment in domestic service across southern Africa's cities, including in Malawi, South Africa, and Zimbabwe.[7] In a study of child domestic workers in Zimbabwe, Michael Bourdillon described the life story of Nomsa. She grew up in poverty during the 2000s in a village 100 km outside of Harare. Her parents were subsistence farmers, and she had been forced to drop out of school aged fourteen because they could not afford her fees. As in Esnart's case, Nomsa's father drank heavily, and this exacerbated the family's precarious situation.[8] Soon after Nomsa dropped out of school, she received a visit from a friend who worked as a maid in Harare. Her friend had been asked by her employer to bring another girl to the city to work in their home. Nomsa left her rural home and moved to Harare to take up this position.[9]

Alongside a need to earn money, girls were also motivated by their hopes for the future. Although Evelyn entered domestic service primarily because of household poverty, she had also hoped that it would provide a stepping stone to better work opportunities in the city. Several interviewees also hoped that working in domestic service would enable them to pursue their education. Grace Musonda explained how she had used her income from working as a live-in maid to pay her school fees. Grace was born in Zambia's Northern Province in 1980. Like Esnart, she was forced to leave school because her parents could no longer afford to pay the fees. During an interview in 2014, Grace lamented, 'there was no money … no life that side'. After Grace dropped out of school, she asked her parents if she could move to Lusaka to join her sister, who had migrated to the city during the late 1980s. Her parents agreed, and she moved to the city to live with her sister in Bauleni. Grace's sister told her that she would need to find a job to pay for her school fees and suggested that she look for work as a maid. Grace described walking around Bauleni, knocking on doors in her search for work. She found a job as a live-in maid in the home of a policeman and his wife. Grace's employers supported her ambition to complete her education, and she used her small cash wage to pay for her school fees.[10] Mercy Banda, whom we first encountered in the Introduction, similarly became a maid in order to earn money for school fees. In her case, she took up a part-time, live-out position, commuting from her Bauleni home to a job in the nearby suburb of Woodlands.[11] Both girls managed to complete their secondary education by working in domestic service.

Niah Mumba also entered domestic service in the hope of paying for school. Niah was born in Lusaka in 1992, the eldest of six children. In the early 2000s, Niah's father became ill and was forced to leave his job in construction. Her mother was unable to support the family on the small income she earned from selling vegetables at the local market. As the eldest child, Niah was forced to leave school and help her mother with market work and with domestic labour and childcare. Niah recalled being out of school for around a year when her parents were approached by a female family friend who asked if she could employ Niah as a maid. The employer in question was a teacher at a boarding school in the Southern Province. Niah described feeling scared by the prospect of moving away from her family but excited about living at a boarding school, which she hoped she would be able to attend alongside her work. Unlike Grace and Mercy, Niah found that her aspirations went unfulfilled. Although her employer had initially said that she would be able to attend the boarding school, Niah's requests to attend lessons were repeatedly refused. Niah's days instead consisted of domestic labour and childcare, in return for which she received accommodation, meals, and a small cash payment.[12] This example of frustrated ambitions mirrors the experiences of many other girl domestic workers in the region. For instance, Bourdillon relates the life story of Tariro, a girl who migrated from her parents' home in rural Zimbabwe to Harare during the 2000s after the death of her father and the premature end of her schooling. Tariro moved to the city to work in the home of a distant relative, who promised to support her through school if she helped around the house. Like Niah, Tariro found that these promises went unfulfilled. Only after Tariro's uncle intervened on her behalf did her employer start sending her to school, highlighting the importance for children of having close relatives who would stand up for and support them.[13]

Some girls entered domestic service after the loss of their parents or guardians. Queen Kangwa was born in Serenje in Zambia's Central Province in 1990, the youngest of three children. Both of her parents died from AIDS-related illnesses before she reached the age of thirteen. Queen explained that her rural relatives had been unable to support the orphaned children and so arranged for them to move to Lusaka to live with their maternal grandmother. Once in Lusaka, Queen found work as a live-in maid in order to help support herself and help her grandmother and siblings.[14] Queen's life story draws attention to the relationship between child domestic work, orphanhood, and the HIV/AIDs pandemic. Rates of orphanhood in Zambia increased throughout the 1990s, primarily as a result of this pandemic. By the early 2000s, when Queen's parents died, an estimated 630,000 Zambian children had lost one or both parents to AIDS-related illnesses, and Zambia had one of the highest rates of orphanhood in Sub-Saharan Africa.[15] In Zambia and across Africa, orphans have often engaged in a higher level of economic activity than their non-orphaned peers. Female children who lost their mothers were often required to take on a high level of domestic labour inside the home, while female children who lost their father or both parents, like Queen, were sometimes required to find employment elsewhere in order to supplement the household income. Additionally, some children became heads of households and pursued employment in order to support their younger siblings.[16] Domestic service was one of the most accessible forms of employment for orphaned children across Africa, because it required no formal education or training and often came with accommodation and meals. In Tanzania, for instance, a quarter of child domestic workers described how they had entered domestic service because they had lost family members to HIV/AIDs and had no one else to take care of them.[17]

## Spatial and social mobility

Spatial mobility was central to many girl domestic workers' life stories, with rural-urban migration a common experience. Esnart's migration from her parents' rural home to Lusaka was prompted by her employment, while Evelyn, Grace, and Queen found work as maids after moving from the countryside to the city. Domestic service provided an entry point to Lusaka for these girls and countless others. This mirrored broader regional patterns, with domestic service facilitating and stimulating girls' and women's migration to urban centres across southern Africa, from Johannesburg to Maputo.[18] Girls' migration into domestic service in Zambia also mapped onto gendered and generational migration trends following independence. As discussed in the introduction, Lusaka consistently attracted female and young migrants from other parts of Zambia during the 1960s to 2010s. Two of the most important drivers of this migration were persistent rural poverty and gendered and generational inequalities within rural communities, with many women and girls migrating to the city in the hope that they could escape patriarchal controls and destitution and secure a better life.

Domestic service not only facilitated girls' migration, it also provided them with a way to support themselves and their dependants. For example, through her labour Esnart supported herself in Lusaka and earned money to send to her family in the Eastern Province. These remittances were her family's only dependable source of cash income. Esnart described her motivation for working as being driven by a desire to send remittances and help her mother.[19] As an adult, her understanding of her motivations as a girl was refracted through her later experiences, including as a mother, and it is possible that she downplayed other factors which led to her employment, including parental pressure. Yet her actions as a child clearly also suggest that she wanted to provide her family with financial support. Girl domestic workers' investments in rural communities have also been observed elsewhere. For instance, Victoria Namuggala observed how girl domestic workers in Kampala used their savings to invest in their rural homes, including by buying livestock.[20] Examples such as these provide new insights into the gender and generational dimensions of urban-rural remittances and the specific contributions made by girls. It is well known that male migrants have historically made a significant economic impact on rural households across Africa through remittances, but the impact that female migrants and children have made is little acknowledged. Interviews with the relatives of migrant female domestic workers confirm the value of such remittances. I interviewed Semu Lameck at his home in Chimusanya village in Lusaka Province in 2014. Semu and his wife were subsistence farmers and also brewed beer which they sold from their home. Their daughter Margaret had been employed in Lusaka as a live-in maid since 2009. She had migrated to the city aged nineteen in search of work after the breakdown of her marriage. Semu explained that Margaret had sent him cash payments of around 200 Zambian kwacha (K; equivalent to approximately 20 US dollars, or USD) twice per year since she had migrated to Lusaka.[21] Semu used this money to buy groceries and fertiliser, goods that he stated he could not have purchased without Margaret's support.[22]

Girl migrants who did not send regular cash remittances to their rural relatives also supported rural households and communities. At the very least, girls' migration relieved their parents and relatives of their material upkeep. For instance, although Evelyn did not send cash remittances to her parents, she undoubtedly still helped them by finding a way to support herself. In the case of Semu and his wife, they struggled to meet their basic living costs after their daughter Margaret returned to live with them after her divorce. Margaret received no financial support from her ex-husband, and Semu and his wife struggled to make their household income and resources stretch to cover another household member. By migrating to Lusaka, Margaret found a way to support herself, relieving Semu and his wife of the need to provide for her. The money that Margaret sent home was a very useful additional benefit of her migration.[23]

Mobility was also a key feature of girl domestic workers' experiences within the city. Some girls travelled across the city daily, commuting between their homes and places of work, while others left their urban homes and went to live with employers in more affluent areas of the city. In 1985, Elizabeth Bwalya moved across Lusaka from her father's house in Chipata compound to the nearby affluent suburb of Roma, where she found work as a live-in maid.[24] Anna Banda also moved across Lusaka, from her parents' home in Matero compound to her maternal aunt's home in Bauleni, where she provided domestic labour in exchange for a place in the household and small cash payments.[25] Domestic service both facilitated and necessitated such intra-urban mobility, as girls and women sought access to employment in the suburbs, and urban employers sought access to cheap female labour from the low-income compounds. Such practices built on long-established patterns of domestic workers moving around the city. In colonial Lusaka, most domestic workers lived in on-site servants' quarters, but a significant number commuted to work. The latter group lived either in the personal servants' compound that was built to house those who could not be accommodated on their employer's property, or in the city's planned and unplanned African compounds. Commuting to work became more common amongst domestic workers during the late colonial period, as the population of Lusaka grew and the supply of housing for all urban residents failed to keep up with demand.[26] These trends continued at pace following independence, as the urban population grew and the housing shortage intensified.[27]

As girl domestic workers like Elizabeth and Anna moved between the city's different neighbourhoods, they experienced and crossed the city's spatial and socio-economic divides. On the one hand, they were able to travel to other parts of the city and access the resources of their employers' homes. Their employment involved the transfer of money, in the form of wages, and goods, in the form of in-kind payments, between the different parts of the city. On the other hand, their mobility exposed the girls involved to the stark differences in wealth and opportunity that distinguished and separated Lusaka's neighbourhoods and residents.

Girl domestic workers were more mobile than their peers. Young and poor Lusakans generally had very low levels of spatial mobility. This resulted from a combination of economic constraints and gendered and gerontocratic hierarchies. Opportunities for education and employment, and the mobility these often required, became increasingly more difficult for young Lusakans to access over time because of shrinking household budgets and the squeezing out of poor urban residents to the margins of the city. These processes had clear gendered and generational dynamics, with girls and women from poor households facing higher barriers to employment and exhibiting lower levels of daily and residential mobility than their male counterparts.[28] In addition, the cost of transportation was a significant barrier to mobility across genders, with few poor young people able to afford to pay for bus fares and instead having to move around the city on foot.[29]

Girl domestic workers' life stories demonstrate how their spatial mobility was facilitated by their participation in kinship networks. In the case of rural-urban migration, we have seen how relationships between female kin created opportunities for women and girls to migrate and shaped their routes into employment in the city. Evelyn, Queen, and Grace all described migrating to the city to live with female relatives. Evelyn found work in domestic service in Lusaka through her aunt, who also worked as a maid in the city, while Queen and Grace found work in domestic service in other ways, using their connections with female kin to establish themselves in the city before looking for work on their own. These connections between kinship, long-distance mobility, and domestic service reflect trends in other African contexts. Belinda Bozzoli's work on Bafokeng migrant domestic workers in Johannesburg and Suzanne Gordon's research on South African domestic workers' life histories both illustrated how 'home girl' networks provided sources of support and information for successive generations of female rural-urban migrants.[30] Namuggala similarly observed how peer networks influenced Ugandan girls' decisions to migrate to the city and become domestic workers.[31] Moreover, relationships with kin also facilitated girl domestic workers' mobility within the city. We have seen, for example, how Elizabeth found work as a maid through her sister's husband, who was employed as a gardener, and how Anna found employment in her maternal aunt's home in Bauleni.[32]

As suggested above, many girls hoped that employment in domestic service might also bring about social mobility. We saw, for instance, how Grace and Mercy pursued education alongside working in domestic service. In Grace's case, her chances of completing her education were much higher in Lusaka than they had been in her rural home in Northern Province. In Zambia, education rates remained higher in urban areas than rural areas following independence. By 1980, school attendance of those aged five and above was just under 40 per cent in urban areas, compared with just over 29 per cent in rural areas. By 1990, this gulf had widened, with the percentage of school attendance in urban areas increasing to nearly 58 per cent and remaining at 29 per cent in rural areas.[33] This divergence can be explained in part by the higher number of schools and educational facilities in urban areas and in part by rural poverty rates, which rendered schooling out of financial reach for many rural households. It also resulted from dynamics within the rural labour force, with children and youth engaged extensively in domestic and agricultural labour to support the household economy. The opportunities for education in the city were somewhat undermined by persistent gender inequality in education, with a higher proportion of male children than female children attending school in both urban and rural areas well into the 1990s. School dropout rates have also historically been higher amongst female students than male.[34] Many parents prioritised the education of male over female members, including in times of hardship, and placed higher demands on girls to help with domestic and care labour within the home. These disparities resulted from and reflected broader gender inequalities at the household level and in wider society.

Aspirations for education shaped female migration strategies into young adulthood. Fridah Njovu's experience is illustrative. She was born in Northern Province in 1970, the eleventh child and only daughter of subsistence farmers. Her father had worked in the copper mines in his youth and had developed long-term health conditions related to this work. He died during the mid-1980s, and this plunged the family into economic difficulty. Like countless other girls, Fridah was forced to leave school because her mother could no longer afford the fees. She soon became engaged to a young man from her village and was married by the age of sixteen. During an interview in 2013, Fridah described the next couple of years as the most difficult of her life. She became pregnant within months of marriage, but her son died just two days after his birth. Soon after their son's death, Fridah's husband took a second wife. Fridah could not adjust to living in a polygynous marriage and decided to separate from her husband. Aged twenty, she left her village and moved to Ndola to live with her maternal grandmother. After several months of helping her grandmother at her small business selling drinks and biscuits at a local market, Fridah decided to find work as a live-in domestic worker. Reflecting on this decision, she explained that she had wanted to find a job that enabled her to support herself and, ideally, save money so that she could go back to school. Over the next five years, Fridah worked as a live-in maid in several homes: first in Ndola, then at her uncle's house in Choma in Southern Province, before finally settling in Lusaka.[35]

Fridah's experiences draw attention to the liminal status of girlhood in post-colonial African societies. As a young woman who had been married and given birth to a child, Fridah had experienced two of the most important stages in the transition to full social adulthood. She likely faced a different set of opportunities and constraints compared with female children and those who had barely entered puberty. Yet despite her more advanced social and chronological age, there are many similarities between Fridah's experiences and those of younger domestic workers. While living with her uncle, Fridah 'earned' her place in the household by cooking, cleaning, and caring for other household members, including her uncle's children, echoing the experiences of my other interviewees. Although Fridah had started along the path to social adulthood, she remained in some senses a girl: she was a female dependant, and her position in the household hinged on her performance of gendered forms of labour. Fridah had hoped that this period of dependency would enable her to improve her prospects, specifically by returning to education, but like Niah and countless other girls, her aspirations were unfulfilled. The liminal nature of girlhood is also illustrated by Namuggala's work on girl domestic workers in Uganda. She explored how domestic service provided a viable source of employment for schoolgirls who fell pregnant and were forced to leave school so that they could earn money to support themselves and their children. She describes these girls as 'child mothers' to highlight their ambiguous status as parents and cultural and legal minors.[36]

Fridah's experiences also highlight how uncommon it was for child domestic workers in post-colonial Africa to succeed in pursuing education alongside employment. Grace and Mercy's experiences were far from the norm, both in Zambia and more broadly. Maxton Tsoka interviewed girl domestic workers in Malawi during the 2000s and found that while most wanted to attend school, very few were enrolled or had attended school beyond primary level. This resulted from a combination of poverty, gendered constructions of childhood which favoured male over female school attendance, the absence of compulsory schooling, and limited educational provision.[37] In Zimbabwe, Bourdillon similarly found that few child domestic workers went to school during the 2000s, while those who did often found that they had little time to complete their homework. The education that child domestic workers who attended school received was also generally of a lower standard than that of their employers' children.[38] In Morocco, domestic service has usually been perceived as an alternative to formal education.[39] An important contrast to these cases is South Africa, where an ILO study from 2002 found that most child domestic workers attended school. This included children engaged in both waged and unwaged domestic service practices, and school attendance rates were similar for girl and boy domestic workers.[40] Perhaps the key reason for high school attendance amongst child domestic workers in South Africa during the 2000s was that education was both free and compulsory for every child up to the age of fifteen years.[41] Although South Africa was in many ways a success story, child domestic workers still faced challenges in pursuing their education. Like child domestic workers elsewhere in the region, South African child domestic workers complained about lack of time to complete homework. Furthermore, 'free' education did not mean the absence of school fees, but that households who were unable to pay school fees should be granted an exemption, a policy which was not always followed, and which excluded some poor child domestic workers from attending school.[42]

## Girls' working and living conditions

Whether they worked for kin or strangers, girl domestic workers' roles involved a wide range of duties. Grace described how in her first role as a maid she had swept the floors, washed and ironed clothes, cooked breakfast and lunch for her employers and their children, washed dishes, bathed her employers' children, and looked after their youngest child.[43] Niah similarly explained that she had done all of the domestic work in her aunt's household and had cared for a small child.[44] In her first role, Esnart was primarily employed to care for her employer's child, but this also involved washing the baby's clothes and preparing his meals, and she was sometimes asked to help her employer to prepare meals for the household.[45] Alongside highlighting the varied labour that girl domestic workers performed, these examples also reiterate the importance of girls as carers of children. Some girl domestic workers also helped their employers with trading and vending. For instance, Anna helped her aunt to cook and sell food from their home in Bauleni.[46]

Some girl domestic workers also sought out work in addition to their main jobs in domestic service. Grace described how she had sometimes had to look for piecework because the wages she received as a maid were very low and not always enough to cover her school fees and other expenses. In her limited time off from her job and school, she walked around her neighbourhood to ask if any neighbours needed help with their laundry.[47] Queen Kangwa also described seeking piecework while working as a maid. At the time of our interview in 2014, she was employed as a live-out maid for three days per week, and she sought piecework on other days. Like Grace, she sought laundry work, and she would also sometimes perform daily cleaning services for employers who could not afford a maid on a more regular basis.[48]

Many of my interviewees described working long hours, stretching from early in the morning to early evening and beyond. Oyaide similarly observed that child domestic workers in Lusaka worked long hours, with many girl domestic workers starting work before five in the morning and finishing after eight at night.[49] These findings mirror broader trends across the continent. In Abidjan, for instance, Mélanie Jacquemin observed that girl domestic workers worked no less than eleven hours per day.[50] In Lusaka and elsewhere, girls who lived with their employers tended to work longer hours than did girls who commuted to work. Oyaide found that live-in workers worked on average just over fifteen hours per day, while live-out workers worked around ten hours per day. Girls who lived with their employers were also often the last people in the household to go to bed, only able to retire once they had finished serving all members of the household.[51] The working day could be especially long for girls who cared for children, particularly if they shared a room with their charges. Anna shared a bed with her aunt's children during the 1980s.[52] Grace similarly described sharing a room with her employers' children during the 1990s.[53] Both described waking up to care for children during the night. Queen's experiences compared favourably with those of other girls who cared for children. During her first role as a maid, Queen began work at seven in the morning and finished at five in the afternoon. She worked from Monday to Saturday and was given Sundays off. She did not share a room with the baby she cared for, and her employer would take care of the baby when she returned from work on weekdays, and for the whole weekend.[54] Girls who did not live with their employers generally worked fewer hours than girls with live-in positions, but they also had to travel to and from work each day, and this added to their working day.

For girls who attended school, the working week was lengthened by time spent on schoolwork. Grace, for example, described working seven days per week in her first role as a maid. Her workload was heaviest on weekdays, when her employers were at work and she had to combine housework and childcare with attending classes in the afternoons. Typically, such days began at around six in the morning and ended after nine at night. She also did housework on Saturdays and helped her employer with childcare over the weekend. She used whatever spare time she had in the evenings and weekend to do her homework, and to look for piecework as described above.[55] Bourdillon related how Tariro similarly faced a long day juggling her employment as a maid in Harare with attending school. In her case, she rose early, cleaned the house, and made breakfast for everyone before going to school in the mornings. When she returned from school in the afternoons, she quickly did her homework and then prepared dinner. She washed the dishes and tried to get in an hour of reading or other schoolwork before bed. On two evenings per week, she also did laundry. On average, she did six hours of domestic work on weekdays, alongside going to school.[56]

During interviews, it was difficult to get a sense of exactly how much girls were paid for their labour. Some girls received cash wages. In addition, some were also given payments in kind, such as food, clothes, toiletries, and other consumer goods. Girls who worked for kin often received part, if not all, of their wages through payments in kind, and parallels can be drawn with other labour practices involving the transfer of children between households, including child fostering. That many girls were paid in kind makes it very challenging to estimate the monetary value of the girls' earnings and to trace how girls' wage rates changed over time. In addition, girls who lived in and were asked to work from early morning or late into the night did not report receiving any form of overtime pay for such work.

Most women could not recall the amount of cash wages they had received as girls. Grace, for example, could not remember how much her cash wage had been but noted that she had to sometimes take on additional work to cover her school fees and have some money to save towards clothes, toiletries, and personal items.[57] Even Esnart, who talked quite explicitly about money, could not recall how much money she had actually sent to her mother.[58] Interviewees' inability to remember how much they had been paid as girls draws attention to the limits of using the retrospective testimonies of adults, though some women were also unable to recall what they had been paid as girls because their employer had sent their wages directly to their parents. For their part, many employers also seemingly could not remember how much they had paid their young employees. Dorothy, for instance, could not recall how much she had contributed toward Anna's school fees.[59] Employers' inability to discuss wage rates conceivably could have resulted from the limits of memory, but may also have been the result of an unwillingness to discuss the issue. As discussed in Chapter 2, it is possible that some employers wanted to disguise the low wages they had offered to the girls they employed, especially after the 2011 introduction of minimum wage legislation for domestic workers and the outlawing of child employment in the sector.

Girls in live-in positions were also provided with accommodation, and this should be taken into account as part of the overall remuneration package they received. The types of accommodation and living conditions that girls experienced varied and depended on the wealth and goodwill of their employer. Some girls described the poor standard of sleeping arrangements they endured. Namuggala related the case of Kate, a girl domestic worker in Kampala, who slept on a one-inch-thick mattress on her employers' sitting room floor, with only a thin sheet for a cover. Kate described how she often struggled to sleep because of the cold and was told by her employer to buy blankets from her wages.[60] Girls' sleeping conditions were also impacted by whether or not they shared a room. As discussed above, Anna and Grace described how they had slept in the same room as their employers' children, practices which built on longstanding spatial divisions within Zambian households, with children and adults occupying separate sleeping spaces.

Girls who worked in the households of Lusaka's higher income residents sometimes accessed a higher standard of living than they had experienced at home. Priscilla Njovu talked about Esther's shock when she arrived in Lusaka from her rural home in Eastern Province and realised that she would have her own bedroom in Priscilla's large suburban home: 'she got scared the first night. She asked, "am I safe? The room is too big for me!"' According to Priscilla, the young maid's astonishment went beyond the size of her bedroom: 'at first just to switch on the lights it was something … exciting to her. To get into the car everyday … when we were going to buy groceries nearby she would want to jump in the car!

Just to be in the car it was exciting for her.'[61] While it is clearly possible that Priscilla wanted to present her treatment of Esther in a favourable light, her home and lifestyle were certainly very different from Esther's parents. For Esther, having her own bedroom, having access to an indoor bathroom, travelling by car, and eating store-bought groceries were luxuries that she had never previously experienced. We can see, therefore, how domestic service provided some girls with access to a wider range of material resources and consumer goods than they had previously. Bourdillon observed a similar phenomenon in Harare, with domestic service offering some children from poor homes access to a higher standard of living.[62]

Despite such examples of increased standards of living, many girl domestic workers experienced negative impacts on their health and well-being. Girls likely suffered from exhaustion due to the length of their working days and the long list of tasks they had to perform, while caring for children through the night likely caused many girls to suffer from sleep deprivation. There were also physical dangers associated with domestic work, such as handling sharp knives and boiling water while cooking, and carrying heavy loads while collecting water. Domestic service could also negatively impact children's mental health. Research with child domestic workers in Kenya showed that they experienced more psychological issues than other children, including insomnia, bed-wetting, withdrawal, and depression.[63] Similar conclusions have been drawn about child domestic workers elsewhere in the world. For instance, child domestic workers in Indonesia were observed to have very low self-esteem and to be able to see no future life for themselves beyond domestic service.[64] As will be explored in further detail below, child domestic workers' health and well-being were significantly impacted by their relationships with employers and relatives.

## Relationships with employers and relatives

Relationships between girl domestic workers and their employers involved many different dynamics. These relationships were grounded in and perpetuated inequality. This is true for all domestic service relationships, and in the case of girl domestic workers and their employers, this inequality was grounded in intersecting hierarchies of gender, generation, kinship, and wealth. Girls' unequal position vis-à-vis their employers was further exacerbated by the private nature of the spaces in which they worked and the fact that many were living away from close family members and dependent upon their employers for accommodation, meals, and other forms of support. We have seen how employers exploited girls' labour, with girls working long hours often in exchange for little or limited remuneration. Moreover, even when the cash and in-kind payments that girls received were of significant value to them and their families, those payments would almost certainly have been lower than what would have been paid to an adult worker for the same labour. In this sense, girls' age and gender, and often their status as junior kin, rendered them less 'valuable' within the marketplace and more easily exploited by employers.

There is evidence from a number of African contexts that domestic service practices involving children became increasingly exploitative over time. This is most clear in relation to kin-based domestic service. Hansen argues that, following independence, the recruitment of Zambian children into domestic service through kinship networks continued to be perceived by many in terms of mutual obligations and dependencies, but increasingly became a means for urban employers to source cheap labour provided by vulnerable young people. She links this to Zambia's economic decline, suggesting that one of the ways urban residents responded to their shrinking household budgets was to exploit the labour of junior kin.[65] This draws our attention to the ways in which formerly voluntary exchanges of labour between kin could become involuntary and coercive in certain cases. Similar trends have been observed elsewhere in post-colonial Africa. Bryceson draws attention to the changing nature of child fostering practices on the continent, arguing that

> the welfare of those being transferred from their natal homes needs to be monitored by a concerned social network of persons dedicated to ensuring the child's well-being in guardianship. Recent evidence suggests that the traditional institution of kin support … has transmogrified in some places towards forced labour or indeed slavery.[66]

Here, Bryceson suggests that the traditional checks and balances which ensured that children in fostering relationships were cared for have been bypassed in certain places, or no longer function effectively. As in the Zambian case, declining economic security was likely to be one of the key drivers of these changes, as urban residents used whatever means they could to secure the labour they needed and exploited children in the process. Organisations including the ILO and Anti-Slavery International have taken a critical line towards kin-based domestic service practices and the related mobility of children, often drawing links between these and forms of trafficking and forced labour.

My findings from Lusaka concur with many of these arguments. I certainly found evidence that some urban employers sought domestic labour through the extended family system because the labour of kin was cheap. I also found evidence of exploitation in kin-based domestic service arrangements, with several interviewees who laboured for relatives describing difficult working conditions, long and irregular working hours, and low remuneration. I found no evidence of forced labour or slavery from oral history interviews or informal observations, though it is of course possible, and indeed likely, that some interviewees who laboured for relatives were coerced into doing so by their parents or senior kin.

Employers' exploitation of girl domestic workers went beyond the economic. During our interview, Niah explained how her employer had shouted at her and sometimes withheld food if she did not finish her day's work. The use of food deprivation as a punishment for child domestic workers has also been observed in other contexts.[67] Niah lamented, 'I was young and couldn't know anything … she gave me too much work and shouted, shouted.' She explained that she only came to realise the extent to which her employer was taking advantage of her labour as she grew older and gathered the courage to discuss the situation with her sister. She said that her sister had sighed and said, 'get used to it, that's how it is'. Niah's understanding of the injustices she had experienced as a girl was likely influenced by her later experiences of working in domestic service; she stated that later employers had paid her a 'fair wage' and that none had shouted at her.[68] Many other interviewees similarly described being shouted at by their employers. Some girl domestic workers were verbally abused by the children of employers, who used terms that marked girls out as low-status and inferior. Priscilla described how her children refused to call their maid Mildred anything other than 'mildew', seemingly to associate the young maid with mould and decay.[69] Examples such as this call to mind the processes of class distancing that have taken place within domestic service arrangements between adult workers and employers.[70]

Employment in domestic service also exposed girls to forms of physical abuse. Several interviewees described being slapped on their faces or legs if they did not finish their work in the allotted time or to the standard expected by their employers. Some interviewees also described being abused by their employer's children or other young dependants in their employer's household. One interviewee explained how her employer's children would spit in her food; she was too frightened to tell her employer and so had to either eat the spoiled food or go hungry. Girl domestic workers were also vulnerable to sexual abuse. This was a difficult issue to explore in depth through oral history interviews. Although many interviewees talked to me about the sexual exploitation of domestic workers in the abstract, few were willing or able to discuss their own experiences. Carol Banda was one such interviewee, and she described an incident that occurred while she worked as a live-in maid for a middle-class family in Lusaka during the late 1970s.

> I shared a room with their daughter. She was thirteen and I was fourteen. The husband would come into the room at night, he pretended he was checking on his daughter, but I knew he was watching me. One day he touched me … I didn't tell the madam. Later I ran from that place.[71]

Carol did not expand on the nature of the assault and I did not probe, as it was clear that she found this to be a distressing topic, even years after the event. Existing studies of child labour in Zambia similarly highlight the vulnerability of girl domestic workers to sexual abuse by male employers.[72] This reflects a broader trend in Africa, and globally, of girl domestic workers suffering sexual abuse at the hands of employers. In Haiti, girl domestic workers are referred to by the Creole term '*la pou sa*', which means 'there for that' and refers to the expectation that girls will be sexually available to male household members.[73] A study in West Bengal during the 2000s found that over 20 per cent of girl domestic workers had been forced into sex with an employer, with more reporting other forms of sexual abuse.[74]

The extent to which female employers in Lusaka were aware of the sexual abuse of girls whom they employed is unclear. None of the female employers interviewed for this project suggested as such. When employers talked about incidents of sexual relations involving girls, coercive or not, they described situations that had occurred in other people's households, stating that they had heard such stories through gossip or the media.[75] It is possible that employers attempted to share their personal experiences by constructing an alternative narrative centred on the experience of a third party, though this cannot be confirmed. But even if female employers had not had personal experiences of the girls they employed engaging in sexual activity with men or boys in their household, fears about the possibility of such activity would have complicated relationships between girls and their female employers. As discussed in Chapter 2, many female employers preferred to hire prepubescent girls precisely because they thought that older girls and young women could pose a threat to marital stability by virtue of their youth and attractiveness.

Sexuality also impacted girl domestic workers' experiences in other ways. Parents' perceptions of their daughters' sexuality could limit girls' access to employment. Oral testimonies demonstrate how some parents sought to stop their daughters from working after they reached sexual maturity. We saw in Chapter 2 how Priscilla's maid Esther was forced to return to her parents' home after falling pregnant. Josephine Phiri's mother feared that her daughter might also engage in premarital sex while working as a maid in Lusaka. Josephine had migrated to Lusaka from her village in the Eastern Province in the late 1970s to work for the kinswoman of her parents' neighbour. She was thirteen years old when she arrived in the city. A year later, she menstruated for the first time, and her mother ordered that she return to her village so that she could live under closer supervision, presumably to prevent premarital pregnancy.[76] Bessie Chanda similarly described how her young maid Jaqueline was forced by her parents to leave her job in Lusaka and return to their village after she entered puberty, where she was soon married to a young man.[77] Each of these cases demonstrates how girls' sexuality could prove a hindrance to their status as workers, as their relatives sought increasingly to control their bodies and options as they matured.

Although girls' relationships with employers were grounded in and perpetuated inequality, girls and their employers were in many ways mutually dependent upon the other. The relationship between a girl domestic worker and her employer could be a resource on which both parties drew to survive personal and household hardship. Moreover, kin-based labour practices mobilised longstanding dependencies within the extended family system, which could act as a form of safety net for children and their parents. For poor rural and urban households, sending a female household member to live with kin and work in their home could provide economic relief in situations of financial hardship arising from failed harvests, drought, poverty, and bereavement. For the girl or woman involved, moving to live with kin could enable survival and, at best, improve educational and employment opportunities. For the household receiving the girl, her labour could greatly contribute to the maintenance of the household and its members.

There is evidence that some girls developed affective feelings towards their employers, be they relatives or strangers. A language of affect and intimacy was used by several interviewees who had worked in domestic service as girls when asked to describe their relationships with employers. Grace, for instance, described her first employers as kind and described the female employer as 'like a sister'. After leaving this job, she stayed in contact with her employers for many years.[78] Agnes Mumba had fond memories of sharing meals with her employers in the evenings, listening to stories and music with her employers' children before she and the children went to bed.[79] These examples suggest how relations between certain girls and their employers seemingly developed beyond mutual social and economic dependency and into affectionate and familial ties. Existing studies have also demonstrated the importance to child domestic workers of developing familial relationships with employers, showing how these relationships contributed to children's happiness in the workplace. Child domestic workers in Zimbabwe were more likely to be happy at work if they ate with their employers and were treated similarly to their employers' children.[80] Being treated like a family member by employers was similarly found to be key to child domestic workers' sense of well-being in Morocco.[81] In Côte d'Ivoire, girl domestic workers were even content to receive presents rather than cash wages if they felt that their employers treated them like family members.[82] Bourdillon suggests that child workers often need more support in the workplace than their adult counterparts, and the weight that child domestic workers have placed on their relationships with employers seems to demonstrate this.[83] Given that so many children entered domestic service due to economic crisis, family breakdown, or bereavement, child domestic workers' emphasis on developing familial ties with employers likely resulted from children's search for stability and security.

Children's descriptions of the relationships they developed with employers should not be interpreted uncritically, of course. In relation to the retrospective oral histories used in this chapter, it is possible that the distance offered by time or feelings of nostalgia led women to cast their youthful experiences of work in a more positive light than they had originally experienced. But the frequency and ease with which certain interviewees described positive relationships in the workplace suggest that a degree of affection was felt by some girls toward their employers. This interpretation is strengthened by the fact that many such interviewees described being aware of their exploitation by employers. For instance, although Grace spoke highly of her former employer during our interview, she also displayed a critical awareness of her past mistreatment, criticising the long working hours she had endured, the low wages she had received, and the fact that she had to seek piecework to earn enough money to cover her school fees. She resented all of this because it reduced the very limited time that she had to spend on her studies.[84] Grace's critique may have been informed by contemporary perceptions of the exploitative nature of child labour, but it also likely provides some insight into her views as a child.

Children's positive perceptions of their relationships with employers complicate our understanding of child domestic workers' experiences. The testimonies of Grace, Esnart, and my other interviewees provide insights into girls' awareness of the difficulties facing their families and themselves, and the ways that girls sought to address these by working in domestic service, even though such work was difficult and often exploitative. The perspectives of girl domestic workers are too often absent from contemporary policymaking on domestic service and child labour, most of which presents girls – and children more broadly – as passive subjects who cannot make informed decisions about their labour and mobility because of their age, gender, and presumed immaturity and vulnerability. However, as Bourdillon perceptively observed, 'although adults often assume that they know what is best for children, children's perspectives often show insights that adults miss. If so many children and their families opt for this kind of situation [domestic service], perhaps it has benefits for children that might at least sometimes override the hazards.'[85] He cites the arresting testimony of a thirteen-year-old girl domestic worker from Senegal, who cautioned delegates at an international conference in Norway in 1997: 'do you understand how you insult me, when you talk of "combating" and "abolishing" the work that I do? I have worked as a domestic servant since I was eight. Because of doing this work, I have been able to go to school (which my parents in the village could not afford); I help my parents with the money I earn. I am very proud of the work I do!'[86] Studies of child domestic workers in Zimbabwe, Côte d'Ivoire, and the Philippines similarly showed that child domestic workers often want better working conditions rather than an end to their employment.[87] Such studies, and the testimonies examined in this chapter, thereby reveal how some children have sought ways to improve their working conditions and opportunities rather than stop working per se.

## Conclusion

Female children and youth have long engaged in domestic service in Lusaka, and across southern Africa's urban centres, cleaning homes, washing clothes and dishes, cooking food, and caring for children. Oral testimonies demonstrate the importance of domestic service to the economic strategies of girls, their families, and their employers, providing all parties with much-needed social and material support. Girls found that perceptions of their gender, age, and sexuality both facilitated and limited their ability to engage in domestic service. On the one hand, girls were sought-after domestic workers precisely because of their gender and youth. The socialisation of children into normative gender roles and longstanding practices of transferring children between households to provide labour and receive care, combined with the cheapness of girls' labour, made them ideal domestic workers in the minds of many employers. On the other hand, once a girl reached puberty, she was widely perceived to have entered a new phase of responsibility and obligation. These dynamics illustrate the liminal status of girlhood. Depending on the situation and those involved, sexually mature girls were perceived variously as maids, as children, as vulnerable, as deceitful, or as sexual objects. For many girls, puberty meant a reduction in their capacity to shape their working and living conditions, as adults sought to control their bodies and choices in various ways.

The impact of intersecting relations of gender, sexuality, age, and kinship on labour relations in post-colonial Lusaka was clearly not limited to girls' experiences. Indeed, girls' employment in domestic service was in many ways similar to that of women, with both groups seeking and securing employment in the sector in unprecedented numbers following independence, and using their kinship networks as sources of employment and support. The tasks that female domestic workers performed built on longstanding gendered divisions of labour present in Lusaka and other southern African cities, according to which domestic labour and childcare were gendered as female responsibilities. These gender divisions of labour were challenged over time in Lusaka and elsewhere in the region, but they were largely maintained, with men reluctant to take on domestic work in their own homes and reliant upon women and girls' labour. Girls and women also had to navigate similar challenges surrounding gender relations within the workplace, including the threat of violence or sexual exploitation at the hands of male household members.

But girl domestic workers' experiences were also distinct from those of women domestic workers. Across post-colonial southern Africa, control over children's labour remained central to generational and gendered power relations within households and communities, with children expected to perform appropriate labour for their parents and elders. Women could command the labour of children, and the two groups had different needs and interests within the hierarchy of the household and wider community. Girls generally performed more domestic chores and care labour than boys, both in their natal homes and the homes of kin. This resulted in large part from the role of labour in gendered socialisation practices for children, with girls assigned chores which would prepare them for their prescribed future gendered roles as wives and mothers.

Overall, by examining the perspectives of women who worked in domestic service as girls, this chapter provides a more complex and nuanced understanding of girls' experiences of working in domestic service. In policymaking and development projects on children's rights and labour in the region, girl domestic workers are largely presented as passive and exploited subjects. The aims of such initiatives of course shape the narratives they construct and promote, with girl domestic workers most frequently discussed as part of campaigns to eliminate child labour and combat child trafficking. Such representations of girl domestic workers are certainly not incorrect. As this chapter has shown, many girls have been exploited and placed in vulnerable positions while working in domestic service. But girls' working lives have also been more complex than a narrow focus on exploitation captures. Employment in domestic service provided a means for girls to access an income, resources, and mobility, even when under exploitative terms. Moreover, oral testimonies also suggest that some girls found ways to challenge exploitative working conditions and shape their own life strategies, despite the massive inequalities they faced.

## Notes

1 Interview with Esnart Lungu, Lusaka, 12 August 2013.
2 See for instance ILO, *Emerging Good Practices on Action to Combat Child Domestic Labour in Kenya, Tanzania, Uganda and Zambia*; ILO, *Ending Child Labour in Domestic Work*; Anti-Slavery International, *Listen to Us! Participation of Child Domestic Workers in Advocacy* (London: Anti-Slavery International, 2013).
3 This representation of girl domestic workers is common in media coverage. See, for example, Banda, 'Zambia Should Save Its Own Children'; Mulenga, 'The Plight of an Exploited Domestic House Maid'; Kayaya, 'Tackling Child Labour in Zambia'.
4 Interview with Evelyn Banda, Lusaka, 2 July 2014.
5 Interview with Esnart Lungu.
6 Oyaide, 'Child Domestic Labour in Lusaka', pp. 23–24. See also Peter Matoka, 'Child Labour in Zambia: An Analysis of the Extent, Nature and Proposed Solutions to the Problem' (PhD dissertation, University of Warwick, 1994), p. 28.
7 Bourdillon, *Child Domestic Workers in Zimbabwe*, pp. 38–40; Debbie Budlender and Dawie Bosch, *South Africa Child Domestic Workers:*

*A National Report. Investigating the Worst Forms of Child Labour No. 39* (Geneva: International Labour Organization International Programme on the Elimination of Child Labour (IPEC), 2002), pp. 8–9, p. 45; Maxton Grant Tsoka, 'Rapid Assessment of Child Domestic Labour in Malawi. Final Report', Vol. 1: Main Report (Zomba: Centre for Social Research, University of Malawi, 2005), pp. iv–vii, p. 2, p. 22, p. 26.

8 Parental alcoholism has broadly been observed as a key factor in pushing children into domestic service. See Jonathan Blagbrough, 'Worst Forms of Child Labor: Child Domestic Labor', in Hugh D. Hindman (ed.), *The World of Child Labor: An Historical and Regional Survey* (Abingdon: Routledge, 2015), p. 87.

9 Bourdillon, *Child Domestic Workers in Zimbabwe*, pp. 28–29.

10 Interview with Grace Musonda, Lusaka, 13 February 2014.

11 Interview with Mercy Banda.

12 Interview with Niah Mumba, Lusaka, 16 February 2014.

13 Bourdillon, *Child Domestic Workers in Zimbabwe*, pp. 20–21.

14 Interview with Queen Kangwa, Lusaka, 25 February 2014.

15 Guarcello *et al.*, 'Orphanhood and Child Vulnerability', p. 2. See also Guest, *Children of AIDS*; Yamba, 'Loveness and Her Brothers', 205–210.

16 Tsoka, *Rapid Assessment of Child Domestic Labour in Malawi*, p. 2, p. 34.

17 Blagbrough, 'Worst Forms of Child Labor', p. 87.

18 See for instance Bozzoli, *Women of Phokeng*; Castel-Branco, 'Legislating Worker Justice', p. 1, p. 17; Suzanne Gordon, *A Talent for Tomorrow: Life Stories of South African Servants* (Johannesburg: Ravan Press, 1985); Miles, 'Working in the City'.

19 Interview with Esnart Lungu.

20 Namuggala, 'Exploitation or Empowerment?', 574.

21 At the time of writing, the conversion rate of K to USD was 9.85 to 1.

22 Interview with Semu Lameck, Chimusanya, 21 June 2014.

23 *Ibid.*

24 Interview with Elizabeth Bwalya.

25 I was not able to interview Anna directly. Her story was told to me by her aunt, Dorothy Phiri. Interview with Dorothy Phiri.

26 On domestic workers' housing and commuting practices under colonial rule, see Hansen, *Distant Companions*, p. 77, p. 156, p. 158, pp. 172–174.

27 *Ibid.*, pp. 240–241; ILO, *Magnitude of Domestic Workers in Zambia*, p. 3.

28 Karen Tranberg Hansen, 'Stuck in the Compound: Some Odds Against Social Adulthood in Lusaka, Zambia', *Africa Today*, 51 (2005), 10; Katherine V. Gough, '"Moving Around": The Social and Spatial

Mobility of Youth in Lusaka', *Geografiska Annaler: Series B, Human Geography*, 90:3 (2008), 250.

29 Hansen, 'Stuck in the Compound', 10, 12; Gough, '"Moving Around"', 247–250. On the Zimbabwean case, see Deborah Potts, '"All My Hopes and Dreams are Shattered": Urbanisation and Migrancy in an Imploding African Economy – the Case of Zimbabwe', *Geoforum*, 37 (2006), 545.

30 Bozzoli, *Women of Phokeng*, pp. 97–98; Gordon, *A Talent for Tomorrow*, p. xviii.

31 Namuggala, 'Exploitation or Empowerment?', 570.

32 Interview with Elizabeth Bwalya; interview with Dorothy Phiri.

33 Republic of Zambia, *1990 Census of Population, Housing and Agriculture. Volume 10.*

34 *Ibid.*

35 Interview with Frida Njovu, Lusaka, 16 August 2013.

36 Namuggala, 'Exploitation or Empowerment?', 569.

37 Tsoka, *Rapid Assessment of Child Domestic Labour in Malawi*, pp. v–vi, p. 2.

38 Bourdillon, *Child Domestic Workers in Zimbabwe*, pp. 60–61.

39 Tone Sommerfelt, 'Petites Bonnes and Their Parents: Experiences and Motivational Factors', in Tone Sommerfelt (ed.), *Domestic Child Labour in Morocco: An Analysis of the Parties Involved in Relationships to 'Petites Bonnes'* (Oslo: Fafo Institute for Applied Social Science, 2003), p. 28.

40 Approximately two-thirds of waged domestic workers were boys, and approximately two-thirds of children doing unpaid domestic work were girls. Budlender and Bosch, *South Africa Child Domestic Workers*, pp. x–xi, p. 13, p. 27, p. 38.

41 *Ibid.*, p. xii, p. 27.

42 *Ibid.*, p. xii, p. 27, p. 34.

43 Interview with Grace Musonda.

44 Interview with Niah Mumba.

45 Interview with Esnart Lungu.

46 Interview with Dorothy Phiri.

47 Interview with Grace Musonda.

48 Interview with Queen Kangwa.

49 Oyaide, 'Child Domestic Labour in Lusaka', pp. 42–43.

50 Jacquemin, 'Children's Domestic Work in Abidjan, Côte d'Ivoire', 385.

51 Oyaide, 'Child Domestic Labour in Lusaka', p. 43.

52 Interview with Dorothy Phiri.

53 Interview with Grace Musonda.

54 Interview with Queen Kangwa.

55 Interview with Grace Musonda.
56 Bourdillon, *Child Domestic Workers in Zimbabwe*, pp. 21–22.
57 Interview with Grace Musonda.
58 Interview with Esnart Lungu.
59 Interview with Dorothy Phiri.
60 Namuggala, 'Exploitation or Empowerment?', 571.
61 Interview with Priscilla Njovu.
62 Bourdillon, *Child Domestic Workers in Zimbabwe*, p. 23; Bourdillon, 'Children as Domestic Employees', 8.
63 N. O. Bwibo and P. Onyango, 'The Final Report of Child Labour and Health Research' (Nairobi: University of Nairobi, 1997), as cited in Blagbrough, 'Worst Forms of Child Labor', p. 88.
64 Jonathan Blagbrough, *Child Domestic Work in Indonesia: A Preliminary Situation Analysis* (Geneva: ILO-IPEC, 1995).
65 Hansen, 'Labor Migration and Urban Child Labor during the Colonial Period in Zambia', pp. 230–231.
66 Bryceson, 'Domestic Work', p. 326.
67 See Bourdillon, 'Children as Domestic Employees', 4.
68 Interview with Niah Mumba.
69 Interview with Priscilla Njovu.
70 See Cock, *Maids and Madams*, p. 69, p. 109; Hansen, *Distant Companions*, pp. 247–251; Bujra, *Serving Class*, pp. 36–49.
71 Interview with Carol Banda, Lusaka, 1 March 2014.
72 Oyaide, 'Child Domestic Labour', p. 3, p. 6, p. 55; Bond *et al.*, *Sweeping the Bedroom*, p. 24, p. 34.
73 Blagbrough, 'Worst Forms of Child Labor', p. 87.
74 Manabendranath Ray and Asha N. Iyer, *Abuse Among Child Domestic Workers: A Research Study in West Bengal* (Kolkata: Save the Children, UK, 2006), pp. 14–17.
75 There was sporadic media coverage of such incidents in post-colonial Zambia. Examples include K. Musonda, 'House Servant Outwits Owner', *Times of Zambia*, 8 January 1985; N. Sichalwe, 'Court Fines Accountant K2m for Impregnating Maid', *The Post*, 19 May 2002; *Lusaka Times*, 'Hubby Caught in Act with Maid', 20 June 2010.
76 Interview with Josephine Phiri, Chipata, 18 July 2014.
77 Interview with Bessie Chanda.
78 Interview with Grace Musonda.
79 Interview with Agnes Mumba, Lusaka, 2 February 2014.
80 Bourdillon, *Child Domestic Workers in Zimbabwe*, pp. 80–81, p. 110.
81 Sommerfelt, 'Petites Bonnes and Their Parents', pp. 33–34.
82 Jacquemin, 'Children's Domestic Work in Abidjan, Côte d'Ivoire', 389, 393.

83 Bourdillon, 'Children as Domestic Employees', 10.
84 Interview with Grace Musonda.
85 Bourdillon, 'Children as Domestic Employees', 6.
86 *Ibid.*
87 *Ibid.*, 6–7; Agnes Zenaida V. Camacho, 'Family, Child Labour and Migration: Child Domestic Workers in Metro Manila', *Childhood*, 6:1 (1999), 70; Mélanie Jacquemin, 'Can the Language of Rights Get Hold of the Complex Realities of Child Domestic Work? The Case of Young Domestic Workers in Abidjan, Ivory Coast', *Childhood*, 13 (2006), 398.

# 4

# Regulation, protection, and exclusion

> (a) The term 'domestic work' means work performed in or for a household or households;
> (b) the term 'domestic worker' means any person engaged in domestic work within an employment relationship;
> (c) a person who performs domestic work only occasionally or sporadically and not on an occupational basis is not a domestic worker.[1]

In 2014, I attended a meeting in Lusaka organised by the ILO to promote its work on domestic worker rights in Zambia. The meeting was held at an expensive chain hotel on the Great East Road in the northern part of the city, near to several affluent suburbs and the University of Zambia. The meeting included attendees from the ILO's Lusaka office, the Ministry of Labour and Social Security (MLSS), the Zambia Congress of Trade Unions (ZCTU), domestic worker trade unions, the Zambia Federation of Employers (ZFE), and maid centres from Lusaka and the Copperbelt. The aims of the meeting were to share knowledge and understanding about labour issues in the domestic service sector and the challenges of improving domestic workers' conditions.[2] It took place three years after the ILO's adoption of Convention 189 and Recommendation 201, which outlined the first international labour standards for domestic workers, including statutory minimum wages and working conditions. The ILO wanted member states like Zambia to ratify the Convention and to develop labour laws in line with the standards it promoted.

The meeting in Lusaka in 2014 followed decades of activism at the national and international levels to introduce labour protections for domestic workers. During the 1990s and 2000s, trade unions and associations for domestic workers were established and existing ones strengthened in countries across the world; international organisations, including the ILO and the International Domestic Workers Network (IDWN), pressured national governments to adopt protective legislation; and governments including Zambia introduced and extended legislation to protect domestic workers. Essentially, all of these efforts involved a fundamental reframing of domestic service. They aimed to formalise and professionalise the sector and to turn it into employment like any other, regulated by labour laws and employment contracts, and with clearly defined roles, responsibilities, and protections for the workers and employers involved. The extract from Convention 189 quoted above epitomises this approach, showing how the ILO has conceptualised domestic service in terms of formal, steady employment.

Policymakers and activists involved in the development and promotion of Convention 189 and other efforts to regulate domestic service have argued that formalisation and protective legislation will positively transform domestic service.[3] But there is debate over the actual impacts of these processes on domestic workers.[4] Some scholars have argued that protective legislation, in its historical and current forms, has and can only have a limited positive impact on domestic workers because of the private and intimate nature of the work and the insufficiency of mechanisms to monitor and enforce labour protections.[5] Other scholars have argued that labour protections have negatively impacted domestic workers. Bryceson states that the introduction of minimum wages for domestic workers has led, in some places, to a race to the bottom in terms of wages and a search for the cheapest available labour.[6] Ally concludes that protective legislation has reduced domestic workers' ability to negotiate with their employers and to mobilise intimate bonds with employers to their advantage.[7] Such studies suggest the complex and often contradictory impacts of labour protections on domestic workers, in southern Africa and beyond. Several issues also warrant further examination. There is scope to examine the extent to which past and present efforts to formalise domestic service and protect domestic workers through legislation have accounted for the breadth of labour relations and workers in the sector, and how they have impacted domestic workers across gender and age groups.

This chapter examines these issues in Zambia, tracing change over time and comparing this case to other examples from southern Africa. Taking colonial labour policies as a starting point, the chapter shows how colonial officials regulated and monitored domestic service as part of broader efforts to discipline workers, police racial boundaries, and maintain social order. Domestic workers in the colonial period were generally excluded from efforts to pay African workers minimum wages and were subject to regulation and punishment under master and servant legislation and similar punitive laws. After independence, the Zambian state's approach to domestic service both built on and departed from colonial labour policies. The Zambian state took a more detached approach towards domestic service than its colonial predecessor, and the sector declined as a topic for official concern. Successive post-independence governments also continued to exclude domestic workers from minimum wage and labour protections until the early 2000s. It was only in 2011 that the Zambian state introduced protective legislation for domestic workers, legislation that was amended in subsequent years to extend its scope. Zambia's approach contrasted with several other southern African nations, including Botswana and Zimbabwe, where protective legislation was extended to domestic service during the 1980s, and Namibia and South Africa, where legal protections for domestic workers were introduced following the transition to democracy in the 1990s. The chapter explores the local, regional, and global contexts within which Zambia shifted from a position of disinterest and exclusion to one of protection, and considers the influence of developments in neighbouring states and at the ILO.

The chapter shows that the protective regulations introduced in Zambia from 2011 have had both positive and negative impacts for domestic workers. On the one hand, labour protections represented real gains for domestic workers, including improvements in wages, regulated working hours and holidays, and social protections such as paid maternity leave. On the other hand, these regulations have not adequately addressed the idiosyncrasies or diversity of domestic service. Some domestic workers have not received improved pay or experienced better working conditions, largely because of limited enforcement and monitoring of the legislation, and parental leave has proved to be more symbolic than practically useful. Moreover, these laws have exacerbated generational inequality in the sector, as large numbers of child domestic workers remain unable to access adequate workers' rights and protections and continue to be entirely dependent on the goodwill of their employers.

## A long and uneven history of formalisation

From the early years of colonial rule in Northern Rhodesia, domestic service was regulated by the state via master and servant laws. The first of these was introduced in the protectorate of North-Western Rhodesia in 1908, before being extended over the amalgamated territory in 1912, with further amendments in 1913 and 1925. This legislation classified as a 'servant' all workers apart from the highly skilled. It specified the obligations of 'masters' (employers) towards their workers, which included the provision of food, medical care, and housing. If an employer could not or did not want to house their worker on site, they provided an allowance for the worker to pay for housing in the African compounds.[8] Live-out domestic workers received 'night passes' to allow them to travel after the curfew that prohibited Africans from moving around European residential areas at night.[9] Northern Rhodesia's master and servant legislation was based on similar laws in Southern Rhodesia, which in turn had developed from South African legislation.[10] This reflected the influence of South African labour law and domestic service practices across British colonial southern Africa. Across these territories, master and servant legislation was adopted as part of broader colonial projects to discipline African workers to new work rhythms and to enforce European authority over Africans.

In 1929, Northern Rhodesia's colonial government replaced the master and servant legislation with the Employment of Natives Ordinance. This Ordinance aimed to more strictly control African workers' labour and mobility in a context of increased urbanisation and a growing urban African labour force. It covered all African workers, including the highly skilled. Criminal punishments could be applied to workers who failed to complete their contracts, and civil punishments could be applied for other transgressions.

Importantly, the Ordinance also allowed workers to pursue criminal procedures against their employers if they withheld wages.[11] During the 1940s, in the context of growing labour unrest, some of Northern Rhodesia's workers, including mineworkers, teachers, and clerks, won improvements to their working conditions.[12] A decade later, minimum wage legislation was introduced for a number of occupations. The colonial government refused to extend minimum wages to domestic workers, however, arguing that it would be unfair to require inspections of private houses. Interestingly, officials also argued that it would be wrong to force all employers to pay the same wage rate because of the variation and breadth of domestic service practices. They highlighted the issue of African employers and child domestic workers, suggesting that African employers would not pay the minimum wage and that children should not be paid an adult wage rate.[13]

During decolonisation in the early 1960s, Northern Rhodesia's colonial government sought to reshape the language of domestic service and to move away from the terminology of servitude. In February 1961, a circular was sent to all Labour Commissioners in Northern Rhodesia instructing them to use the term 'garden hands' rather than 'garden boys'. On the eve of independence in 1964, an amended version of the 'Employment Services Manual' was issued which included a more dramatic shift in language from 'garden boys' to 'garden workers'.[14] These attempts to alter the language of domestic service failed to produce either an immediate or a lasting change, however. Colonial officials continued to use terms including 'domestic servant', 'housemaid', and 'garden boy' in their documentation and in conversation.[15] These terms also persisted in usage after independence, reflecting the enduring discursive power of colonial constructions of work and of workers.

Elsewhere in southern Africa, the regulation of domestic service proceeded along different paths. In colonial Mozambique, domestic service regulations mirrored practices elsewhere in the region but were also distinguished by the characteristics of the Portuguese colonial labour regime. Domestic workers were required to carry a range of documentation to prove their right to work and live in urban areas, including identification cards from 1914 and *caderneta* (passbooks) detailing their employment history and tax obligations from 1926. A stricter urban registration system was introduced from 1944 to more tightly control all workers' wages and mobility. The regulation of domestic service was also shaped by the liberation struggle. In 1966, Mozambique's colonial government passed new regulations for domestic service, which introduced a number of protections for workers, including minimum wages and rights to holidays and paid sick and maternity leave. These regulations also set out to protect the rights of employers and stipulated that domestic workers behave with respect, loyalty, and obedience. As under earlier laws, domestic workers were required to carry passes and register with the administration. The colonial government monitored and enforced these laws, including by carrying out inspections in private homes and fining employers who violated the law.[16] In apartheid South Africa, government officials built on earlier master and servant legislation and developed one of the most oppressive and exploitative systems of domestic service anywhere in the world. Domestic workers, of whom the majority were Black women, had almost no legal rights under apartheid and were subject to strict racialised laws governing their labour, mobility, and urban residence.[17]

Across colonial southern Africa, domestic workers were vulnerable to various forms of legal punishments. In Northern Rhodesia, a servant could be fined or imprisoned if they were deemed to have breached their contract of employment. Some prisoners were also made to do hard labour. The legislation defined 'breach of contract' in broad terms and included a range of minor infractions, such as unauthorised absence from work, poor work performance, and refusing to obey an employer's orders. Hansen describes an incident in Livingstone in 1912 in which three adult domestic workers were punished for playing music and dancing in public on a Sunday afternoon. The magistrate reprimanded them for disturbing 'the white man's day of rest' and sentenced them to a fine or three days in prison with hard labour.[18] In Mozambique, domestic workers were subject to corporal punishment, including for minor issues such as breaking crockery or burning laundry while ironing. Between 1953 and 1957 alone, 1,000 domestic workers in Lourenço Marques, nearly three-quarters of whom were young people below the age of twenty, received forms of corporal punishment.[19]

Alongside regulating domestic service via legislation, colonial officials across southern Africa also gathered and analysed information about domestic service. As discussed in Chapter 1, in Northern Rhodesia officials calculated estimations of the number of domestic workers employed and included these figures in monthly and annual labour reports. Officials also gathered information about wage rates and the estimated the number of domestic workers employed in specific roles, including as cooks, maids, and 'garden boys'. During the late colonial period, labour reports also included a breakdown of employment figures in domestic service by gender and, to a lesser extent, by age. These efforts to gather knowledge about domestic service were made by colonial officials across the region and were part of broader projects to monitor the African labour force. But this was about more than labour policy. It was also about controlling interactions between colonised workers and their employers and policing the racial and social boundaries upon which colonialism was built and depended.[20]

Alongside official efforts to regulate and monitor domestic service, the sector was also shaped by a range of cultural practices and social conventions. For instance, Emily Bradley, a writer and wife of a British colonial official, drew on her experiences of running households across the British Empire and wrote three household management manuals aimed at settler women. She advised her readers about a wide range of issues and had specific advice on how to hire, interact with, and manage domestic workers.[21] Branches of the Women's Institute in Northern and Southern Rhodesia developed pamphlets on household management to advise new settlers on 'proper' servant-keeping practices.[22] These pamphlets emphasised the need for women to be firm and direct when dealing with African domestic workers, and some also contained warnings that servants were prone to breaking things, stealing, and lying.[23] Colonial officials promoted these efforts and sought to work with women's organisations and individual female settlers who were held in high esteem like Bradley. Conversation manuals and phrase books also provided colonial readers with guidance on servant management. Sheldon's research on phrase books written during the colonial period in Mozambique shows, for example, how such texts instructed their readers on how to command and direct the labour of domestic workers and punish them for poor performance of their duties.[24] The impacts of phrase books, pamphlets, and household management manuals on colonial societies should not be underestimated. They promoted an idealised model of domesticity that had long-lasting consequences for housekeeping practices in southern Africa, and more broadly across the colonial and former colonial world. Crucially, they promoted a model of labour relations that was grounded in racism, patriarchy, and assertions of difference between colonial employers and colonised workers.

Following independence, the Zambian state's approach to domestic service both built on and departed from its colonial predecessor. Decolonisation brought full citizenship rights and some improvements in labour policy for domestic workers. The 1929 Employment of Natives Ordinance was repealed and replaced by the 1965 Employment Act. This Act prohibited discrimination not only on the basis of race but also due to sex, tribal affiliation, and religion, amongst other protected characteristics. The Act resulted not only from efforts to decolonise labour law but also to implement legislation in line with the international labour standards promoted by the ILO.[25] From 1966, domestic workers became eligible for pensions under the ZNPF. This was a compulsory savings scheme for private sector employees based on contributions from both workers and employers. As noted in Chapter 1, however, it seems that only a minority of domestic workers were ever registered for ZNPF coverage.

Despite some improvements to their legal status following independence, domestic workers continued to be treated differently to other workers under the law. Notably, although UNIP introduced labour protections and minimum wages for various occupational groups during the 1960s and 1970s, it excluded domestic workers from these reforms. The state's failure and unwillingness to extend equal rights to domestic workers meant that they were unable to claim the full range of rights accessible to other Zambian citizens. This impacted domestic workers across gender and age groups. In addition, as part of UNIP's efforts to move away from paternalist colonial labour relations, domestic workers lost certain privileges. Specifically, domestic workers had been entitled to food rations as part of their remuneration package under colonial law, but this was legally abolished at independence. Although many employers continued to provide meals or food rations to their domestic workers, this was no longer legally required.[26] More broadly, state interest in domestic service declined markedly following independence, exemplified by UNIP's exclusion of domestic service from labour reports and statistics from 1970 onwards.

UNIP's apparent disinterest in domestic service and its exclusion of the sector from equal provision in labour law likely resulted from several intersecting factors. The government's priorities regarding the regulation of labour were different from its colonial predecessor. The colonial government's focus on domestic service was part of its core role of preserving the racial and political order. After independence, the government was not concerned with policing labour relations along racial lines, though racial distinctions continued to distinguish domestic workers and employers in many households. Domestic service increasingly became an institution grounded in class-based and gendered inequality, two issues in which the UNIP government seemed largely unwilling or unable to intervene. UNIP also faced declining political support from the late 1960s and economic instability during the 1970s. Although UNIP portrayed itself as being both popular and unchallenged during its time in power, there is clear evidence to the contrary. As Miles Larmer shows, UNIP's authority and position were challenged by dissent within the party and by a range of opposition movements. Larmer argues that Zambia became a one-party state in 1972 in large part because UNIP was struggling against rising political opposition and failing to meet the social and political expectations of the population.[27] The economic shocks of the 1970s exacerbated the problems facing the party. Subsequent reductions in government spending and the need to address rising labour unrest meant that the MLSS lacked capacity to monitor and address many labour issues, let alone the relatively politically unimportant domestic service sector.

During the 1980s, UNIP's attention was directed at stemming the economic crisis and exerting control over organised labour. Its capacity to regulate employment, in domestic service and many occupations, was also undermined during this period by the increased casualisation and informalisation of work. During the 1990s, the relationship between the state and workers shifted again, as the MMD government's radical programme of liberalisation had wide-ranging impacts for the economy and employment. The aggressive pursuit of privatisation and deregulation led to further reductions in formal employment and the expansion of informal employment largely beyond the bounds of state regulation and monitoring.

Broader policy developments around women's rights and gender relations during the 1980s and 1990s appear not to have paid any serious attention to domestic service, despite its importance as a source of employment for poor women and girls and of labour for working women across the nation.[28] Zambian gender activists, policymakers, and legislators were certainly aware of the exploitative working conditions and low pay that many domestic workers endured, not least because most were employers themselves. But they were either unable or unwilling to pursue this cause. Those engaged in gender-based activism or social justice campaigning were perhaps uncomfortable with acknowledging their participation in domestic service. As other scholars have observed, whilst feminists in Africa and beyond have denounced domestic service because it reproduces gendered, class, and racial privilege, many have remained silent on their own employment of domestic workers.[29]

Elsewhere in southern Africa, several states sought to more closely regulate domestic service during the 1980s. At independence in Zimbabwe in 1980, domestic workers' conditions were still governed by master and servant legislation adopted in 1903. The Zimbabwe African National Union – Patriotic Front (ZANU–PF) government investigated the situation facing domestic workers as part of a broader commission of inquiry into labour issues and took steps to improve domestic workers' conditions. In 1981, it passed legislation that introduced minimum wages for domestic workers for the first time; regulated working hours, overtime, food, accommodation, and conditions for hiring and dismissal; and made it legal for domestic workers to form and join trade unions. This legislation also provided unprecedented support for working women, requiring employers to provide maternity leave regardless of a woman's marital status. As part of broader policy changes, domestic workers also gained access to wider social services, including healthcare and education. The impacts of these legal changes were significant, with the new minimum wage amounting to a 100 per cent increase in income for most domestic workers. Moreover, the legal regulation of working conditions meant that, in theory at least, domestic workers were no longer dependent on the goodwill of their employers and could assert their rights to minimum standards of employment.[30] More limited rights were extended to domestic workers in Botswana, where parts of the 1982 Employment Act were extended to domestic service. Like other workers, domestic workers became entitled to a written or oral contract, maximum working hours, mandatory rest days, and sick pay. They were excluded, however, from the sections of the Act which regulated minimum wages, paid holidays, recruitment, and health and safety issues.[31]

Further efforts to regulate domestic service in southern Africa occurred during the 1990s. In post-independence Namibia, a new Labour Act was passed in 1992 which applied to all workers, including domestic workers. The Act introduced a range of rights and protections including a forty-five-hour working week, overtime pay, and maternity leave after twelve months' continuous service. The Act also made provision for the establishment of wage commissions at the request of employees or employers to determine minimum wages.[32] The most remarkable attempts at formalising domestic service occurred in South Africa following the end of apartheid and the transition to democracy. In 1996, South Africa's labour laws were extended to cover domestic workers for the first time, and a state agency was established to monitor labour practices in the sector. In 2002, the government introduced a statutory minimum wage and made annual salary increases mandatory. The 2002 legislation also regulated working hours, leave, and sick and severance pay, and made formal written contracts compulsory. Ally suggests that these laws represented 'quite possibly, the world's most progressive state effort to regulate paid domestic work'.[33] The South African state's efforts to formalise domestic service also had a clear emphasis on professionalisation, illustrated by the development of the Domestic Worker Skills Development Project to provide accredited training to domestic workers.[34] The impact these respective legislative changes had on domestic workers in the region is examined below.

## Developing protective state legislation for domestic workers during the 2000s

It was only during the 2000s that a post-independence Zambian government began to intervene explicitly and purposively in the domestic service sector. In 2011, the MMD introduced minimum wages and a range of labour protections for domestic workers for the first time.[35] Statutory Instrument No. 3 of 2011 stipulated that domestic workers were entitled to receive a minimum monthly wage of K250 (approximately USD25) and that domestic workers who earned in excess of this minimum when the legislation came into force had the right to retain their higher wage. Domestic workers who lived over 3 km from their place of employment and who were not provided with transport by their employer were also entitled to a monthly transport allowance of K102 (approximately USD10). The 2011 legislation also stated that the working week should not exceed forty-eight hours and that additional hours worked should be paid at a rate of one-and-a-half times the normal hourly rate or through time in lieu; that two days of paid leave per month were to be awarded after six months of continuous service; and that one month's paid sick leave was available upon presentation of a medical certificate, after which point their employer had the right to terminate a domestic worker's employment if they could not return to work. Mothers also had the right to take leave to care for sick children who required hospitalisation, and they were entitled to take up to 120 days' unpaid maternity leave after two years' continuous service. If a domestic worker's contract was terminated for any reason other than resignation or summary dismissal, they had the right to a month's full basic pay for every two years' continuous service. Finally, the legislation stipulated that no person below the age of fifteen years should be employed in domestic service.[36] These wide-ranging provisions addressed many key issues relating to pay and working conditions. They involved both a return to explicit state regulation of domestic service and a break from the past, with the state's approach focusing on protecting rather than disciplining workers.

In 2012, the newly elected PF government sought to further expand protective regulations for domestic workers. To do so, it introduced Statutory Instrument No. 45 of 2012 to increase the minimum wage to K420 (approximately USD43) per month.[37] Six years later, in 2018, the PF government extended protective regulations for domestic workers even further. Statutory Instrument No. 69 of 2018 doubled the minimum wage to K840 (approximately USD85) per month. The transport allowance was also increased, to K153 (approximately USD16) per month. The 2018 legislation also made important improvements for parents and carers. Mothers were entitled to receive half of their regular pay during maternity leave.

New provisions for fathers were introduced, with male domestic workers entitled to five days' unpaid paternity leave after twelve months' continuous service and presentation of proof of paternity. Any employee with 'a sick spouse, child or dependent' could take up to fifteen days' paid leave per twelve months to carry out caring responsibilities. Finally, the 2018 legislation revised the legal definitions of domestic work and domestic workers. Adopting the definitions outlined in ILO Convention 189, it defined a domestic worker as 'a person engaged in domestic work in an employment relationship' and domestic work as 'work performed in or for a household or households', and stated that the legislation did not apply to those 'who perform domestic work only occasionally and not on an occupational basis'.[38] The introduction of these definitions is important, because it marked Zambia's legal adoption of a narrow and in many senses exclusionary conceptualisation of domestic service which was at odds with the realities of labour relations in that context.

In neighbouring Mozambique, labour protections for domestic workers were also adopted for the first time by a post-independence government during the 2000s. Following independence, Frelimo had sought to create a workers' state and to formally organise Mozambican workers but had consistently excluded domestic workers from its efforts. This was partly because Frelimo saw domestic service as a relic of colonialism and also because it focused on developing and organising the public sector, industry, and agriculture, and took a narrow approach towards women's emancipation and feminism.[39] Only in 2008 did the Mozambican government adopt legislation to provide domestic workers with basic protections under the law. These included the right to a contract, set working hours, breaks from work, annual leave, and social protections, including maternity leave and pensions. This legislation marked an important step in domestic worker rights in Mozambique, but it was weaker than comparable laws adopted in neighbouring countries, including Zambia. Crucially, a minimum wage was not introduced, and regulations around the working week, working hours, breaks, contracts, and health and safety were also weaker than elsewhere in the region.[40]

As in Mozambique, the Zambian government's decision to explicitly intervene in domestic service through legislation in 2011, and again in 2012 and 2018, marked a clear shift in approach. This shift resulted from a combination of economic and political factors. On the one hand, the government's introduction of stricter state regulation of domestic service appeared to be out of line with the broader economic climate of the period. The Statutory Instruments introduced 2011, 2012, and 2018 were adopted at a time when state intervention in the wider economy had markedly diminished in comparison with earlier decades, in line with the broad efforts towards liberalisation and privatisation that had been pursued in Zambia since the 1990s. Somewhat paradoxically, these policies of liberalisation likely facilitated the regulation of domestic service. Castel-Branco persuasively argues for the case of Mozambique that 'domestic workers were recast as engines of economic growth, capable of boosting employment in the context of massive unemployment'.[41] She suggests that Frelimo extended labour protections to domestic and other informal sector workers during the 2000s in the hope of increasing the formalisation of employment and increasing its potential tax base. These arguments are also relevant for understanding events in Zambia, where the decline of formal sector employment from the late 1970s onwards had resulted in the vast majority of employment taking place within the informal sector and beyond the reaches of state tax collection.

Politically, too, there were a number of reasons for the MMD and PF governments to more closely regulate domestic service. One was to increase support for the government from those who would benefit most from the reforms – domestic workers and their dependants – and also from the broader urban working poor. Officials from UHDWUZ suggested that the MMD introduced the 2011 legislation in an attempt to garner support from the poorer members of Zambian society in the run-up to the general election.[42] It is likely that the MMD government did feel under pressure to take a more interventionist approach to reducing poverty in order to counter the pro-poor, populist message of the opposition PF during that election campaign. These arguments have their limits, however. While this legislation may have boosted support for MMD amongst the poor, it was much less popular amongst middle-class and wealthy Zambians, who were required to pay their domestic workers according to the government's minimum wage. Newspaper coverage from 2011 and from 2012 suggests there was considerable discontent amongst employers towards the legislation for precisely this reason.[43] This argument also minimises the intentions of Zambian politicians who sought to reform the domestic service sector to fight inequality and social injustice. Apart from the appeal of the 2011 policy amongst certain parts of the electorate, at least some members of the MMD government must also have wanted to improve wages and conditions for domestic workers, who are widely recognised in Zambia as being amongst the most exploited workers in society. The PF's extension of protective legislation for domestic workers in 2012 and in 2018 likely also resulted from a combination of motives.

For their part, many of the domestic workers that I interviewed criticised the lack of interest shown by politicians towards them at any time other than the run-up to elections. Custom Banda, a retired cook in his late seventies when we met in 2013, criticised the government for doing too little to create decent jobs for poor urban residents and suggested that only persons with family connections to government or business could secure employment in the formal sector.[44] This sentiment was echoed by many interviewees. Monica Zimba, a widow in her early fifties when we met in 2014, had moved between domestic service and a number of low-paid jobs over the years. When asked about the Zambian government's approach to the economy and employment issues, she sighed and said, 'the rich are getting rich and the poor are getting poorer. Widows, vulnerable children, the elderly, we are left behind by the government … they take money for projects, but nothing happens.'[45] Such critiques reflected the frustrations that domestic workers felt as members of the urban working poor and merged with more specific arguments about the Zambian state's neglect of domestic workers. Monica's comments also seemed to suggest a critique of the relationship between the government and donors, with the latter providing funding for development projects that never materialised or were unsuccessful in helping the poor.

Interviews with officials from Zambia's domestic worker trade unions also highlighted feelings of powerlessness and lack of influence on the government in relation to labour and other issues. Although the unions were involved in meetings with government officials and key stakeholders in the run-up to and following the passing of the 2011 legislation, the extent to which the unions' activities had prompted ministers to introduce this legislation was likely minimal. As will be examined in detail in Chapter 5, domestic worker trade unions in Zambia have never been in a strong position and have had minimal contact with and influence over the government.

Regional developments around domestic worker rights may have had some influence on the Zambian government's shift in policy during the 2000s. The legislation introduced in Zambia through the 2010s shared common features with the legislation adopted in Zimbabwe and in South Africa in earlier decades. It is possible that Zambian government officials, especially those with a background in the labour movement or social justice campaigning and links to relevant regional organisations, were influenced by developments in Zimbabwe and South Africa. A parallel example from Mozambique suggests the possibilities of such regional influence. The Comité da Mulher Trabalhadora (Working Women's Committee, or COMUTRA) of the state-sponsored Organização dos Trabalhadores Moçambicanos (Mozambican Workers' Organisation, or OTM) told Castel-Branco that the South African Domestic Service and Allied Workers Union (SADSAWU) played a key role in Mozambique's adoption of protective legislation for domestic workers in 2008.[46]

The introduction of protective legislation for domestic workers in Zambia also resulted from international developments. As described in the Introduction, there was an explosion of interest in domestic service amongst labour movements and policymakers operating at the international level during the early 2000s. This built on growing international interest from the 1990s onwards in the issues of formalising informal work and advancing women's and children's rights. Focus on these issues within the ILO created an environment in which productive discussions could be had about regulating domestic service and protecting domestic workers. By the 2000s, the ILO came to view domestic service as a key part of its Decent Work agenda, which aimed to promote productive, fair, and secure employment in a range of sectors.[47] These developments within the ILO also resulted in large part from national and transnational activism and lobbying by domestic workers' organisations such as the IDWN and by supportive feminist and labour organisations.[48] Together, these organisations created what Boris and Fish have described as 'a united front for domestic worker rights within the ILO' and succeeded in securing access to ILO structures and voting seats on national delegations.[49] This united front, combined with the broader interest in domestic workers' issues within the ILO, led to the drafting and adoption in 2011 of Convention 189 and Recommendation 201.

After adopting these instruments, the ILO began working with a range of stakeholders to align national labour laws and employment practices with the new international labour standards for domestic service. Evans Lwanga, the coordinator of activities on domestic workers' issues at the ILO's Country Office for Zambia, Malawi, and Mozambique, played a key role in this process. During an interview in 2013, Lwanga explained that the ILO first began working with the Zambian government on domestic worker rights in 2009. It promoted its Decent Work agenda to the government and worked with the MLSS to develop the legislation adopted in 2011. It also worked with the ZFE to develop a set of guidelines for employers of domestic workers that reflected the Decent Work agenda and Zambia's labour laws. In 2013, the ILO worked with the MLSS and the Central Statistical Office of Zambia to conduct the survey into domestic service in rural and urban Zambia discussed in Chapter 1, the results of which were disseminated to key stakeholders at the 2014 meeting in Lusaka described in the opening of this chapter.[50]

It would be incorrect to attribute the Zambian government's decision to introduce legislation on domestic worker rights entirely to external actors like the ILO. As has been discussed, there were several political and economic factors at play. That said, the ILO, working alongside donors and transnational workers' organisations, clearly shaped the content and timing of the legislation adopted. It was no coincidence that the 2011 legislation was passed in the same year that Convention 189 was endorsed by ILO members or that the content of Zambia's legislation reflected the content of Convention 189 and the aims of the Decent Work agenda. Since Zambia's adoption of the 2011 legislation, ILO officials have continued to push the government to revise and expand legislative protections for domestic workers. The impacts of the ILO's lobbying are clearly illustrated by the content of Zambia's 2018 legislation, which replicated verbatim the narrow definitions of 'domestic work' and 'domestic worker' used in Convention 189.

## The impacts of protective state legislation on domestic workers

The dramatic shift in approach towards domestic workers that was pursued by the MMD in 2011 and by the PF from 2012 had the potential to positively transform the sector in several important ways. It is difficult to make a definitive assessment of how transformational the legislation was, however, because of a lack of systematic monitoring of or reporting on these laws by either government or other relevant organisations. Oral interviews provide some insights, though, into domestic workers' perceptions of these laws and how they have shaped individuals' working conditions. The picture that emerges is one of positive transformation alongside continued gaps in protection and limited enforcement of the law.

Several of the adult domestic workers that I interviewed felt that their working conditions had improved since the legislation was introduced. The most discussed improvement was higher wages. Matilda Banda, who worked for a Black Zambian couple in Chilenje at the time of our interview in 2014, described how her employers had increased her wage from K300 to K350 after the minimum wage was introduced in 2011, and from K350 to K520 in 2012. As she lived at a distance from her employers' home, her total pay included the mandatory transport allowance of K102.[51] In 2014, Betty Zimba received K700 per month as a live-in domestic worker for a Zambian family in Kabulonga. After the 2011 legislation was introduced, her employer had increased her salary from K500 to K600, and in 2012 her pay was increased to K700. Betty's employer had told her that she wanted to pay more than the minimum wage in order to deter Betty from seeking better paid work elsewhere.[52] Cecilia Phiri similarly described how her salary had increased significantly since the introduction of the minimum wage in 2011. She started working for her employer in 2010 and was initially paid K350 per month. By the time of our interview in 2014, her monthly salary had increased to K800 per month. Her employer was a lawyer, and Cecilia thought she had increased her wages because she was keenly aware of her obligations under the law.[53] Research from Harare similarly found that domestic workers perceived their wages to have improved in the years immediately following the introduction of protective legislation in 1981.[54] In South Africa, too, real wages increased by around 20 per cent in the two years following the introduction of the minimum wages for domestic workers in 2002. During the same period, the number of people earning less than the minimum wage reduced from 75 per cent to 63 per cent of domestic workers.[55] These examples suggest that protective legislation has had a positive impact on wages for some domestic workers in southern Africa's cities.

Evidence from maid centres also suggests that at least some employers adhered to the minimum wage legislation. As discussed in Chapter 3, maid centres have mushroomed in Lusaka since the 1990s and appear to have increased in appeal amongst employers. I visited five maid centres while conducting fieldwork in Lusaka and was able to ask their staff members about the impacts of protective legislation on their business model and approach. Staff at all five maid centres stated that they required employers to pay their employees at least the national minimum wage and to follow the law regarding other working conditions. Moreover, if an employer violated the terms of the employment contract, for example by failing to pay the minimum wage, the worker involved could return to the maid centre for support. If a dispute with an employer could not be resolved, the contract would be terminated, and the maid centre would help the worker to find another position.

A number of maid centre staff that I interviewed clearly appeared to see themselves as playing an important role in upholding the law and promoting domestic worker rights. Veronica Tembo of Aunty Veronica's Maid Centre in Kabulonga stressed that she felt responsible for protecting domestic workers from exploitation by ensuring they entered into contracts that upheld their legal rights.[56] Patricia Bwalya, manager of the maid centre at the Abundant Life Fellowship in Kabulonga, made similar comments. She explained that it was the duty of her staff to inform the domestic workers and employers they worked with about the protective legislation for domestic workers and to ensure the law was followed.[57] It is possible that both interviewees presented an exaggerated or false image of benevolence towards domestic workers, but there is evidence to suggest that such statements were at least partly true and that maid centres were engaged in conversations with local and international campaigns for domestic worker rights. The walls of Veronica's office were covered in ILO posters promoting Convention 189 and the Decent Work agenda. The ILO sought to develop relationships with maid centres as part of its broader strategy of promoting domestic worker rights at an institutional level and invited maid centres to its events. Domestic worker trade unions also pursued relationships with maid centres as part of their efforts to promote domestic worker rights and ensure compliance with the new labour laws.

The MLSS and the Industrial Relations Court (IRC) were key state institutions responsible for regulating and enforcing protective legislation for domestic workers. Discussion with IRC staff and trade union officials revealed that some domestic workers have pursued cases against their employers through the courts and the MLSS.[58] Discussing this during an interview in 2014, Justice Musona of the IRC stated that protective legislation had bolstered the legal position of domestic workers and had also enabled lawyers and trade union officials to make specific references to infractions of conditions of employment such as unfair dismissal and non-payment of wages. Although Justice Musona had not presided over many cases involving domestic workers, he had on several occasions ordered employers to make payments to domestic workers in line with the new labour laws.[59]

**Figure 4.1** Domestic workers wait to register at Beverly Hills Maid Centre, 6 February 2014.

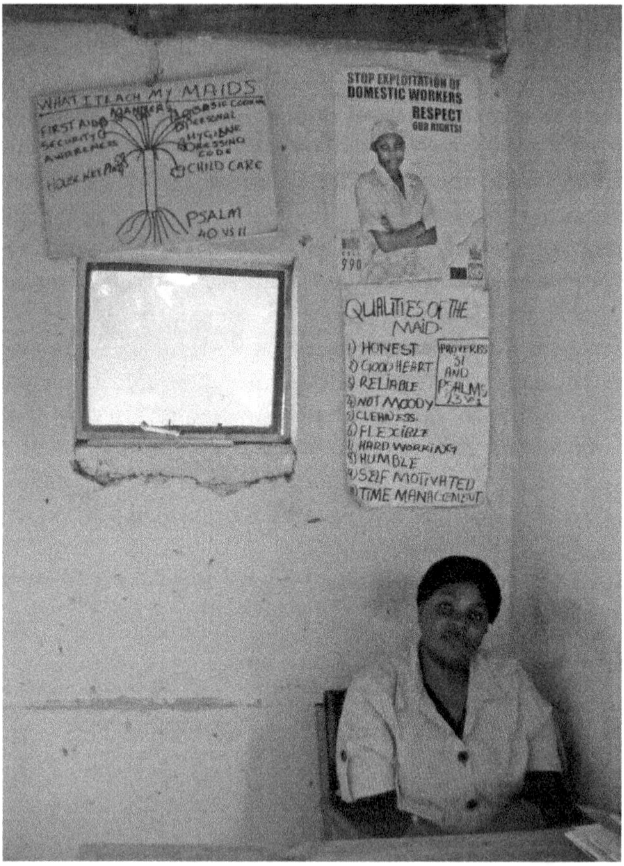


**Figure 4.2** Veronica Tembo in her office at Aunty Veronica's Maid Centre in Kabulonga, Lusaka, 6 August 2014.

Overall, examples of increased wages and of domestic workers pursuing their legal rights illustrate the potential for protective legislation to improve domestic workers' conditions and their position within the labour force and wider society. Moreover, they show how protective legislation led to the creation of working conditions that were in line with international labour standards. These positive developments notwithstanding, many domestic workers did not experience positive change following the introduction of protective legislation because of a range of limitations in the formulation and implementation of these laws, as will now be explored.

Some interviewees stated that they were not paid the minimum wage. When we met in 2014, Rebecca Phiri worked as a live-out maid in Chalala, a middle-class suburb of Lusaka. She received K400 per salary per month, K20 lower than the monthly minimum. She also did not receive the mandated transport allowance of K102 per month and had to commute on foot, a journey of around one-and-a-half hours each way.[60] Niah Mumba, whom we first encountered in Chapter 3, highlighted the difficulty for domestic workers of challenging such practices. Even when domestic workers knew they were being paid below the minimum wage, she explained, many would not complain for fear of losing their jobs.[61] Regardless of the illegality of such an act, unequal power dynamics with employers would understandably cause many domestic workers to stay silent and endure their exploitation.

For their part, several of the employers that I interviewed complained that they could not afford to pay the minimum wage and had consequently changed how they employed domestic workers. When asked about the impacts of the minimum wage, Priscilla Njovu stated 'I am a victim of that one. I used to have a gardener who was working Monday to Friday. I used to give him K400 but now the minimum wage is K520 with transport allowance … what I can't afford.' She explained how she had now employed her gardener for three rather than five days per week. He made up his hours by working for three days per week for another employer. According to Priscilla, many of her friends had also reduced their domestic workers' hours in order to avoid paying higher full-time wage rates.[62] This appears to have been a broader response by employers in the region to the introduction of minimum wages. In his research into the formalisation of domestic service in South Africa, Tom Hertz found that many employers reduced their domestic workers' hours or stopped employing them altogether.[63] Benson Nguni, a pastor at a Pentecostal church in Bauleni, criticised employers who refused to pay their domestic workers the minimum wage. He drew attention to the hypocrisy of those government employees whose minimum wages had been increased in recent years but who did not pay their domestic workers the legal minimum.[64]

More broadly, a number of domestic workers that I spoke with felt that the minimum wage was too low. Niah argued, 'K450 is not enough I'm telling you.' She felt that the minimum wage should be increased to at least K700 and that even that would not be enough because 'it is difficult to get by on less than K1,100'.[65] Mayben Banda reflected on his time working as a gardener from 2008 to 2009. Although he then earned K250 per month, equal to the minimum wage introduced in 2011, he said that this was not enough: 'Even K550 doesn't make up for how you are treated … I felt like a slave to that family.'[66] Herbert Bwalya, husband of Elizabeth Bwalya, whose experiences were discussed in Chapter 1, similarly complained about the low level of wages. He received K600 per month as a guard in Woodlands but explained that he worked around sixty hours per week for this, well in excess of the working hours outlined in the legislation and without any overtime pay or time in lieu.[67] Pastor Nguni noted that the complaint he heard most frequently from domestic workers in his congregation was that their salaries were too low. He empathised with his congregants, not least because he had worked as a gardener in his youth during the 1980s: 'Rents are high, the work they do is hard. Government must increase salaries to a reasonable rate', he argued. He gave the example that the rental cost of a two-room house in Bauleni was around K450 per month in early 2014. This exceeded the monthly minimum wage for domestic workers and would have been unaffordable without other wage-earning members of the household.[68]

Alongside the payment of substandard wages, it is clear that many domestic workers also continued to labour under conditions that did not comply with legal regulations. Interviewees who engaged in both kin-based and waged domestic service stated that they worked long hours and with few breaks. As discussed previously, a substantial minority of interviewees reported enduring verbal abuse, with female domestic workers also reporting physical abuse and sexual harassment. Evidence from elsewhere in the region also shows that protective legislation for domestic workers did not always translate into improved working conditions. In Zimbabwe, for example, domestic workers interviewed in Harare during the late 1980s and early 1990s complained of working far longer than the legal limits and of being housed in poor-quality accommodation by their employers.[69]

One of the reasons for the failure of protective legislation to translate into concrete improvements for domestic workers is the weakness of state monitoring mechanisms. In Zambia, few cases make it to the IRC. In large part this is because disputes between domestic workers and employers are settled informally between the two parties. This reflects the longstanding informality and intimacy of the domestic service relationship, the lack of awareness amongst domestic workers of their legal rights, and, for those who are aware of their rights, the prohibitive cost of taking legal action. In the case of unionised domestic workers, disputes were more likely to be settled through informal or formal mediation facilitated by their union. Moreover, only cases that have been through such mediation make it to the IRC. The situation is similar in Mozambique, where Castel-Branco found that most domestic workers and employers were unaware of the legislation passed in 2008 and tended to settle disputes informally or through mediation and union channels rather than the law courts.[70]

Many of my interviewees also criticised the MLSS for failing to proactively and adequately monitor the law. Given the highly decentralised and widespread nature of the domestic service sector, regular workplace inspections would be extremely labour intensive and costly for the government. But the lack of labour inspections also reflects a broader lack of capacity within Zambia to monitor labour laws. The MLSS instead relies on employers and domestic workers to comply with the legislation and to report any infractions to the local labour office. But many domestic workers in Lusaka stated that they would not pursue a dispute through official channels because they thought that labour officers were corrupt. Interviewees suggested that labour officers were likely to accept bribes from employers and to give out confidential information in exchange for payments. Although such arguments may have been mere speculation, the limited mechanisms that do exist to enforce the new legislation will undoubtedly not be effective without the trust of domestic workers. A similar situation developed in Mozambique where the state relies on domestic workers and workers' organisations to report infractions of the law.[71] By contrast, in South Africa labour inspectors have the right to inspect private homes and to carry out raids in order to apprehend exploitative employers.[72]

The MLSS was also limited in its capacity to monitor the activities of maid centres. Some of the maid centres that I visited stated that they were legally registered, but others did not comment on this, and it is likely that many small operations are not. Even those maid centres that were registered appear not to have much interaction with government. For example, Beverly Hills Maid Centre had been operational for almost twenty years in 2014 and was officially registered with the MLSS. Martha Banda explained that in the eight months she had worked full-time at the centre, she had never encountered any form of communication from government officials.[73] Patricia, of the Abundant Life Fellowship maid centre, which was also registered, similarly noted that the centre had never been visited or inspected by government officials.[74]

The lack of government oversight of maid centres is problematic for several reasons. Although the maid centres I visited purported to follow and promote the law, without adequate government oversight there is clearly scope for these centres to do otherwise and even to exploit domestic workers. Most domestic workers in Lusaka had received limited education, and it is likely that many were unable to fully understand the precise details of their written contracts, which were provided only in English. Even if maid centre staff offered oral translation, domestic workers relied upon those staff to accurately inform them of the conditions they were agreeing to. Many workers also reported that they were not provided with a written copy of the employment contract they had signed, making it difficult for them to check the terms of the contract once they had started work. Although the staff of all five maid centres stated that they provided copies of contracts to all parties involved, it seems plausible that domestic workers were not provided with the same level of support and information as employers, who were often in a more powerful economic and social position than themselves and maid centre staff.

The failure of protective legislation to bring about positive transformations for domestic workers is also about more than the lack of state monitoring and enforcement of the law. There is persuasive evidence that the protective legislation introduced for domestic workers in a number of African states has had a negative rather than positive impact on domestic workers because it has undermined their ability to mobilise the informality and intimacy of their relationship with their employers and informally negotiate pay, terms, and conditions. Ally persuasively argues this in the case of South Africa, where she suggests that the state extended new forms of disciplinary control over domestic workers in its will to 'empower' them. Crucially, in its efforts to formalise and depersonalise domestic service and turn it into work 'like any other', the South African state reduced domestic workers' ability to use the close and personal character of the labour process to their advantage.[75] Domestic workers in Zambia have similarly sought to use the ambiguities of the labour process to their advantage, even when faced with exploitative employers and limited circumstances. While the enactment of protective legislation is a crucial step in the process of securing fair wages and decent working conditions, it is important to recognise that formalisation can also increase state power and reduce domestic workers' autonomy and ability to shape the labour process for themselves. Partly due to the various limitations of existing labour protections, domestic workers also pursued individual strategies of defiance within the workplace and various methods of collective worker organising, all issues that are examined in the next chapter.

There is also evidence of formalisation leading to increased casualisation and demand for cheap labour. As Bryceson has observed, in many African contexts 'wage control intensified the demand for cheap domestic labour options that were disempowering rather than empowering for domestic workers'.[76] In Lusaka, many domestic workers sought to hold onto their jobs in the face of intense competition from large numbers of unemployed jobseekers, including young workers and kin who are often paid low to no wages or entirely in kind. This process had especially disempowering impacts upon child domestic workers and those employed in kin-based arrangements.

This is suggestive also of the broader limitations of the existing legislation in relation to working children's rights. In Zambia, the employment of children below the age of fifteen in domestic service was made explicitly illegal under the 2011 legislation. Although this aimed to reduce instances of child labour and the exploitation of children, it meant that the legislative gains won by adult domestic workers were inaccessible to working children. It also encouraged employers to conceal their young employees, making it harder for government officials, workers' organisations, and children's rights organisations to reach and support these young workers. Since 2011, child domestic workers have been in the difficult position of needing and, for some, wanting to work whilst being ineligible for the same rights and respect as adult domestic workers under the law. These issues have had a particularly significant impact on girls, who, as has been shown, generally outnumber boys in domestic service.

The lack of attention paid to the needs of child domestic workers in Zambia's legislation reflects a broader issue in policymaking on domestic service. Zambia's laws were developed in relation to the international labour standards outlined in Convention 189, which state that children below the national minimum age for employment should not be employed as domestic workers. These standards have implications for millions of working children across southern Africa and the wider world, as ILO member states are expected to develop laws in line with its conventions. The ILO itself estimated that around 15.5 million children aged between five and seventeen years of age were engaged in domestic work in 2008, a figure that counted for over 5 per cent of children's employment globally.[77] Domestic workers' organisations and trade unions have similarly focused on the needs of adult workers and framed child workers as vulnerable subjects who should be kept out of the workplace.[78] By casting children in these roles, the ILO and workers' organisations have ignored the reality that many children around the world depend on employment in domestic service for survival and deserve protection as workers. As shown in Chapter 3, it is a mistake to assume that working children are not cognisant of the challenges they face or capable of contributing to policymaking that shapes their working conditions and options.

Finally, protective legislation for domestic workers in Zambia continues to be limited in terms of parental rights. The rights to maternity leave introduced in 2011 were an important step forward for working women and parental rights more broadly, but they were limited in terms of their practical utility. Only women who had two years' continuous service were eligible, and the leave was unpaid.[79] Few of the women I interviewed could afford to lose four months' income. Furthermore, many women feared that their employers would simply replace them after they went on maternity leave. Although this was technically illegal, many women may well have lost their jobs if they took their full allowance of maternity leave given the lack of monitoring of the legislation. The government sought to address some of these issues through the 2018 legislation, which stipulated that female domestic workers on maternity leave were entitled to half of their regular pay. In a similar vein, while the right to paternity leave granted by the 2018 legislation was another important development in parental rights, the fact that this leave was unpaid made it inaccessible to many male domestic workers.[80]

The regulatory mechanisms for domestic service also do nothing to address the challenges faced by female domestic workers with regard to sexual harassment in the workplace. During an interview in 2013, Elizabeth Bwalya described how her current employers, a Zambian couple, paid her more than the minimum wage and adhered to the broader regulations surrounding working conditions outlined. At the same time, however, the male employer subjected her to consistent sexual harassment when his wife was away from the house. He offered to increase her wage from K750 to K1,500 or even K2,000 per month if she would have sex with him. She confided in her husband but would not go to the government labour officials or the police.[81] Such forms of sexual harassment are illegal under the Employment Act, but it is likely that many women workers like Elizabeth do not feel confident, safe, or able to report their employers to the authorities.

## Conclusion

This chapter has illustrated the deep and uneven history of formalisation of domestic service in Zambia. Under colonial rule in Northern Rhodesia and across southern Africa, governments monitored and regulated domestic service as part of broader efforts to control workers, enforce racial hierarchies within the workplace and the city, and secure colonial power. The regulation of domestic service was about disciplining, not protecting, workers. Following independence in Zambia, the government's approach both reflected and differed from that of its colonial predecessors. On the one hand, successive post-independence governments' decisions to exclude domestic workers from minimum wage legislation and other labour protections built on longer-standing policies of marginalising domestic workers under the law seen since the colonial period. On the other hand, UNIP and its successors in the MMD took a more detached approach to domestic service, exemplified by their exclusion of the sector from key official labour reports and publications. Post-independence governments' approaches to domestic service were also motivated by different factors than colonial governments. The economic crises facing the Zambian state from the mid-1970s undermined its capacity to monitor labour relations in domestic service and many other sectors. More broadly, the sector declined as an area of focus because the government was unwilling or unable to intervene in the wealth- and gender-based inequalities that domestic work came to symbolise and perpetuate.

It was only in 2011 that a post-independence government in Zambia pursued significant legal interventions into domestic service. The adoption of Statutory Instrument No. 3 in 2011 introduced protective state regulations for domestic workers for the first time, with amendments in 2012 and 2018 extending the scope and scale of protections. The introduction of these laws marked a dramatic shift in Zambian state policy towards domestic service and resulted from a combination of local political and economic pressures and regional and international developments in the field of domestic worker rights. The ILO encouraged and supported the state and workers' organisations in Zambia and across southern Africa in these endeavours as part of its Decent Work agenda. Overall, these findings show how efforts to formalise domestic service practices across the region shifted over time in relation to broader changes in labour regimes and associated legal frameworks, and wider political and economic transformations.

My findings also reveal the mixed impacts of protective state regulations on domestic workers in Lusaka and beyond. Interviews with domestic workers and others show that labour protections did lead to real gains for individual workers, including higher wages and social protections such as maternity leave. However, these gains were neither consistent nor equally accessible to all workers within the sector. Some domestic workers did not experience improved pay or working conditions, with many interviewees lamenting the low rate of the minimum wage and employers' unwillingness to pay what they should. There were also clear limitations for female domestic workers, with maternity protection proving to be more symbolic than accessible, and sexual harassment continuing unabated. These laws were specifically limited in relation to working children's rights, with large numbers of child domestic workers unable to access parity in workers' rights and protections, and thus left at the mercy of their employers. In order for all domestic workers to benefit from protective state legislation, such laws must not only be upheld through better inspection and enforcement – they also need to be applicable to the diversity of working arrangements in which children, women, and men engage. The latter will require expanding the scope of existing legislation or introducing supplementary measures so that children can access workers' rights and entitlements to minimum wages and working conditions. Without a more nuanced and sensitive approach to formalisation that accounts for the realities of domestic service, interventions developed by national governments and international organisations aimed at improving domestic workers' rights will continue to exclude large numbers of domestic workers and exacerbate existing gendered and generational inequalities in the sector.

Protective legislation is, of course, only one part of securing decent employment and fair treatment for domestic workers. Domestic workers in Zambia and beyond have long pursued their own strategies to improve their working conditions and challenge exploitation. Part of this has involved domestic workers trying to leverage the intimate dynamics of domestic service to their advantage, mobilising their relationships with employers to at best secure improvements in their conditions and at worst hold onto their jobs in the face of competition. It has also involved individual acts of defiance and non-compliance in the workplace and formal and informal collective organising with other domestic workers. Let us now turn to examine the varied strategies that Zambia's domestic workers have pursued to improve their conditions.

## Notes

1 ILO, C189 – Domestic Workers Convention, 2011 (No. 189).
2 Observations by the author, Lusaka, 21 February 2014.
3 Such arguments are outlined more fully in ILO, *Decent Work for Domestic Workers*. ILO, *International Labour Conference, 100th Session* (Geneva: ILO, 2011), pp. 1–78.
4 Manuela Tomei, 'Decent Work for Domestic Workers: Reflections on Recent Approaches to Tackle Informality', *Canadian Journal of Women and the Law*, 23:1 (2011), 185–211; Nisha Varia, '"Sweeping

Changes?" A Review of Recent Reforms on Protections for Migrant Domestic Workers in Asia and the Middle East', *Canadian Journal of Women and the Law*, 23:1 (2011), 265–287; Sarah van Walsum, 'Regulating Migrant Domestic Work in the Netherlands: Opportunities and Pitfalls', *Canadian Journal of Women and the Law*, 23:1 (2011), 141–165.

5 Jennifer N. Fish, 'Engendering Democracy: Domestic Labor and Coalition Building in South Africa', *Journal of Southern African Studies*, 32:1 (2006), 107–127. See also Alison J. King, *Domestic Service in Post-Apartheid South Africa: Deference and Disdain* (Aldershot: Ashgate, 2007).

6 Bryceson, 'Domestic Work', p. 325.

7 Ally, *From Servants to Workers*, pp. 13–15, pp. 94–118.

8 Hansen, *Distant Companions*, pp. 50–51.

9 *Ibid.*, pp. 65–66.

10 *Ibid.*, p. 50. On the longer history and broader application of master and servant legislation in the British Empire, see Douglas Hay and Paul Craven (eds), *Masters, Servants, and Magistrates in Britain and the Empire, 1562–1955* (Chapel Hill, NC: University of North Carolina Press, 2004).

11 Hansen, *Distant Companions*, p. 76.

12 *Ibid.*, pp. 166–167.

13 *Ibid.*, p. 169.

14 The shift from 'garden boys' to 'garden hands' is suggested in NAZ, MLSS1/19 17, Labour Exchanges and Agencies General, 1961–1964, notice to Employment Exchanges, February 1961. The suggestion to use the term 'garden workers' is found in NAZ, MLSS1/19 18, Employment Exchange General 1962–1964, Employment Services Manual, August 1964.

15 This can be seen, for instance, in the monthly reports submitted by labour officers in Lusaka in 1964. Examples include NAZ, MLSS1/15 126, Labour Officer Monthly Reports Lusaka, 1963–1965; monthly labour report for Lusaka, August 1964; monthly labour report for Lusaka, October 1964.

16 Castel-Branco, 'Legislating Worker Justice', pp. 28–30. For further discussion of the Portuguese colonial labour regime, see Jeanne Marie Penvenne, *African Workers and Colonial Racism: Mozambican Strategies and Struggles in Lourenço Marques, 1877–1962* (Johannesburg: Witwatersrand University Press, 1994); Bridget O'Laughlin, 'Class and the Customary: the Ambiguous Legacy of the Indigenato in Mozambique', *African Affairs*, 99 (2000), 5–42.

17 For further discussion, see Cock, *Maids and Madams*; Ally, *From Servants to Workers*; Ginsburg, *At Home with Apartheid*.

18 Hansen, *Distant Companions*, pp. 50–51.
19 Castel-Branco, 'Legislating Worker Justice', p. 28.
20 Hansen, 'Introduction: Domesticity in Africa', pp. 4–5.
21 Emily G. Bradley, *A Household Book for Africa* (Oxford: Oxford University Press, 1939); Emily G. Bradley, *A Household Book for Tropical Colonies* (Oxford: Oxford University Press, 1948); Emily G. Bradley, *Dearest Priscilla: Letters to the Wife of a Colonial Civil Servant* (London: Max Parrish, 1950).
22 Examples include NAZ, MLSS1/9 33, Conditions of Employment in Certain Industries and Services: Domestic Servants, 1944–54, The Federation of Women's Institutes of Northern Rhodesia, 'Hints to Settlers', Lusaka, 1949.
23 *Ibid.* See also Alison K. Shutt, *Manners Make a Nation: Racial Etiquette in Southern Rhodesia, 1910–1963* (Rochester NY: University of Rochester Press, 2015), p. 83, pp. 87–90.
24 Kathleen Sheldon, '"Rats Fell from the Ceiling and Pestered Me": Phrase Books as Sources for Colonial Mozambican History', *History in Africa*, 25 (1998), 352–355.
25 Evance Kalula, 'The Influence of International Labour Standards on Zambian Legislation', *International Labour Review*, 124:5 (1985), 594.
26 Hansen, *Distant Companions*, p. 255.
27 Larmer, *Rethinking African Politics*, p. 5.
28 During the 1980s, there was a gradual increase in the attention paid to women's issues in government policy, reflecting broader global turns towards women's rights and the incorporation of women into official decision-making processes. Such initiatives gathered pace from the mid-1990s under the MMD, which made gender more central to policymaking. Increased attention was paid to gender-based violence, gendered imbalances in political participation and representation, and the gendered dimensions of poverty. See Republic of Zambia, *National Gender Policy* (Lusaka: Gender in Development Division, 2000).
29 Bujra, *Serving Class*, p. 5, pp. 45–46; Johnson, *Women on the Frontline*, p. 146. For further discussion, see Wrigley, 'Feminists and Domestic Workers'; Schwartz: *Feminism and the Servant Problem.*
30 Pape, 'Still Serving the Tea', 388–390.
31 Republic of Botswana, Employment Act 1982 (Cap 47:01) (Act 29, 1982) (Gaborone: Government Printer, 1982), available at www.ilo.org/dyn/natlex/natlex4.detail?p_lang=en&p_isn=842 (accessed 31 July 2021). Republic of Botswana, Employment (Domestic Employees) Regulations 1984. No. 156 (Gaborone: Government Printer, 1985), available at www.ilo.org/dyn/natlex/natlex4.detail?p_lang=en&p_isn=1249 (accessed 31

July 2021). For further discussion, see Sejoe and Magula, *Domestic Workers in Botswana.*

32 Østreng, *Domestic Workers' Daily Lives in Post-Apartheid Namibia*, pp. 68–72.

33 Ally, *From Servants to Workers*, p. 3.

34 *Ibid.*, p. 68, p. 70.

35 Some watchmen or guards were already entitled to minimum wages under a statutory instrument adopted in 2006. Republic of Zambia, Statutory Instrument No. 57 of 2006. The Minimum Wages and Conditions of Employment Act (Laws, Vol. 15, Cap. 276). The Minimum Wages and Conditions of Employment (General) Order, 2006 (Lusaka: Government Printer, 2006), available at www.ilo.org/dyn/natlex/natlex4.detail?p_lang=en&p_isn=96082&p_classification=12.02 (accessed 2 March 2022).

36 Republic of Zambia, Statutory Instrument No. 3 of 2011.

37 Republic of Zambia, Statutory Instrument No. 45 of 2012.

38 Republic of Zambia, Statutory Instrument No. 69 of 2018.

39 Castel-Branco, 'Legislating Worker Justice', p. 31.

40 *Ibid.*, p. 69.

41 *Ibid.*, p. 32.

42 Interview with Kevin Liywalii; interview with Martha Kasaro. As discussed in Chapter 5, Liywalii and Kasaro were members of a breakaway branch of UHDWUZ referred to elsewhere in this thesis as U-FFTUZ.

43 K. Chimpinde, 'Govt Sets New Minimum Wage for Shopkeepers, Domestic Workers but ZFE Dismisses It as Absurd', *The Post*, 12 July 2012; Editorial, 'Opposing Minimum Wage', *The Post*, 18 July 2012; K. Chimpinde, 'Propose Alternative Minimum Wage, Shamenda Tells ZFE', *The Post*, 20 July 2012.

44 Interview with Custom Banda, Lusaka, 13 July 2013.

45 Interview with Monica Zimba, Lusaka, 2 February 2014.

46 Castel-Branco, 'Legislating Worker Justice', p. 35.

47 Boris and Fish, 'Decent Work for Domestics', pp. 532–542. For further discussion, see Adelle Blackett, 'Making Domestic Work Visible: The Case for Specific Regulation', Labour Law and Labour Relations Programme, Working Paper 2 (Geneva: International Labour Office, 1998); Asha D'Souza, *Moving Towards Decent Work for Domestic Workers: An Overview of the ILO's Work* (Geneva: International Labour Office, 2010); ILO, *Promoting Decent Work for Domestic Workers: ILO in Action* (Geneva: International Labour Office, 2014).

48 Boris and Fish, 'Decent Work for Domestics', p. 531.

49 *Ibid.*, p. 543.

50 Interview with Evans Lwanga, Lusaka, 12 August 2013.

51 Interview with Matilda Banda, Lusaka, 16 February 2014.
52 Interview with Betty Zimba, Lusaka, 18 February 2014.
53 Interview with Cecilia Phiri, Lusaka, 23 February 2014.
54 Pape, 'Still Serving the Tea', 394–395.
55 Tom Hertz, 'The Effect of Minimum Wages on the Employment and Earnings of South Africa's Domestic Service Workers', Working Paper 05/99, University of Cape Town Development Policy Research Unit (2005), p. 1.
56 Interview with Veronica Tembo.
57 Interview with Patricia Bwalya.
58 Interview with Oscar Cheupe, Lusaka, 27 August 2014; interview with Hon. Mr Justice Edward Luputa Musona, Lusaka, 1 September 2014.
59 Interview with Hon. Mr Justice Edward Luputa Musona.
60 Interview with Rebecca Phiri.
61 Interview with Niah Mumba.
62 Interview with Priscilla Njovu.
63 Hertz, 'The Effect of Minimum Wages on the Employment and Earnings of South Africa's Domestic Service Workers', p. 23.
64 Interview with Pastor Benson Nguni, Lusaka, 13 February 2014.
65 Interview with Niah Mumba.
66 Interview with Mayben Banda, Lusaka, 13 February 2014.
67 Interview with Herbert Bwalya, Lusaka, 13 February 2014.
68 Interview with Pastor Benson Nguni.
69 Pape, 'Still Serving the Tea', 395–397.
70 Castel-Branco, 'Legislating Worker Justice', pp. 53–59.
71 *Ibid.*, p. 69.
72 ILO, *Guide to Design a Law for Domestic Workers* (Geneva: ILO, 2012).
73 Interview with Martha Banda.
74 Interview with Patricia Bwalya.
75 See Ally, *From Servants to Workers*, pp. 15–17, pp. 94–118.
76 Bryceson, 'Domestic Work', p. 325.
77 ILO, *Domestic Workers Across the World*, p. 22.
78 This will be examined in detail in Chapter 5.
79 Republic of Zambia, Statutory Instrument No. 3 of 2011.
80 Republic of Zambia, Statutory Instrument No. 69 of 2018.
81 Interview with Elizabeth Bwalya.

# 5

# Collective organising and the limits of unionisation

My mother was a kitchen girl,
My father was a garden boy,
That's why, I'm a unionist, I'm a unionist, I'm a unionist.[1]

On 16 June 2014, a group of domestic workers marched through the backstreets of central Lusaka to commemorate the ILO's adoption of Convention 189, which had come into force the previous year.[2] Members of UHDWUZ, they carried placards bearing ILO slogans, wore union-branded T-shirts, and sang songs that proclaimed their commitment to the agenda of formalisation that Convention 189 epitomised. These actions and the language of the songs that UHDWUZ members sang at the march, an example of which can be seen above, reflect the transnational links between domestic worker organisations in the region and internationally.[3] But they also betrayed the challenges inherent in organising and formalising domestic service. As has been illustrated throughout this book, the labour relations of domestic service are often highly personalised, informal, and, in post-colonial cities like Lusaka, grounded in a history of racialised, gendered, and generational inequalities. Supporters of the formalisation agenda have struggled to address these challenges, both today and in the past.

The image of domestic workers coming together and marching to demand greater rights stands in stark contrast to the common stereotype of these workers as atomised and passive, incapable of organising collectively because of the private and personalised nature of their work. This stereotype does not represent domestic workers in the contemporary world, nor does it characterise their experiences in the past. From Robyn Pariser's work on domestic workers in colonial Tanganyika to Shireen Ally's study of domestic service in post-apartheid South Africa, studies of domestic service in Africa have variously drawn attention to the capacity of domestic workers to organise formally, to ally themselves with other workers, and to pursue legislative reform.[4] In the Zambian context, domestic workers have engaged with the formal labour movement since at least the 1930s, with small groups of workers seeking to establish worker associations and trade unions in Lusaka and on the Copperbelt beginning in the early 1950s. Formal organisations for Zambian domestic workers emerged during the 1950s, 1960s, and 1970s, though these were short-lived and intermittent. Zambian domestic workers had more success with formal organising from the late 1990s, culminating in the registration of UHDWUZ as an official trade union in 2000. Although existing studies have done much to highlight African domestic workers' engagement with collective organising, several issues warrant further examination. There is scope to expand understandings of the challenges facing formal organisations for domestic workers, the capacity of domestic workers to organise outside the formal labour movement model, and the gender and generational dynamics of worker organising. The broad definition of domestic service used in this book allows for examination of each of these issues. Can labour movements represent and address the needs of a wide range of workers, from adult men to female children? How have trade unions sought to organise workers engaged in informal and highly personalised working arrangements, including those between kin or involving children?

This chapter examines the varied ways in which domestic workers in Lusaka and other southern African cities have pursued collective organising, from efforts to establish formal associations and trade unions to participation in informal strategies of joint action. In doing so, it both builds on existing studies of domestic service and engages with recent scholarship on work and labour movements in Africa. The chapter shows that, in the Zambian case, despite the efforts of successive groups of domestic workers and labour activists, formal organisations have failed to secure broad support amongst the labour force or to achieve significant improvements in domestic workers' rights. This resulted from the limited financial and organisational capacity of such organisations, the government's dismissive attitude towards the sector, and the failure

**Figure 5.1** Members of the United House and Domestic Workers Union of Zambia (UHDWUZ) march to commemorate International Labour Organization Convention 189 and Recommendation 201, 16 June 2014.

of workers' organisations to tailor their interventions to reflect the breadth of domestic service practices. Formal worker organisations were dominated by adults engaged in wage labour, with no efforts to organise working children and limited engagement with kin-based domestic workers, most of whom were female and, often, young. The formal labour movement model was also unsuccessful because male and female domestic workers of all ages could pursue alternative solutions to their grievances at work, from individual strategies of resistance to informal collective organising.

In Lusaka and across urban southern Africa, informal relations of solidarity developed between domestic workers through a range of associations and in the neighbourhoods in which they worked and lived. Through these relationships, domestic workers became aware of each other's challenges and developed ways to support each other. They created accessible and popular spaces to share grievances and developed tangible strategies of material and emotional support from which collective and individual action sprang.

Scholars have examined domestic workers' participation in associations and organised social activities in southern Africa's urban centres but have generally interpreted these in relation to the maintenance of rural-urban connections, principally through ethnicity, and the building of urban-based communities.[5] This chapter builds on such studies by illustrating the ways in which domestic workers' participation in urban associations and social networks helped to foster labour solidarity and inspire collective responses to workplace exploitation.

## Collective organising before independence

Forms of collective organising amongst domestic workers in southern Africa can be traced from the late nineteenth century. Charles van Onselen has shown how a group of Zulu houseboys formed a secret society in Johannesburg during the 1890s 'to protect their interests "without recourse to a law court"'.[6] Known as the *izigebengu* or Ninevites, this secret society later became a criminal gang, but it had its roots in worker organising. The Ninevites inspired the formation of the *Amalaita*, a gang on the Witwatersrand which recruited members primarily from amongst houseboys. Like the Ninevites before them, the *Amalaita* engaged in criminal activity and not in traditional forms of worker organising. But van Onselen is keen to stress the gang's importance to the workers involved, describing it as 'a movement which sought to give its members who labored in alienated colonial isolation a sense of purpose and dignity'.[7] During the 1920s and 1930s, as proletarianisation extended in South Africa, domestic workers also engaged in more traditional forms of worker organising, joining established trade unions and founding new organisations including the African Domestic Servants League.[8] Notably, these efforts constituted some of the earliest labour unions in South Africa.[9]

In Northern Rhodesia, domestic workers participated in collective action from at least the 1930s to advance demands for higher wages, better working conditions, and reductions in racial and economic inequality. Numerous domestic workers took part in the mineworkers' strikes on the Copperbelt in 1935 and 1940, offering support to fellow urban workers and passing on information about the strikes that they overheard in the homes of their European employers. The proportion of domestic workers who engaged in such activities was often high. In Luanshya, for instance, around 50 per cent to 60 per cent of domestic workers voluntarily joined the 1935 strike.[10] Domestic workers' participation in such activities in Northern Rhodesia's towns suggests the development of broader relations of solidarity amongst African urban workers. This was likely based on shared experiences of life in town and the struggles for survival facing urban waged workers under colonial rule.[11]

Northern Rhodesia's labour movement grew in size and strength from the late 1940s, with a number of trade unions for African workers being granted official status. During the early 1950s, groups of domestic workers in Lusaka and in the mining towns of Kitwe and Broken Hill (now Kabwe), inspired by these reforms, sought to formally organise into associations and trade unions. These early efforts at formal organisation, however, largely failed. The domestic workers' associations that were established in both Kitwe and Lusaka appear to have dissipated during the later 1950s, while the workers in Broken Hill do not seem to have ever registered as an official union.[12] It is likely that the relative isolation of domestic workers, their lack of free time, and the personalised nature of many domestic service arrangements each played a role in limiting the success of these formal organisations. The dismissive attitude of labour officials also significantly limited the effectiveness of domestic workers' attempts to formally organise. The colonial government's stance towards domestic workers' demands for union representation remained inflexible until independence and, as discussed in the previous chapter, domestic workers were excluded from improvements to colonial labour regulations such as minimum wages.

The efforts of domestic workers in Northern Rhodesia to establish formal associations and trade unions during the 1940s and 1950s were part of a broader trend of organising amongst African domestic workers in the post-war period. For example, domestic workers formed the first African labour union in Tanganyika in 1945, the African Cooks, Washermen, and House Servants Association (ACWHSA).[13] A notable exception to this trend is South Africa, where collective organising by domestic workers declined from 1948 because the apartheid regime ruthlessly constrained the activities of trade unions and political activists.[14]

Domestic workers in Northern Rhodesia finally succeeded in forming a registered trade union during the early 1960s. The National Union of Catering, Hotel and Domestic Workers (NUCHDW) was founded around 1960 and continued to be active on the Copperbelt and in Lusaka until 1965. The records of NUCHDW do not appear to have survived, but government records offer some insight into the scope and scale of the union's activities. NUCHDW membership seems to have expanded quickly, with colonial records suggesting an increase from seven members in 1960 to 1,145 by 1961 and 7,027 by 1962.[15] Membership of NUCHDW was open to workers in various hospitality and service industries, and the proportion of members who were domestic workers is unknown. But several sources suggest the seriousness with which the union campaigned for domestic worker rights. In 1963, for instance, NUCHDW published an article in Northern Rhodesia's leading newspaper, the *Northern News*, criticising the low wages and poor conditions of employment for domestic workers. The article specifically criticised European mineworkers, arguing that these employers should provide free medical care to their domestic workers.[16] On the eve of independence in 1964, NUCHDW put sustained pressure on the government to introduce an official minimum wage, using press coverage and regular correspondence with government officials.[17] The timing here is significant, for although the colonial government had excluded domestic workers from labour laws, the context of imminent independence likely made union activists hopeful about the legislative gains that might be achieved for domestic workers in the coming years.

Across colonial southern Africa, domestic workers' engagement in collective organising to secure better wages and working conditions were shaped by gendered and generational dynamics. Collective organising amongst male domestic workers was often part of broader struggles to preserve manhood and honour. Van Onselen argues that the *Amalaita* should be understood as 'the "houseboys" liberation army fighting to reassert its decolorized manhood during one of the first major waves of South African proletarianization'.[18] Pariser also draws a link between domestic worker organising and masculinity. She explores how domestic service in Tanganyika was transformed during the 1940s and 1950s from a well-paid, skilled occupation for men into one of the lowest paid and least respectable sectors of employment. She argues that this transformation directly threatened male domestic workers' masculinity because it limited their 'ability to achieve the financial and social capital required to achieve senior status and respect within the African community'.[19] The formation of ACWHSA in 1945 was an attempt by men to secure and enhance their occupational status and, with it, their manhood. Given the male dominance of waged domestic service across most of colonial Africa, Pariser's arguments are helpful for understanding collective organising amongst male domestic workers in other colonial societies. The 1935 strikes on the Copperbelt were sparked by proposed increases to taxation which would have reduced waged workers' disposable income. By participating in these strikes, men domestic workers were in part fighting for their ability to provide for their wives, children, and other dependants. During the 1940s and 1950s in Northern Rhodesia, relations between domestic workers and employers became increasingly strained. The booming post-war mining economy attracted large numbers of White immigrants to the protectorate, many of whom were inexperienced at employing domestic workers and developed fractious relationships with their male employees. The cost of living also increased significantly in this period, while domestic workers' wages remained stagnant.[20] In this context, many male domestic workers likely pursued collective organising to secure improvements to their working conditions and wages so that they could both provide for their families and defend their status as workers and as men.

Using the available documentary sources, it is difficult to know how far women and child domestic workers participated in formal collective organising in Northern Rhodesia. Written sources suggest that men dominated NUCHDW and the formal associations for domestic workers which developed during the 1940s and 1950s. This certainly reflects the broader dominance of men in wage labour and the labour movement at that time. Moreover, given their prominence in kin-based labour and in African households, the types of collective organising in which women and child domestic workers engaged likely looked different to the strategies pursued by men. For instance, they were more likely to engage in informal collective organising than join a trade union. Such strategies would have been less visible to labour officers and organised labour and, in any event, were likely of little to no interest to such groups. Women and child domestic workers' general absence from formal organising in the colonial period draws our attention to some of the blind spots of trade unionism, with men fighting for better wages and working conditions for waged workers, and women and children largely excluded from the debate or spoken for by others. As will be examined below, these dynamics would continue to shape formal collective organising amongst domestic workers after independence. An interesting exception to this general trend comes from South Africa, where a short-lived association for female domestic workers was established during the 1930s. The Bantu Girls Domestic Servants Association sought to represent girls and women who had attended boarding schools and been trained for domestic service.[21]

Alongside efforts to formally organise, domestic workers across colonial southern Africa came together through various associations and organised social activities in urban centres. These included savings and burial societies, religious organisations, and dance clubs. Peter Delius noted the 'rich variety of associations' which developed amongst Pedi migrant workers on the Rand in the 1940s and 1950s, including the boxing clubs that were dominated by young male domestic workers.[22] Eleanor Preston-Whyte and Belinda Bozzoli each examined the friendships that developed amongst women domestic workers in the White suburbs under apartheid.[23] Hansen discussed the importance of ballroom dancing clubs to the development of an 'occupational subculture' amongst domestic workers in Northern Rhodesia's urban centres.[24] Established in most towns during the 1930s and 1940s, these clubs organised weekly practices and monthly competitions. The clubs also served a broader purpose, providing members with access to various forms of financial support, including payment of funeral expenses and funding towards travelling home on leave or for moving to another town. While Hansen acknowledges the social and economic functions of ballroom dancing clubs, she stresses that these were 'first and foremost dance clubs'.[25] Thus, her analysis does not consider the extent to which these clubs or other urban associations provided spaces for domestic workers to come together to discuss workplace grievances. That club members supported each other with funeral costs and other personal expenses shows that ballroom dancing clubs fostered collective action. It is clearly possible that domestic workers shared stories about the challenges they faced at work and that they collectively developed solutions to such problems, for example sharing information about alternative jobs or offering advice on how to manage difficult employers. Deborah James' work on *Kiba* dance societies, for instance, points to the potential for domestic workers to share such information with fellow members.[26] The support that domestic workers provided to each other through such organisations may also have lessened their interest in establishing or joining a formal workers' organisation, which only ever had limited success in these colonial societies. It is important to consider the gender dynamics of socialising at the ballroom dancing clubs, such as the extent to which these clubs enabled male domestic workers to assert forms of masculinity or provided women domestic workers with spaces to share workplace grievances and source advice. Domestic workers' engagement in informal strategies of collective action is addressed in further detail in the final section of this chapter.

## Collective organising since independence

NUCHDW remained active in Lusaka after independence and appeared to be in a strong position into 1965, with international ties linking it to workers' movements around the world. In May 1965, Dulizani Banda, NUCHDW's Lusaka Regional Secretary, even travelled to Cuba to meet with Fidel Castro.[27] The origins of this Cuba connection are unknown, but it is possible that the visit was arranged through either left-leaning unionists within the Zambian labour movement or through one of the southern African liberation movements in exile which were resident in Lusaka in the 1960s and had connections to Cuba.[28] Although NUCHDW clearly achieved a degree of longevity and prestige that eluded its predecessors, it also faced a number of challenges. By mid-1965, NUCHDW had collapsed amid rumours of alleged misappropriation of funds by its officials, reflecting a tendency towards fission that such nascent worker organisations have consistently struggled to overcome. The union's campaign to introduce minimum wages for domestic workers and improve working conditions was ultimately unsuccessful in legislative terms, illustrating my argument about the limited effectiveness of domestic workers' formal organisations.

More broadly, the 1960s was a period of extensive industrial action. UNIP was concerned about the impact of strikes and stoppages on productivity and economic stability and set out to curb the power of organised labour. Through the Trade Unions and Trade Disputes (Amendment) Act of 1965, UNIP sought to influence and weaken trade union structures. The Act led to the founding of ZCTU to replace the United Trade Union Congress, which was established before independence.[29] UNIP's attempts to control the labour movement resembled similar moves elsewhere in post-colonial Africa. In Tanzania, for example, formerly active workers organisations, including for domestic workers, were increasingly silenced by the incorporation of all trade unions into the state-controlled National Union of Tanganyika Workers.[30] In Zambia, state attempts to curb trade union power intensified during the late 1960s with the nationalisation of key industries, including the copper mines.[31]

By the early 1970s, the activities of trade union members were increasingly constrained by the strengthening of state control through ZCTU and the gradual closing down of political space. UNIP ruthlessly suppressed its political opponents during 1971 and 1972, including by detaining members of the United Progressive Party, who had received considerable support from mineworkers on the Copperbelt.[32] When Zambia officially became a one-party state in 1972, it became increasingly difficult to express criticism of state policy on labour or other issues. After this point, workers continued to organise and to pursue their grievances, but this commonly took place outside formal union channels.[33]

Despite the increasingly repressive political environment of the 1970s, domestic workers continued to pursue formal methods of organisation. In 1973, a group of domestic workers in Lusaka formed the National Domestic Houseservants' Association of Zambia (NDHAZ). The association campaigned for higher wages and better working and living conditions, and encouraged employers to register their domestic workers with the ZNPF. NDHAZ struggled, however, to build a broad membership and to establish a sound structural base. Moreover, although the association's name stated that it was a national body, it failed, like earlier organisations for domestic workers, to expand its activities beyond the capital. NDHAZ collapsed in 1979 after its leader left the organisation, reflecting the tendency towards fission discussed above.[34] The gender and age dynamics of NDHAZ are not traceable using the available source material, but, given the continued male dominance of waged domestic service during the 1970s, it is likely that the union was dominated by male, adult members engaged in wage labour.

During the 1980s, unofficial industrial action on the Copperbelt continued and often became violent, as workers rejected the deterioration of living conditions, increased prices, and shortages of basic commodities that resulted from economic decline and structural adjustment.[35] During this period, the labour movement also played a key role in campaigning for the reintroduction of multi-party politics. Indeed, it was the Chairman of ZCTU, Frederick Chiluba, who first called for Zambia to reinstate multi-party elections in December 1989.[36] Between 1989 and 1991, the labour movement joined with other advocates of democracy and civil liberties to form a movement for democratic reforms. In 1991, the MMD was formally established as a political party, with Chiluba as its elected leader. The actors campaigning for multi-partyism were certainly reacting to the increasingly repressive policies and economic failures of UNIP, but they were also likely inspired by general shifts in global politics, notably the fall of the Berlin Wall in 1989 and the collapse of one-party communist states in Eastern Europe.

Elsewhere in southern Africa, domestic worker organising expanded during the 1970s and 1980s. In neighbouring Zimbabwe, domestic worker organising was transformed following independence. The Zimbabwe Domestic and Allied Workers' Union (ZDAWU) was established in 1980 with government support and comprised over 5,000 members by 1981. Given Pape's estimation that domestic service had become a female-dominated occupation in Zimbabwe by the 1980s, it is possible that the majority of ZDAWU members were women. ZDAWU pursued various strategies to recruit members and inform them of the legal rights for domestic workers passed by the newly elected ZANU–PF government. This included organising meetings, going from house to house to speak with domestic workers, and the production of radio programmes. Although it succeeded in attracting members and had government backing, ZDAWU at times struggled to turn legislative and political change into concrete improvements for domestic workers. This was especially true during the early 1980s when, as discussed in Chapter 4, many employers fired their domestic workers to avoid paying the newly introduced minimum wage. While the union successfully negotiated on behalf of some members, its overall efforts were hampered by employer resistance and by domestic workers' efforts to work outside of union channels and secure jobs which paid below the legal minimum wage. Despite such challenges, ZDAWU continued to grow during the 1980s, and it expanded beyond Harare, establishing offices in cities across Zimbabwe. By the end of the decade, however, the union's reputation was tainted by charges of fraud and corruption, and it nearly entered bankruptcy.[37]

In South Africa, collective organising by domestic workers had been limited for decades due to the apartheid regime's restrictions on organised labour. During the 1970s, though, domestic worker organising increased in intensity. The Domestic Workers and Employers Project (DWEP) was founded in Johannesburg in 1972 to foster greater understanding between domestic workers and employers and to improve domestic workers' working conditions, wages, and status. DWEP was a White liberal organisation and faced criticism that it was dominated by White women employers rather than the Black women workers they sought to support. DWEP's composition reflected the broader trend discussed in the Introduction of feminist employers, activists, and scholars seeking to formalise and organise domestic service. The South African Domestic Workers Association (SADWA) grew out of DWEP and involved a move away from White liberal leadership. SADWA was instead established and run by Black women domestic workers. In 1986, SADWA merged with four other domestic workers' unions to form the South African Domestic Workers Union (SADWU). Ally argues that SADWU reflected both strands of collective organising of domestic workers in South Africa: the organising of domestic workers by White liberal women employers and the organising of domestic workers by domestic workers themselves. Although weaker than other labour unions in South Africa, SADWU was strong in comparison with domestic worker organisations elsewhere in the region and became the largest union for domestic workers in South Africa's history to that point, with 85,000 members by the early 1990s.[38] Domestic workers in Namibia, which was under *de facto* South African control until 1990, also successfully established a union during the 1980s.[39] The Namibia Domestic and Allied Workers Union (NDAWU) was founded in Windhoek in 1987 by a subcommittee of the National Union of Namibian Workers. NDAWU organised domestic workers in Windhoek and nine other urban centres during the late 1980s, before being formally registered as a trade union following independence in 1990. By the mid-1990s it had around 5,000 members.[40] Like SADWA and SADWU, NDAWU was a predominantly female organisation, with women constituting 70 per cent of its leaders and members.[41] The gender composition of domestic workers' organisations in Namibia and South Africa reflected trends across southern Africa's urban centres in this period.

In Zambia, the ending of the one-party state in 1991 signalled dramatic changes in the nation's politics, including for organised labour. Although the newly elected MMD government owed much of its support to labour movement activists and workers, its pursuit of extensive and aggressive economic liberalisation policies once in power severely weakened trade unions. Trade union membership and revenue declined substantially because of formal-sector job losses, undermining both the demographic and financial base of the labour movement.[42] Moreover, efforts to incorporate the growing number of informal sector workers into the labour movement were limited. Such challenges faced labour movements across southern Africa in this period. For instance, membership of OTM declined significantly during the 1990s as Mozambique's economy was restructured, constitutional reforms encouraged the democratisation of the labour movement, and OTM declared independence from Frelimo.[43]

Despite the economic and political challenges facing labour movements across the region, new organisations for domestic workers emerged. UHDWUZ, discussed at the beginning of the chapter, grew out of a smaller association for domestic workers that was founded in Lusaka in 1998. This association has an unlikely beginning, developing out of a friendship between a retired engineer, Edward Chitalu, and a widowed clerical worker, Joyce Phiri. Chitalu and Phiri met in 1998, when Chitalu was working in domestic service to supplement his small pension. After conversations about the exploitative conditions that Chitalu and others experienced, he and Phiri decided that they would establish and run an association to represent domestic workers in disputes with employers.[44] The association began operating in 1998 and was expanded and registered as a trade union in 2000. Chitalu was elected President and Phiri was elected Deputy General Secretary for Finance, before replacing Chitalu as Acting President when he retired in 2006.[45] By the 2010s, UHDWUZ had allied to ZCTU, employed ten staff and had almost 3,500 registered members. Reflecting the female dominance of domestic service in Zambia during the 2010s, the majority (two-thirds) of UHDWUZ's members were female. In neighbouring Mozambique, three unions for domestic workers were registered during the 2000s. Maputo's first trade union for domestic workers, the Associação das Mulheres Empregadas Domésticas (Women's Association of Domestic Workers, or AMUEDO), was formally registered in 2006. OTM had long excluded domestic workers because it saw them as too dispersed and difficult to organise. In 2006, however, it founded the Associação de Empregados Domésticos de Moçambique (Mozambican Domestic Workers' Association) as part of broader efforts to incorporate informal sector workers and boost its declining membership base. A third union for domestic workers, the Sindicato Nacional de Empregados Domésticos (National Union of Domestic Workers, or SINED), was registered in 2008.[46] These unions were distinguished from each other by their allegiance to different trade union federations, and by AMUEDO's distinct position as a trade union for women domestic workers.

The female dominance of many of the domestic worker trade unions that emerged in post-colonial southern Africa is reflective of both the broader feminisation of domestic service across the region during this period and the enduring appeal of formal methods of collective organising. These findings support the arguments of numerous feminist scholars that female workers are no more passive than their male counterparts and have often engaged with organised labour.[47] They suggest that the feminisation of employment, in domestic service and other sectors, in post-colonial Africa has not in itself brought about a decline in the size and power of organised labour. Such decline was driven instead by government efforts to weaken organised labour and the disastrous impacts on workers organisations of economic decline and liberalisation as these led to decreased formal employment and increased casualisation. The traditional labour movement model has largely proved ill-equipped to deal with and adapt to the changing nature of work and labour relations in post-colonial Africa, in domestic service and other sectors. This is notable in relation to the expansion of kin-based labour and children's employment, as these practices involved workers and labour relations which sat outside organised labour's traditional and narrow focus on adult (male) workers and wage labour.

## The limits of unionisation

The trade unions established for domestic workers across southern Africa following independence organised themselves as traditional trade unions, with formal constitutions and administrative structures and processes. UHDWUZ outlined its structure and aims through its constitution, adopted in 2000. This specified that the union sought to organise domestic workers, to campaign on their behalf for better wages and working conditions, and to put pressure on the state to introduce legislative change in the interest of its members. Members were to be issued with membership cards in exchange for a registration fee, a monthly membership fee, and an annual renewal fee.[48] During the early 2000s, the union focused on the first two aims and sought to expand the membership base and advocate for workers. Union officials went from door to door in different areas of Lusaka to inform domestic workers about the union and its aims, to inform workers of their rights, and to recruit them as formal union members.[49] UHDWUZ also sought to expand its structures and membership beyond Lusaka. The union's constitution outlined its plans to establish branches on the Copperbelt and in Southern Province and to hold regular conferences to bring together branch leaders from across the country.[50]

Unfortunately, UHDWUZ's ambitious aims for expansion were not fulfilled. In large part, this was due to sustained financial challenges and staffing issues. UHDWUZ struggled to maintain sound finances from its inception. Due to their low wages, many domestic workers were unable to pay their membership fees or declined to join the union because of the costs involved. The union's difficult financial position also limited its capacity to employ the staff needed to conduct recruitment drives in the city and expand the membership base. When I interviewed UHDWUZ officials in 2013 and 2014, they were employed solely on a voluntary basis, at best receiving sporadic payments when members made contributions.[51] Financial weakness was a challenge faced by domestic workers' organisations across the region. In Namibia, for example, NDAWU reported in 1990 that only 5 per cent of its members managed to pay their monthly membership fees.[52] UHDWUZ's financial weakness also reflected longer-term problems for not only domestic workers' trade unions but Zambia's labour movement more broadly. As Mulenga notes, ZCTU was 'plagued by financial problems' from its creation, and even the powerful mineworkers' unions had historically struggled with financial problems.[53]

UHDWUZ was also weakened by internal conflicts. Between 2005 and 2006, it went through a period of crisis that resulted in a split into two rival organisations. The crisis was the result of a disagreement about the use and control of union funds, the precise details of which were difficult to establish through union documentation or interviews. What is clear is that a small group of union officials left UHDWUZ and founded a breakaway organisation under the leadership of ex-UHDWUZ official Kevin Liywalii. Liywalii and colleagues insisted that they were the legitimate representatives of UHDWUZ and continued to operate under the same name. The breakaway organisation allied with the Federation of Free Trade Unions of Zambia (FFTUZ), in part to distinguish themselves from UHDWUZ, which was allied to ZCTU.[54] This distinction will be used to differentiate between the two unions, with the breakaway organisation hitherto referred to as U-FFTUZ. The splintering of UHDWUZ reflected longer-term problems of disunity and fission within Zambia's labour movement, discussed above, and also resulted from legal changes that occurred during the 1990s. The 1993 Industrial and Labour Relations Act abolished an earlier principle of 'one union, one industry' and allowed for the creation of rival trade unions. This policy change resulted in the splintering of many existing unions and the formation of new ones. The Industrial and Labour Relations (Amendment) Act passed in 1997 allowed for the formation of new trade union federations, such as FFTUZ. Mulenga argues that 'as a direct result of this liberalisation of the law on freedom of association, there emerged a crop of small unions that faced problems of lack of resources, poor organisation and general instability'.[55] UHDWUZ and U-FFTUZ certainly fit this description.

By the 2010s, U-FFTUZ had become the more successful of the two unions, with a permanent office in the FFTUZ headquarters in central Lusaka and several full-time salaried employees. In interviews, Liywalii stressed that all members of the U-FFTUZ executive are former domestic workers and criticised UHDWUZ for failing to ensure the same.[56] U-FFTUZ keeps extensive records, including membership lists and a logbook of disputes between members and their employers. Consulting these records during our interview, Martha Kasaro, U-FFTUZ Deputy General Secretary, stated that U-FFTUZ had 1,377 female members and 845 male members.[57] These figures suggest that women comprised just over 62 per cent of U-FFTUZ's total membership, giving the union a similar gender composition to UHDWUZ. U-FFTUZ faced similar financial challenges to UHDWUZ and earlier formal organisations for domestic workers. Liywalii acknowledged that collecting monthly subscriptions from members has consistently been a problem because of the low wages that most domestic workers receive.

As workers' organisations, both UHDWUZ and U-FFTUZ arguably have a responsibility to develop strategies that reflect their members' wants and needs. The extent to which members have shaped the objectives and activities of either union is, however, unclear. Due to lack of funding and low staffing levels, neither union communicates with its members in a systematic or regular way. Interviews with union members suggest they often had to take the initiative in keeping in touch with union officials, for instance by visiting their offices in person or by contacting them by telephone.[58] Even if this were not the case, and the unions contacted their members regularly, the memberships of both unions represent only a minority of the large number of domestic workers currently employed in Lusaka, let alone nationally. The available data suggests that at least 100,000 children, women, and men were employed in domestic service in Zambia in late 2013, far more than the unions' then combined membership of about 5,700 adult men and women.[59]

The unions also did not represent the many children employed in domestic service in Lusaka. During an interview in 2013, Joyce Phiri described being aware of the many children who engaged in kin-based and waged domestic service. She acknowledged that union staff struggled to identify child domestic workers: 'it is not easy to identify them ... they do not show themselves as workers, they hide'. Despite child domestic workers' hesitancy, Phiri stated that she and other union officials could sometimes identify them: 'from the way the child looks, you may know'.[60] Throughout this discussion, Phiri referred to the children concerned using the pronoun 'she', reflecting both the prevalence of female children in domestic service and the gendering of child domestic service as female.

Overall, the limited membership of both unions, coupled with their financial and administrative limitations, illustrate my argument that formal organisations for domestic workers have consistently struggled to establish a broad following within the labour force. Given this, the extent to which either union is representative of domestic workers in Zambia is doubtful.

The accountability of union officials to members appears more questionable when the issue of external funding is considered. As both unions have struggled to maintain an adequate income through membership subscriptions, they have relied heavily on the support of local and foreign donors, especially the ILO. UHDWUZ and U-FFTUZ have each engaged with the ILO's Decent Work agenda and have sought to access the resources available through participation in ILO initiatives. U-FFTUZ has been the more successful in this regard, working with the ILO on several projects, including a 2011 ILO-United Nations anti-trafficking project for which it secured funding reported of K123,019 (approximately USD12,489).[61] By working with the ILO, U-FFTUZ gained access to resources that were out of the reach of both its predecessors and UHDWUZ. Nevertheless, it is significant that such projects appear to have been determined by the aims of the ILO rather than by members of U-FFTUZ, despite the involvement of U-FFTUZ officials as the 'voice' of local domestic workers and the good intentions of local ILO staff. Interviews with domestic workers suggest that poor working conditions and low wages were their key issues of concern, rather than trafficking or forced labour. Some other domestic workers' organisations in the region were also successful in securing external funding. In Namibia, NDAWU received funding from Trade Union Solidarity of Finland and Oxfam. This funding was channelled into a basic education program and a cooperative project. Notably, these two initiatives appeared to be in line with

Namibian domestic workers' concerns to bolster their skills and possibilities to support themselves alongside or as an alternative to domestic service.[62]

UHDWUZ has been less successful than U-FFTUZ in securing external support. The 2014 march to commemorate Convention 189, discussed at the beginning of this chapter, is a key example. UHDWUZ had initially tried to organise an exhibition at the Lusaka National Museum to commemorate the first anniversary of the passing of Convention 189. After these plans failed, union officials decided to hold a march.[63] On the day of the event, a small group of union members met at Phiri's place of work in central Lusaka, where they changed into their union T-shirts and collected placards bearing ILO slogans. Phiri was keen to portray the union as successful and proactive and had organised for the event to be filmed and photographed for publicity purposes. Unfortunately, as officials had not secured the permit required to hold a march on a public street, members were unable to march down busy Cairo Road as they had planned, and instead decided to march in the back streets hidden from public view.[64] UHDWUZ officials' ambitions and outward-looking self-presentation contrasted markedly with the realities of the situation, as a small number of union members sang to themselves along empty back streets rather than to a public audience.[65]

Both U-FFTUZ and UHDWUZ have had fairly limited contact with the Zambian government. The unions' role in the development of protective legislation for domestic workers during the 2010s was limited because of their lack of organisational capacity and public presence. Although both unions were invited to meetings with government officials and other key stakeholders during the development of the legislation, the unions played only a minor role in proceedings. They were invited to be the 'voice' of domestic workers (a role that we may question considering the discussions above) but had little influence over the content or timing of the legislation. The most sustained form of contact between either union and the state has been through the judicial system. The unions settled most disputes with employers through informal negotiation, but they also pursued a small number of cases through the IRC, as discussed in Chapter 4.[66]

Given the provisions of the new legislation and increased state intervention in the domestic service sector, both UHDWUZ and U-FFTUZ will need, in the coming years, to address the challenge of how to remain relevant, both to their members and as workers' organisations. It is possible that the role of formal organisations for domestic workers will be considered increasingly unimportant by both the state and domestic workers themselves. As Ally has illustrated in the South African context, the extension of full democratic and legal rights to domestic workers can have negative consequences for workers' organisations. In 1996, the South African government finally recognised SADWU's status as a trade union after years of repression by the apartheid government and introduced extensive protective legislation for domestic workers. Yet, in this context of increased domestic workers' rights, SADWU unravelled. Ally argues that the post-apartheid state directly and indirectly usurped the role of SADWU and cast itself as the representative voice of domestic workers' interests.[67] The decline of SADWU was likely exacerbated by domestic workers' perception that there was less need for a union after the legislative changes. The apparent relationship between increased state intervention and a decline in union support has clear implications for the Zambian context, not least because both UHDWUZ and U-FFTUZ were in a far weaker position in 2011 and since than SADWU had been in 1996.

U-FFTUZ and UHDWUZ will each need to develop strategies not only to maintain their relevance but, ideally, to increase their influence. They could do this in several ways. First, they could step up their efforts to monitor the implementation of the legislation for domestic workers and to call out those who violate the law. As discussed in Chapter 4, during interviews many domestic workers criticised the lack of any mechanism to monitor or enforce the new legislation. While the Zambian government relies on employers and domestic workers to comply with the law and to report any infractions to the local labour office, many of my interviewees stated that they would not pursue a dispute through official channels because they feared that labour officers would accept bribes from employers and give out confidential information in exchange for payments. The unions could play the vital role of monitoring the reporting of incidents to local labour offices and following up on complaints.

More broadly, both unions could extend their monitoring of the implementation of the legislation to help domestic workers access their legal rights.

The unions could also push for improvements to the current legislation, using their links with international organisations such as the ILO to pressure the government to extend existing provisions. This is especially clear in relation to gender and parental rights. While the 2018 protective legislation for domestic workers provided greater protections to new mothers than had previous laws, and extended some protections to new fathers, there is still work to be done. Specifically, men on paternity leave would likely struggle to work unpaid, and many women would still probably have difficulty making ends meet on half pay. The 2018 legislation also does nothing to improve the monitoring of these laws.[68] The unions could campaign for improvements in parental rights and for better monitoring of their implementation. This could have specifically important impacts on women for whom the birth of a child may no longer mean a substantial loss of income, or a rushed and emotionally and physically harmful return to work. The unions' failure to develop more active and forceful campaigning on such issues likely resulted from their limited capacity and political capital. But it also demonstrates how gendered blind spots have persisted in domestic workers trade unionism since independence, despite the increased involvement of women in the labour movement and the female dominance of many domestic worker trade unions.

Finally, U-FFTUZ and UHDWUZ have scope to actively engage with the political agenda concerning children's rights and child labour. To date, both unions have focused overwhelmingly on representing adult workers, even though children have been employed in waged and kin-based domestic service in significant numbers throughout both unions' existence. Because the employment of children under the age of fifteen in domestic service became illegal under the 2011 legislation, the legislative gains for domestic workers are effectively irrelevant to the large number of child domestic workers. The unions could listen to and amplify the voices of child domestic workers and encourage their participation in worker organising and advocacy. More broadly, they could highlight to policymakers and employers that children perform essential work within and beyond the home and are deserving of rights and respect under labour laws.

UHDWUZ's and U-FFTUZ's lack of action on children's issues is not unusual and represents a broader trend within labour movements in Africa and elsewhere of failing to organise or effectively advocate for working children. Historically, child workers have at worst been seen by labour movements as a threat to adult workers and at best as victims to be spoken for and protected by adults. There are, however, some examples of trade unions engaging meaningfully with child domestic workers, and these could be used as a model by domestic worker trade unions such as UHDWUZ and U-FFTUZ. During the 1990s, the Kenya Union of Domestic, Hotels, Educational Institutions, Hospitals and Allied Workers (KUDHEIHA) and Tanzania's Conservation, Hotels, Domestic and Allied Workers Union (CHODAWU) began working with child domestic workers as part of campaigning against children's exploitation. CHODAWU also supported child domestic workers to leave abusive employment situations and enrol in school, and provided vocational training for older children.[69] KUDHEIHA and CHODAWU have also worked with the ILO's International Programme on the Elimination of Child Labour (IPEC) to develop a handbook and training module on the prevention of child labour in homes, aimed at those who employ children.[70]

As these collaborations with the ILO and IPEC suggest, domestic worker trade unions' engagement with child workers has often developed out of collaborations with IGOs and NGOs engaged in children's rights promotion. Such organisations have developed a range of programmes to organise and educate child domestic workers. During the 2000s, WAO-Afrique began establishing Advisory Committees of child domestic workers in Togo to advise NGOs and policymakers on children's employment in domestic service.[71] In Tanzania, Kivulini Women's Rights Organization established similar Advisory Committees.[72] One of these, WoteSawa (meaning 'all equal' in Swahili), became an NGO in its own right and, at the time of writing, continues to organise child domestic workers in Tanzania. WoteSawa focuses on the legal and economic empowerment of child domestic workers, provides psychological and social support, monitors abusive employment practices, and advocates for policy reform.[73] There have been similar successful efforts by NGOs to organise child domestic workers elsewhere in Africa and beyond, including in Brazil, Bangladesh, India, and Senegal.[74]

## The potential of informal worker organising

A more enduring challenge facing trade unions is that most domestic workers are either unaware of their existence or have found ways to act outside of formal labour-movement channels. In Hansen's research with domestic workers in Lusaka in the 1980s, for instance, none of her interviewees knew that formal organisations like NDHAZ had existed.[75] In my own research in Lusaka in 2013 and 2014, most of my interviewees were unaware that unions for domestic workers existed in Zambia, and only a handful had heard of either UHDWUZ or U-FFTUZ. The only union members that I met were men and women with whom I made contact through a union official. Other studies have similarly reported low levels of awareness about trade unions amongst southern Africa's domestic workers. Domestic workers' lack of knowledge of such organisations probably resulted from the highly sporadic nature of such organisations and their limited financial and organisational capacity, as noted above. But it also reflects the highly personalised nature of domestic service and the capacity for domestic workers to pursue alternative solutions to workplace challenges. Associations and organised social activities have provided spaces for the development of informal relations of labour solidarity amongst domestic workers, for instance through domestic workers' membership of ballroom dancing clubs in the colonial context; similar processes also occurred outside of formally organised activities and associations, as I now explore using oral histories.

In Lusaka and urban centres across the region, domestic workers developed an awareness of each other's personal problems and workplace grievances in the neighbourhoods in which they worked, as they socialised with each other during breaks, when hanging out the washing or gardening, and as they commuted. Previous scholarship on domestic service in Africa has acknowledged the importance of such neighbourhood interactions. Preston-Whyte's study of domestic service in apartheid South Africa, for instance, examined the significance of informal gatherings and visits as sources of companionship to Black women domestic workers in the White suburbs. Her study outlined how domestic workers forged and sustained relationships despite the seemingly atomised nature of their work. Preston-Whyte did not, however, examine the ways in which such neighbourhood interactions also fostered labour solidarity. She acknowledges that such relationships were sources of 'mutual aid' but portrays the information that domestic workers exchanged regarding working conditions, wage rates, and employers as gossip.[76] Although such communication was exchanged as part of broader conversations about what was going on in the neighbourhood, it also contained valuable information about labour relations and conditions. With this information, women could compare their rates of pay and conditions with others and know who was a good employer and who should be avoided. Through such conversations, women probably also exchanged information about vacancies and how to manage their relationships with employers, vital sources of information for workers vulnerable to exploitation.

Neighbourhood interactions between domestic workers in Lusaka certainly fostered the development of labour solidarity. Oral testimonies provide important insights into how domestic workers engaged in and perceived such interactions. During an interview in 2014, Clarence Chiteta described how she had recently turned to other domestic workers for help with managing an abusive employer. Clarence had been working as a live-out maid for a Swiss woman in Kabulonga. She had been deeply unhappy in this job because her employer regularly shouted at her and accused her of stealing household items. She stated that one of the only advantages to the job was that she had built good relationships with other women and men who worked as maids and gardeners on the same housing development. These workers would sit together in a secluded part of the development at quiet points in the working day to share food and chat. Clarence would join them when she could and regularly sought advice on how to manage her employer's temper. Several of the workers encouraged her to take radical action, by leaving the position without giving any notice in order to 'pay back' her employer for her mistreatment.[77] Studies of domestic service in Africa have drawn attention to the use of this strategy as a last resort by domestic workers who faced difficult working conditions, but they tend to frame such actions as individual acts of resistance.[78] As Clarence's experience suggests, such seemingly individual strategies of resistance could involve both a collective element and solidarity across gender lines.

The relationships that developed between domestic workers in the neighbourhoods in which they worked could also be sources of emotional support. Clarence, for instance, felt that the relationships that she had developed with other domestic workers had given her the confidence and the support that she had needed to leave her job and find something else. This was no small thing. As a single mother and sole provider for her household, it had serious financial and practical implications. Clarence described how women who worked on the development had told her about vacancies in the area. By the time we met, she had followed up on these leads and found a new position.[79] Here, parallels might be drawn with the ways in which kinship networks functioned as sources of support and information for rural-urban migrants in the region. Bozzoli's observations about the functions of 'homegirl' and 'homeboy' networks amongst domestic workers in Johannesburg are also relevant.[80] Although there are clear differences between these examples, each suggests how domestic workers turned to each other for help with finding employment and escaping exploitative situations.

Neighbourhood interactions between domestic workers also fostered the development of collective strategies to overcome economic hardship. Limited access to food was a consistent theme in interviews with domestic workers, a challenge which resulted from a combination of low wages and inadequate in-kind payments. Several interviewees explained how they had helped each other to overcome this challenge. Cecilia Phiri described how she had shared her food provisions with a gardener while working as a maid in the 1980s. At the time, she was a live-in maid in Woodlands and was paid through a combination of meals, accommodation, and a small cash wage. The gardener, who was employed at the same property, commuted to work and was not given meals. Phiri shared her provisions with him and, when she could, she also gave him the leftovers from their employers' meals.[81] Augustine Mulanda, Andrew Banda, and Teophilous Mufonko, all guards in the suburb of Kabulonga, also described how they helped each other to secure adequate supplies of food. Although the group were meant to receive monthly rations of maize flour and vegetables from the management of the housing development on which they worked, such provisions were often not issued or were inadequate to last for the whole month. The group shared what food they had and received supplies from several women who worked as maids on the development.[82] Although unequal access to food and resources within the workplace likely also bred resentment and competition between domestic workers, these examples show how at least some domestic workers responded to such inequalities by forging solidarities and developing informal collective responses.[83]

Informal collective organising amongst domestic workers also had a political element. While observing conversations between domestic workers during their breaks from work, I became aware of the extent to which men and women took the opportunity to debate and discuss politics and socio-economic inequality. Interviewees were highly aware of the grievances they shared with other poor urban residents, and many criticised the unequal structures of gender, class, and status that shaped both their working conditions and the broader urban social structure.

This book's discussion of informal organising amongst domestic workers has focused on the activities of adults, not because child domestic workers did not engage in such activities, but because this topic did not arise in oral history interviews. There is clear evidence from other contexts of child domestic workers developing solidarities with other workers and engaging in informal collective action. Bourdillon describes how, in Senegal, older child domestic workers have negotiated with the employers of younger children to try and improve their conditions.[84] It is likely that child domestic workers in Zambia and elsewhere also developed informal relations of labour solidarity amongst themselves and with adult workers. This may have occurred through everyday neighbourhood interactions or while participating in organised social activities, NGOs working on child welfare and development in Kenya and Uganda organised drama, dance, music, and sport activities to enable child domestic workers to meet and socialise with other children.[85] Solidarities between child domestic workers also developed through their participation in NGO activities in other ways. For example, child domestic workers joined the Advisory Committees of WAO-Afrique and Kivulini and acted as links between the committees and their peers, talking with fellow child workers and feeding back these children's ideas and concerns. Anti-Slavery International, which worked with WAO-Afrique and Kivulini to establish the committees, noted how the children involved displayed a strong sense of solidarity not only with each other but with all child domestic workers.[86] Examples such as these highlight the links between informal and formal organising, and the potential for each to inform and strengthen the other. This applies not only to organising of child domestic workers but to domestic workers of all ages.

## Conclusion

This chapter has examined the history of collective organising and solidarity amongst domestic workers in Lusaka and beyond. Domestic workers in southern Africa have engaged in forms of collective organising since at least the 1890s. In Zambia specifically, there is evidence of domestic workers engaging with the labour movement from the 1930s and of domestic workers attempting to establish their own organisations from the early 1950s. During the 1960s and 1970s, trade unions for domestic workers were established in Zambia, though each of these organisations was short-lived and achieved only limited success. Zambia's domestic workers had more success with formal organising from the 1990s, with the establishment of a workers' association and, later, a trade union that continues to operate in Lusaka at the time of writing.

The chapter has shown that, despite the efforts of workers and activists, formal workers' organisations have failed to deliver lasting, meaningful gains for Zambia's domestic workers. Each of the organisations discussed in this chapter struggled to establish a significant base of support, with membership rates that only ever represented a fraction of the many thousands of adults and children who were engaged in domestic service at a given time. Trade unions and associations for domestic workers have also played only a limited role in improving domestic workers' rights at an official level. This was the result of both their limited financial and organisational capacity and the consistent marginalisation of domestic service as an area of concern by colonial and post-colonial governments. It also reflects a more fundamental problem: the failure of workers' organisations to tailor their interventions to suit the diversity of labour relations and workers in domestic service, specifically in relation to kin-based labour practices and the employment of children. By incorporating gender and age into the analysis of worker organising, this chapter has highlighted longstanding and enduring blind spots in trade unionism when it came to understandings of work and of workers.

Domestic workers were more likely to pursue informal strategies of resistance, both individual and collective, than to join a formal organisation. As has been discussed, this was the result of a lack of awareness that such formal organisations existed and reflected the ability of domestic workers to act outside of formal channels. In Lusaka and beyond, domestic workers developed an awareness of each other's personal problems and workplace grievances through participation in urban associational life and while socialising with each other in the neighbourhoods in which they worked. Through such channels, domestic workers developed ways to support each other, developing informal collective solutions to exploitative working conditions, abusive employers, and economic hardship. These informal relations of solidarity were significant to those involved and provided sources of much-needed material and emotional support.

Collective organising amongst domestic workers forms part of a broader phenomenon of collective organisation by urban workers in Africa's informal economies. Such initiatives have proliferated and diversified since the 1980s as workers responded to neoliberal policies, limited formal employment, and the increased casualisation and precariousness of work.[87] Existing studies have shown how a wide range of workers, including street vendors, market traders, small-scale manufacturers, textile workers, and dock workers, amongst many others, have organised themselves through a range of pre-existing and newly established mechanisms, such as market associations, credit associations, cooperatives, and various societies.[88] Though hampered by a wide range of structural and practical limitations, such organisations have created opportunities for informal sector workers to voice grievances, express interests and, in some cases, foster political influence. This chapter builds on such studies by demonstrating the significance and potential, as well as the challenges, of collective organising amongst domestic workers. It has shown how, even in the face of structural constraints and personal challenges, domestic workers have come together, both within and outside of the formal labour movement, to help each other, express grievances, and challenge their exploitation.

## Notes

1 This song was performed by UHDWUZ at a march in Lusaka on 16 June 2014. Observations by the author, Lusaka, 16 June 2014.
2 ILO, C189 – Domestic Workers Convention, 2011 (No. 189).
3 These lyrics were adapted from a South African hymn and have been used at events by organised domestic workers and other workers' organisations in the southern African region. For example, Castel-Branco observed domestic workers singing a similar song in Maputo in 2012. See Castel-Branco, 'Legislating Worker Justice', p. 68.
4 Pariser, 'Masculinity and Organized Resistance in Domestic Service in Colonial Dar es Salaam'; Ally, *From Servants to Workers*. See also Bujra, *Serving Class*, pp. 67–72, pp. 156–171, p. 175; Castel-Branco, 'Legislating Worker Justice'; Hansen, *Distant Companions*, pp. 166–170, p. 255, pp. 286–287; Sharon B. Stichter, 'Trade Unionism in Kenya, 1947–52: The Militant Phase', in Peter Gutkind, Robin Cohen, and Jean Copans (eds), *African Labour History* (London: Sage, 1975), pp. 155–174.
5 See, for example, Peter Delius, 'Sebatakgomo; Migrant Organisation, the ANC and the Sekhukhuneland Revolt', *Journal of Southern African Studies*, 15:4 (1989), 588–599; Deborah James, *Songs of the Women Migrants: Performance and Identity in South Africa* (Edinburgh: Edinburgh University Press, 1999), pp. 50–52, pp. 58–61; Lee, *African Women and Apartheid*, pp. 128–154; Laura Phillips and Deborah James, 'Labour, Lodging and Linkages: Migrant Women's Experience in South Africa', *African Studies*, 73:3 (2014), 420–424.
6 Van Onselen, *Studies in the Economic and Social History of the Witwatersrand*, p. 55.
7 *Ibid.*, p. 59.
8 Ally, *From Servants to Workers*, pp. 149–150.
9 Baruch Hirson, *Yours for the Union: Class and Community Struggles in South Africa, 1930–1947* (London: Zed Books, 1990), p. 61.
10 Hansen, *Distant Companions*, p. 158.
11 *Ibid.*, pp. 159–161.
12 *Ibid.*, pp. 166–169.
13 Pariser, 'Masculinity and Organized Resistance in Domestic Service in Colonial Dar es Salaam', 109.

14 Ally, *From Servants to Workers*, p. 150.
15 NAZ, MLSS1/23 86, Department of Labour Annual Report 1960; NAZ, MLSS1/23 92, Department of Labour Annual Report 1961; NAZ, MLSS1/26 73, National Union of Hotel, Catering and Domestic Workers 1952–1965, return for the year 1962.
16 NAZ, MLSS1/26 73, National Union of Hotel, Catering and Domestic Workers 1952–1965, 'Free Medical Aid Sought by Union', *Northern News*, 14 November 1963.
17 NAZ, MLSS1/26 73, National Union of Hotel, Catering and Domestic Workers 1952–1965, 'Wages Move But Mass Sackings Feared', *Northern News*, 18 August 1964.
18 Van Onselen, *Studies in the Economic and Social History of the Witwatersrand*, p. 59.
19 Pariser, 'Masculinity and Organized Resistance in Domestic Service in Colonial Dar es Salaam', 110.
20 See Hansen, *Distant Companions*, pp. 170–176.
21 Deborah Gaitskell, '"Upward All and Play the Game": The Girl Wayfarers' Association in the Transvaal 1925–1975', in Peter Kallaway (ed.), *Apartheid and Education: The Education of Black South Africans* (Johannesburg: Ravan, 1984), p. 128.
22 Delius, 'Sebatakgomo', 589–592.
23 Eleanor Mary Preston-Whyte, 'Between Two Worlds: A Study of the Working Life, Social Ties and Inter-Personal Relationships of African Women Migrants in Domestic Service in Durban', Vol. 2 (Durban: Institute for Social Research, University of Natal, 1969), pp. 307–311; Bozzoli, *Women of Phokeng*, pp. 100–101.
24 Hansen, *Distant Companions*, pp. 161–166.
25 *Ibid.*, p. 162.
26 James, *Songs of the Women Migrants*, pp. 56–57.
27 NAZ, MLSS1/15 126, Labour Officer Monthly Reports – Lusaka, 1963–1965, Department of Labour Monthly Report – Labour Officer, District: Lusaka, May 1965.
28 On the history of liberation movements in exile in Lusaka, see Stephen Ellis, *External Mission: The ANC in Exile, 1960–1990* (London: Hurst, 2012); and Hugh MacMillan, *The Lusaka Years: The ANC in Exile in Zambia, 1963 to 1994* (Auckland Park: Jacana Media, 2013).
29 Larmer, *Mineworkers in Zambia*, p. 63.
30 Bujra, *Serving Class*, pp. 164–165.
31 Larmer, *Mineworkers in Zambia*, pp. 83–85.
32 Larmer, *Rethinking African Politics*, pp. 78–80.
33 Larmer, *Mineworkers in Zambia*, pp. 110–114.
34 Hansen, *Distant Companions*, pp. 286–287.

35 Larmer, *Mineworkers in Zambia*, pp. 5–6.
36 *Ibid.*, p. 55.
37 Pape, 'Still Serving the Tea', 391–393.
38 Ally, *From Servants to Workers*, pp. 150–152.
39 Walvis Bay and the Penguin Islands remained under South African control until 1994.
40 Østreng, *Domestic Workers' Daily Lives in Post-Apartheid Namibia*, p. 76.
41 Magano Nagombe, 'The Namibia Domestic and Allied Workers Union', in Margaret Hosmer Martens and Swasti Mitter (eds), *Women in Trade Unions: Organizing the Unorganized* (Geneva: International Labour Office, 1994), pp. 45–46; Kathleen Sheldon, *Historical Dictionary of Women in Sub-Saharan Africa* (Oxford: Scarecrow Press, 2005), p. 201.
42 Friday E. Mulenga, 'Fighting for Democracy of the Pocket: The Labour Movement in the Third Republic', in Jan-Bart Gewald, Marja Hinfelaar, and Giacomo Macola (eds), *One Zambia, Many Histories: Towards a History of Post-Colonial Zambia* (Leiden: Brill, 2008), pp. 247–249.
43 Castel-Branco, 'Legislating Worker Justice', p. 34.
44 Interview with Joyce Phiri, Lusaka, 11 July 2013.
45 Papers of the United House and Domestic Workers Union of Zambia (UHDWUZ Papers), letter from P. Simfukwe, Principal Labour Officer of Lusaka, to the Ministry of Labour and Social Security, 25 February 2002.
46 Castel-Branco, 'Legislating Worker Justice', p. 33, p. 35.
47 See, for instance, Iris Berger, 'Sources of Class Consciousness: South African Women in Recent Labor Struggles', in Claire C. Robertson and Iris Berger (eds), *Women and Class in Africa* (New York, NY: Africana Publishing Co., 1986), pp. 216–236; Susan Geiger, *Tanu Women: Gender and Culture in the Making of Tanganyikan Nationalism, 1955–1965* (Portsmouth, NH: Heinemann, 1997); Aili Mari Tripp, 'Deindustrialisation and the Growth of Women's Economic Associations and Networks in Urban Tanzania', in Sheila Rowbotham and Swasti Mitter (eds), *Dignity and Daily Bread* (London: Routledge, 1994), pp. 139–157.
48 UHDWUZ Papers, Constitution of the United House and Domestic Workers Union of Zambia (November 2000).
49 Interview with Joyce Phiri.
50 UHDWUZ Papers, Constitution.
51 Interview with Joyce Phiri.
52 Nagombe, 'The Namibia Domestic and Allied Workers Union', p. 47.
53 Mulenga, 'Fighting for Democracy of the Pocket', p. 248.
54 Interview with Kevin Liywalii.
55 Mulenga, 'Fighting for Democracy of the Pocket', p. 252.

56 Interview with Kevin Liywalii.
57 Interview with Martha Kasaro.
58 I interviewed six members of UHDWUZ and one member of U-FFTUZ. Contact was made through officials from each organisation and interviews were conducted at their respective offices in Lusaka city centre. Interviews with Irene Kamau, Alice Phiri, Theresa Chanda, Riberia Chambanenge, Rose Chanda, and Harriet Mukololo (all members of UHDWUZ), Lusaka, 16 June 2014; interview with Fisher Chowa (member of U-FFTUZ), Lusaka, 29 August 2014.
59 ILO, *Magnitude of Domestic Workers in Zambia*, p. 2.
60 Interview with Joyce Phiri.
61 Interview with Kevin Liywalii.
62 Nagombe, 'The Namibia Domestic and Allied Workers Union', p. 47.
63 Interview with Joyce Phiri.
64 Observations by the author, Lusaka, 16 June 2014.
65 The outward-looking approach of both UHDWUZ and U-FFTUZ can be understood as an example of 'extraversion' as defined and discussed by Jean-Francois Bayart. See Jean-François Bayart, *The State in Africa: The Politics of the Belly* (London: Longman, 1993), pp. 20–32, pp. 196–200.
66 Interview with Oscar Cheupe; interview with Hon. Mr Justice Edward Luputa Musona.
67 Ally, *From Servants to Workers*, p. 147, pp. 153–160.
68 Republic of Zambia, Statutory Instrument No. 69 of 2018.
69 Anti-Slavery International, *Child Domestic Workers: A Handbook on Good Practice in Programme Interventions* (Horsham: The Printed Word, 2005), p. 71.
70 UNICEF, *Innocenti Digest. No. 5: Child Domestic Work* (Florence: UN, UNICEF, 1999), p. 10.
71 WAO-Afrique's name reflects its history as a branch of the World Association of Orphans (WAO). It became an autonomous organisation in 1985. Further information about WAO-Afrique is available at www.waoafrique.tg/ (accessed 21 November 2021).
72 Anti-Slavery International, *Listen to Us!*, p. 12.
73 Further information about WoteSawa is available at www.wotesawa.or.tz/index.php (accessed 8 April 2021).
74 Bourdillon, 'Children as Domestic Employees', 13–14. For further discussion, see Maggie Black, *Child Domestic Workers: Finding a Voice. A Handbook on Advocacy* (London: Anti-Slavery International, 2002); Leslie Groves, *Good Practice in Working Children's Participation: A Case Study from Brazil* (London: International Save the Children Alliance, 2003).

75 Hansen, *Distant Companions*, pp. 286–287.
76 See Preston-Whyte, 'Between Two Worlds', pp. 307–311.
77 Interview with Clarence Chiteta, Lusaka, 5 June 2014.
78 On individual strategies of resistance, see Cock, *Maids and Madams*, p. 37, p. 103, pp. 105–106; James, *Songs of the Women Migrants*, pp. 56–57; Ginsburg, *At Home With Apartheid*, pp. 61–62, pp. 108–109, pp. 157–163.
79 Interview with Clarence Chiteta.
80 Bozzoli, *Women of Phokeng*, pp. 97–98, p. 123, p. 132, pp. 157–158.
81 Interview with Cecilia Phiri, Lusaka, 4 February 2014.
82 Interview with Andrew Banda; interview with Teophilous Mufonko; interview with Augustine Mulanda, Lusaka, 12 August 2014.
83 Resentment and unequal access to food and resources between domestic workers in Lusaka is a key theme in M. Haimbe, 'Madam's Sister', *Granta*, 4 June 2019, available at https://granta.com/madams-sister/ (accessed 10 June 2021).
84 Bourdillon, 'Children as Domestic Employees', 14.
85 Anti-Slavery International, *Child Domestic Workers*, pp. 45–46.
86 Anti-Slavery International, *Listen to Us!*, p. 4.
87 Ilda Lindell, 'Introduction: The Changing Politics of Informality – Collective Organizing, Alliances and Scales of Engagement', in Ilda Lindell (ed.), *Africa's Informal Workers: Collective Agency, Alliances and Transnational Organizing in Urban Africa* (London: Zed Books, 2010), pp. 2–3. For further discussion, see Arne Tostensen, Inge Tvedten, and Mariken Vaa (eds), *Associational Life in African Cities: Popular Responses to the Urban Crisis* (Uppsala: Nordic Africa Institute, 2001); and Aili Mari Tripp, 'Non-Formal Institutions, Informal Economies, and the Politics of Inclusion', Discussion Paper no. 2001/108, UNU-WIDER (Helsinki: UNU-WIDER, 2001).
88 For an excellent selection of such studies, see contributions to Lindell, *Africa's Informal Workers*.

# Conclusion

> I help Elina in the house; washing the curtains, washing the walls and dabbing paint over the worst bits ... Never has it smelt so clean, of soap and fresh air; never have the floors and windows sparkled quite like this ... I walk the five miles home, trying to ignore the pebbles slipping into my shoe through a hole in my sole. I'll have to get a new second-hand pair after payday.[1]

So narrates Cephas, the protagonist of Mbozi Haimbe's prize-winning short story, 'Madam's Sister'. Published just a few years after I completed interviews for this book, the story puts domestic service in the spotlight and, in so doing, illuminates what remains one of the most ubiquitous yet overlooked forms of work in urban southern Africa. Set in contemporary Lusaka, the story follows Cephas as he goes about his work as a gardener for a middle-class Black Zambian household and tries to provide for his wife and children. Cephas's narration of his experiences at work, of his daily commute, and of his life in the fictional compound in which he lives perfectly captures the realities of work and life for domestic workers in Lusaka and vividly reminded me of the testimonies of so many of my interviewees. 'Madam's Sister' is a story of inequality and poverty, of the exploitation and undervaluing of domestic workers' labour and the efforts of poor urban residents to care for their loved ones. It is also a story of domesticity and aspiration, and of the ways in which southern Africa's urban residents are entangled in and marginalised from local and global patterns of consumption, mobility, and opportunity.

Like 'Madam's Sister', my intention in this book has been to place domestic service at the centre of the story. Specifically, I wanted to show the significance of domestic service and of domestic workers to individual and household survival strategies and to broader economies in southern Africa. I have also presented a new theoretical approach to domestic service that, with productive and critical engagement, can reshape historical understandings of and contemporary policymaking on domestic labour practices in Africa and beyond. In this concluding chapter, I summarise my key findings, illustrate their broader significance, and point towards future avenues for research.

The innovative theoretical approach that I developed and utilised throughout *Home economics* provides a historically informed and culturally sensitive framework for interpreting domestic service in southern Africa's past and present. Unlike the narrow approaches towards domestic service utilised in much extant scholarship and policymaking, the book's inclusive approach allows for analysis of waged and kin-based labour, forced and free employment, performed by adult and child workers. It considers domestic service to include all forms of domestic labour performed in a household or for a household in exchange for payments in cash or kind. This approach brings the diverse range of labour relations and workers involved in domestic service in southern Africa's cities into a single frame of analysis for the first time. Oral history interviews with domestic workers, employers, trade unionists, and urban residents provided insights into the variety of labour relations and workers in domestic service and the ways in which urban residents across the socio-economic spectrum managed domestic labour in their homes. Crucially, these testimonies demonstrated the importance of kin-based domestic labour and female and child workers, all of which are largely excluded from existing documentary sources and scholarly writing on domestic service in Zambia and, to a larger extent, the broader region.[2] A household survey and informal observations reinforced these findings, whilst archival work provided additional insights into longer-term and broader trends in labour relations, work, and the economy, and the approaches of policymakers at the national and international levels.

*Home economics* shows that novel domestic service practices emerged in southern Africa's urban centres following independence and the end of apartheid, as workers and employers responded to a range of social pressures and economic crises and sought ways to make ends meet and maintain their households. An increasing number of households needed help to perform the necessary tasks of maintaining the home and its members. This growing need resulted in large part from increasing demand amongst Black urban householders, and especially from Black working women who had to balance working beyond the home with the demands and expectations of marriage, motherhood, and domesticity, as shown in Chapter 2. To meet their domestic labour needs, Black urban householders utilised and reworked existing models of domestic service that were grounded in colonial labour relations and the gendered and gerontocratic hierarchies of kinship. The racialised and gendered colonial models of domestic service that were adopted in colonial households across southern Africa emphasised wage labour by male workers. These models remained prevalent in Lusaka and other southern African towns and cities following independence, and the gendered constructions of labour and class they promoted continued to shape domestic service practices and employer preferences for decades to come. Waged domestic service was gradually undermined, however, by Black employers' increased reliance on kinship-based labour relations. This built on longstanding practices of kin-based domestic service in Black urban households that had persisted throughout the colonial period and primarily involved women and children's labour. Kin-based domestic service practices were also reconfigured in the post-colonial period, as employers responded to economic decline and used their kinship networks as sources of cheap labour. Overall, *Home economics* shows how labour relations in Black households were shaped by a diverse set of historical and contemporary ideals and pressures, from colonial gendered constructions of the ideal worker to the gendered and generational hierarchies of kinship and marriage, and the immediacy of economic hardship. Through all of these configurations, domestic labour continued to underpin daily and generational reproduction and capital accumulation.

Female labour became increasingly central to domestic service practices in Lusaka in the decades following independence. A slow and steady process of feminisation occurred, and male domestic workers found their dominant position in the sector gradually eroded as women and girls engaged in waged and kin-based domestic service in increasing numbers. As shown in Chapter 1, this process of feminisation needs to be understood in relation to broader regional dynamics. Domestic service was gradually but unmistakably feminised across southern Africa during the twentieth century, a process that occurred differently in different places according to a number of factors. Historically, these factors included demand for male labour in other key sectors such as mining and farming, the presence of White settlers, the workings of racialised constructions of sexuality and labour, and the supply of female labour. In Lusaka specifically, the gradual feminisation of domestic service resulted from a combination of a growing supply of and increased demand for women and girls' labour. Domestic service was a vital source of paid work for Lusaka's women and children, who generally faced gendered, age-based, educational, and economic barriers to accessing most other forms of employment. Women and children could draw on skills developed in their own homes and use their kinship and friendship networks to find work, as we saw in Chapters 2 and 3. Demand for female labour rose alongside broader increases in female labour force participation because many working women sought out and depended upon other women and girls to perform domestic and care labour in their stead, as shown in Chapter 2. Combined, these processes eroded the male dominance of domestic service in Lusaka that had been established during the colonial period and resulted in the female dominance of the sector by the 2010s.

The feminisation of domestic service in Lusaka and other southern African urban centres involved the reorganisation of labour along gendered lines. Women and girls experienced an expansion in opportunities for employment in domestic service and came to dominate indoor roles that involved cleaning, cooking, and childcare. Conversely, male domestic workers experienced a gradual narrowing over time of opportunities in domestic service and became concentrated in outdoor roles as gardeners and guards. These processes had contradictory impacts on the children, women, and men employed in the sector. Overall, male workers generally lost more than they gained, with reduced opportunities for employment and fewer occasions to develop strong and positive relationships with an employer and to access resources. These findings provide useful insights for thinking about the broader gender and age dynamics of work in southern Africa and the ways in which male and female adults and children have been differentially incorporated into household, formal, and informal economies.

Extant approaches to regulating employment and labour relations do not account for the complex realities of domestic service in urban southern Africa. Since the 1990s, there has been a growing effort at the international and national levels to formalise domestic service and to introduce or extend protective state legislation for domestic workers. These efforts culminated in the ILO's adoption of Convention 189 and Recommendation 201 in 2011, which outlined international labour standards for domestic workers and stimulated legislative change amongst ILO member states, including in southern Africa. As Chapter 4 showed, these processes of formalisation and legislative intervention brought about meaningful gains for many domestic workers, including improvements in wages and working conditions, but they also had negative and negligible impacts. Many domestic workers did not experience improvements in their pay and conditions due to inadequate mechanisms to monitor and enforce the law, an unwillingness amongst employers to comply with the law, and domestic workers' limited trust in state officials and fears that challenging their employers would result in dismissal. More than this, the way that domestic service has been conceptualised in national laws in southern Africa has excluded a wide range of domestic workers and common domestic service practices. This is especially clear in relation to child workers and kin-based labour, both of which are marginalised under current legal systems in the region which focus on adult workers and steady, formal employment. These limitations both mirror and result from the narrow conceptualisation of domestic service in current international labour standards.

Domestic workers' organisations and trade unions that have operated in southern Africa have also largely failed to tailor their approach to reflect the diversity of workers and employment practices in the sector, as shown in Chapter 5. These organisations have focused on adults engaged in wage labour, with inadequate efforts to organise those in kin-based employment or to reach out to and organise working children. The efficacy of these organisations has also been impacted by their limited financial and organisational capacity and by the dismissive attitudes of successive colonial and post-independence governments towards domestic service. The impetus for domestic workers to pursue formal organising methods despite these challenges and limitations needs to be understood in relation to the broader history of labour movements in the region. In Zambia specifically, the labour movement enjoyed significant support amongst large numbers of the workforce from the late colonial period onwards. After independence, governments in Zambia and elsewhere on the continent did much to dismantle the power of organised labour, especially during the 1990s, but labour solidarity continued to exert a significant influence on the ways in which many Africans conceptualised the relationship between employers and workers, and workers and the state.[3] But it is evident that trade unions and other workers' organisations have generally not succeeded in securing widespread support amongst domestic workers in southern Africa. An important exception is South Africa, where domestic workers' organisations secured large memberships during the 1980s and 1990s, though membership of such organisations declined massively by the early 2000s.[4] Interviews with domestic workers show that they were much more likely to cultivate informal relations of solidarity with fellow workers than to be members of formal workers' organisations. As Chapter 5 showed, informal relations of solidarity could be the basis for developing collective and individual strategies for addressing exploitation in the workplace and personal hardship. These informal solidarities provided material and emotional support and appeared to be of great significance to those involved.

These findings make important contributions to the broader fields of African labour history and gender history. The approach and findings presented in this book challenge normative assumptions in much existing labour history that privilege formal employment beyond the home and adult male workers, and overlook domestic labour and women and child workers. As has been shown throughout this book, such assumptions limit our understanding of how female and male adults and children have responded to economic opportunities and challenges, how the nature of work has changed and persisted over time, and, ultimately, how household, formal, and informal economies have functioned. Here, I want to elaborate on several key issues.

In Lusaka specifically, the post-independence years entailed an initial period of economic growth and an expansion of education and employment opportunities, followed by sharp economic decline and contraction from the late 1970s. As the economy went into decline, employment stagnated, and it became increasingly difficult to hold onto or find wage labour jobs. Structural adjustment during the 1980s and liberalisation during the 1990s exacerbated the decline of the formal sector and drove the growing casualisation and informalisation of work. As many men struggled to find employment to support themselves and their dependants, increasing numbers of women and children had to find ways to generate income and support their households, resulting in significant gendered and generational shifts in employment and resource flows. There were also important transformations in kin-based labour practices, as urban employers used kinship networks as sources of cheap labour and commodified the labour of junior kin. As in earlier periods, kinship networks still connected urban and rural areas and provided junior kin with a means to migrate to the city, but the relations of obligation and service that underpinned these networks shifted as urban and rural residents dealt with new and changing economic and social pressures. These developments in Lusaka reflected broader trends across the region's urban centres, with declining formal sector employment accompanied by increased casualisation, precarity, and female and child employment.

Selling domestic labour provided one of the only means for women and children to support themselves and their dependants in the face of pervasive gendered and generational barriers to accessing employment, declining opportunities for waged work, and increased casualisation. This was true for women and children who lived in the region's urban centres, and for rural residents who migrated to towns and cities in the hope of securing an income and a means to survive. Interviews with female domestic workers and employers provided important insights into the ways in which women and girls looked for and secured employment in domestic service, their working and living conditions, and their relationships with employers and fellow workers. We know too little about how southern Africa's women and children have responded to the challenges of economic decline, structural adjustment, and liberalisation, and the findings presented in this book provide important insights upon which future research must build.

There is also clear scope to expand understandings of the working lives of women and girls in southern Africa's post-colonial cities. This is especially true for girls, who remain marginal figures in extant labour and broader histories of the region. By exploring the working lives of girls in domestic service and demonstrating the importance of girls to household and broader economies across the region, *Home economics* challenges this historiographical omission. It also engages with the representation of African child workers as passive and exploited subjects, an approach that is common in children's rights discourses and development projects in the region. Such approaches rightly highlight and seek to challenge the exploitation and abuse that many African working children have experienced. At the same time, by focusing on passivity and victimhood, such approaches also obscure the complexity of children's working lives and their roles in southern Africa's economies. *Home economics* shows that girls' employment in domestic service could be a rational survival strategy and a means for girls to access mobility, resources, and the support of senior kin. Moreover, as we saw in Chapter 3, despite the gendered, generational, and economic inequalities they faced, some girls found ways to challenge abusive employers and shape their own life strategies. Policies that seek to exclude children from employment in domestic service or other sectors by virtue of wanting to protect them from exploitation need to reckon with the fact that many children will seek and be drawn into such work, regardless of legal restrictions and levels of protection. These realities provoke important ethical and practical questions for scholars and policymakers to address in the future.

In terms of women's history, although women's work beyond the home has been vital to household economies and survival strategies in post-colonial southern Africa, only a few studies have explored how women balanced employment with the necessary labours of social reproduction. Providing detailed insights into working women's lives in Lusaka and revealing broad trends across southern Africa's cities, *Home economics* demonstrates how working women constructed local care chains to help them to manage their domestic responsibilities. These care chains were shaped by and reinforced unequal gender divisions of labour and gendered and gerontocratic hierarchies within urban society and kinship networks, with most women dependent upon poorer women and girls from within the city and the countryside to provide the labour they needed. These findings have relevance for scholarship and policymaking around gender and women's empowerment. By exploring the ways in which women have attempted to balance the pressures of employment and motherhood in contexts of widespread gender inequalities, the book has shown that female employment can entrench gender divisions of labour and intensify class inequalities between women. This is intensely clear in relation to childcare, which remains predominantly a private issue to be negotiated within families and organised by the mother, despite the necessity of childcare for broader social and economic development.[5] Further historical research is needed into unequal gender distributions of household labour in post-colonial Africa and the impacts of this on women and girls, including on their ability to access education or employment. Such research could contribute to much-needed policy interventions that acknowledge the economic and social value of domestic labour and contribute towards reducing the burdens facing women and girls across Africa. Such policies could help to reduce gender inequalities, increase female educational and employment levels, and generate more inclusive development in the region.

Overall, the ways in which women and girls' economic and social roles have shifted in urban southern Africa since independence and the end of apartheid cannot be understood without consideration of domestic service, in its many forms. Nor can we understand the ways in which urban households have maintained themselves on a daily and generational basis without examining the performance and management of domestic labour.

*Home economics* also speaks to broader debates around the regulation and organisation of labour. The book's findings enrich our understanding of collective organising by urban workers in Africa's informal economies. They demonstrate how southern Africa's domestic workers have used alternatives to the formal labour movement model to address exploitation at work, economic hardship, and political grievances. Moreover, the book's analysis of the impacts of state-led formalisation of domestic service highlights the limits of existing approaches in the region and internationally. Chapter 4 showed how the current formalisation agenda risks creating a bifurcated labour market in which adults in waged and steady employment can gain access to rights and protection, while children and adults engaged in kin-based and irregular employment remain invisible to the state and excluded from protection. Without a more nuanced and inclusive approach to formalisation, and legislation that accounts for the realities of work and labour relations in the region, interventions aimed at improving domestic workers' rights and conditions will continue to be limited and ineffective. With efforts to formalise domestic service and other sectors currently being promoted across southern Africa and beyond, this is more than a Lusakan story: lessons can be learned by governments and international organisations working to improve the rights and working conditions of (domestic) workers across the world. Further research could deepen our understandings of the impacts of protective state legislation on working children and on kin-based employment practices within the home and beyond, and the ways in which workers' organisations have engaged with child workers and those in kin-based employment.

It is unlikely that domestic service will decline in importance as a source of labour and of employment in urban southern Africa. It is part of the fabric of social life, bound up with complex relations of service, obligation, dependency, and inequality that have connected and continue to connect households in urban and rural areas over successive generations. Domestic workers will continue to sell their labour to support themselves and their dependants and to further their aspirations, and employers will continue to depend on their labour. What remains to be seen is whether southern Africa's domestic workers will continue to be taken for granted and their labour exploited, or whether they will be able to take advantage of and expand their legal rights and secure both better working conditions and public recognition of their importance to social and economic life.

## Notes

1 Haimbe, 'Madam's Sister'.
2 South Africa is an exception, with numerous important studies of women domestic workers under apartheid and since the transition to democracy. These include Cock, *Maids and Madams*; Gaitskell *et al.*,

'Class, Race and Gender'; Ally, *From Servants to Workers*; Ginsburg, *At Home with Apartheid*.

3 For further discussion, see Mulenga, 'Fighting for Democracy of the Pocket'.

4 See Ally, *From Servants to Workers*, pp. 147–154.

5 Dimova *et al.*, 'Intimacy and Inequality', 173.

# Bibliography

## Interviews


Andrew Banda, Lusaka, 12 August 2014
Carol Banda, Lusaka, 1 March 2014
Custom Banda, Lusaka, 13 July 2013
Edwin Banda, Lusaka, 30 January 2014
Evelyn Banda, Lusaka, 2 July 2014
Jennifer Banda, Lusaka, 28 July 2013
Justina Banda, Lusaka, August 5, 2013
Mariana Banda, Lusaka, July 29, 2013
Martha Banda, Lusaka, 6 February 2014
Matilda Banda, Lusaka, 16 February 2014
Mayben Banda, Lusaka, 13 February 2014
Mercy Banda, Lusaka, 13 July 2013
Veronica Banda, Lusaka, 16 February 2014
Elizabeth Bwalya, Lusaka, 13 February 2014
Herbert Bwalya, Lusaka, 13 February 2014
Patricia Bwalya, Lusaka, 18 February 2014
Riberia Chambanenge, Lusaka, 16 June 2014
Bessie Chanda, Lusaka, 7 July 2014
Hope Chanda, Lusaka, 16 July 2014
Patricia Chanda, Lusaka, 1 August 2013
Rose Chanda, Lusaka, 16 June 2014
Theresa Chanda, Lusaka, 16 June 2014
Oscar Cheupe, Lusaka, 27 August 2014
Paul Chipeta, Lusaka, 17 June 2014
Mary Chirwa, Lusaka, 4 February 2014
Clarence Chiteta, Lusaka, 5 June 2014
Fisher Chowa, Lusaka, 29 August 2014
Jane Kafula, Kitwe, 10 February 2014

Bridget Kalobwe, Lusaka, 5 July 2014
Imelda Kalobwe, Lusaka, 13 February 2014
Irene Kamau, Lusaka, 16 June 2014
Queen Kangwa, Lusaka, 25 February 2014
Martha Kasaro, Lusaka, 27 August 2014
Rebecca Keyala, Lusaka, 5 July 2014
Semu Lameck, Chimusanya, 21 June 2014
Kevin Liywalii, Lusaka, 27 August 2014
Evans Lwanga, Lusaka, 12 August 2013
Evaristo Mubanga, Lusaka, 4 February 2014
Teophilous Mufonko, Lusaka, 12 August 2014
Harriet Mukololo, Lusaka, 16 June 2014
Mikala Mukongolwa, Lusaka, 2 August 2013
Augustine Mulanda, Lusaka, 12 August 2014
Agnes Mumba, Lusaka, 2 February 2014
Diana Mumba, Lusaka, 25 February 2014
Niah Mumba, Lusaka, 16 February 2014
Hon. Mr Justice Edward Luputa Musona, Lusaka, 1 September 2014
Grace Musonda, Lusaka, 13 February 2014
Grace Mwale, Lusaka, 29 May 2014
Chombe Nachula, Lusaka, 18 February 2014
Pastor Benson Nguni, Lusaka, 13 February 2014
Frida Njovu, Lusaka, 16 August 2013
Priscilla Njovu, Lusaka, 22 August 2013
Alice Phiri, Lusaka, 16 June 2014
Cecilia Phiri, Lusaka, 4 February 2014
Dorothy Phiri, Lusaka, 10 August 2013
Josephine Phiri, Chipata, 18 July 2014
Joyce Phiri, Lusaka, 11 July 2013
June Phiri, Lusaka, 9 August 2013
Howard Phiri, Lusaka, 17 June 2014
Rebecca Phiri, Lusaka, 23 February 2014
Stella Soko, Lusaka, 29 May 2014
Veronica Tembo, Lusaka, 6 August 2014
Betty Zimba, Lusaka, 18 February 2014
Monica Zimba, Lusaka, 2 February 2014

## Archive collections

Geneva, International Labour Organization Archive
London, The British Library

Lusaka, Central Statistical Office of Zambia Library
Lusaka, International Labour Organization Country Office for Zambia, Malawi, and Mozambique Library
Lusaka, National Archives of Zambia
Lusaka, United House and Domestic Workers Union of Zambia Papers
Oxford, Oxford University, Bodleian Library, Special Collections

## Periodicals

*Lusaka Times*
*The Atlantic*
*The Post* (Zambia)
*Times of Zambia*
*Zambia Daily Mail*

## Unpublished research papers

Castel-Branco, Ruth Kélia, 'Legislating Worker Justice: The Formalisation of Paid Domestic Work in Maputo, Mozambique' (MA thesis, University of KwaZulu Natal, 2012).

Evans, Alice, '"Women Can Do What Men Can Do": The Causes and Consequences of Growing Flexibility in Gender Divisions of Labour in Kitwe, Zambia' (PhD dissertation, the London School of Economics and Political Science, 2013).

Guarcello, Lorenzo, Scott Lyon, and Furio Camillo Rosati, 'Orphanhood and Child Vulnerability: Zambia', Understanding Children's Work Project Working Paper Series (Rome: University of Rome, 2004).

Matoka, Peter, 'Child Labour in Zambia: An Analysis of the Extent, Nature and Proposed Solutions to the Problem' (PhD dissertation, University of Warwick, 1994).

Oyaide, Omolara Dakore, 'Child Domestic Labour in Lusaka: A Gender Perspective' (MA dissertation, University of Zambia, 2000).

Preston-Whyte, Eleanor Mary, 'Between Two Worlds: A Study of the Working Life, Social Ties and Inter-Personal Relationships of African Women Migrants in Domestic Service in Durban', Vol. 2 (Durban: Institute for Social Research, University of Natal, 1969).

Sefalafala, Thabang, 'Precarious Work: A Case Study of Security Guards in Johannesburg' (MA dissertation, University of the Witwatersrand, 2012).

Tsoka, Maxton Grant, 'Rapid Assessment of Child Domestic Labour in Malawi. Final Report', Vol. 1: Main Report (Zomba: Centre for Social Research, University of Malawi, 2005).

## Published sources

Abrams, Lynn, *Oral History Theory* (New York, NY: Routledge, 2010).

Ahmad, Attiya, *Everyday Conversions: Islam, Domestic Work, and South Asian Migrant Women in Kuwait* (Durham, NC, Duke University Press, 2017).

Ally, Shireen, *From Servants to Workers: South African Domestic Workers and the Democratic State* (London: Cornell University Press, 2009).

Andall, Jacqueline, *Gender, Migration and Domestic Service: The Politics of Black Women in Italy* (Aldershot: Ashgate, 2000).

Anti-Slavery International, *Child Domestic Workers: A Handbook on Good Practice in Programme Interventions* (Horsham: The Printed Word, 2005).

Anti-Slavery International, *Listen to Us! Participation of Child Domestic Workers in Advocacy* (London: Anti-Slavery International, 2013).

Baker, Bruce, 'Living with Non-State Policing in South Africa: The Issues and Dilemmas', *The Journal of Modern African Studies*, 40:1 (2002), 29–53.

Barchiesi, Franco, *Precarious Liberation: Workers, the State, and Contested Social Citizenship in Postapartheid South Africa* (New York, NY: State University of New York Press, 2011).

Barchiesi, Franco, 'Precarious and Informal Labour', in Stefano Bellucci and Andreas Eckert (eds), *General Labour History of Africa: Workers, Employers and Governments, 20th–21st Centuries* (Woodbridge: James Currey, 2019), pp. 45–75.

Barnes, Teresa, *We Women Worked So Hard: Gender, Urbanization and Social Reproduction in Colonial Harare, Zimbabwe, 1930–56* (Portsmouth, NH: Heinemann, 1999).

Bates, Robert H., *Unions, Parties, and Political Development: A Study of Mineworkers in Zambia* (New Haven, CT: Yale University Press, 1971).

Bates, Robert H., and Paul Collier, 'The Politics and Economics of Policy Reform in Zambia', in Robert H. Bates and Anne O. Krueger (eds), *Political and Economic Interactions in Economic Policy Reform: Evidence from Eight Countries* (London: Blackwell, 1993), pp. 387–443.

Bayart, Jean-François, *The State in Africa: The Politics of the Belly* (London: Longman, 1993).

Becchio, Giandomenica, *A History of Feminist and Gender Economics* (Abingdon: Routledge, 2019).

Beck, Julie, 'The Concept Creep of "Emotional Labor"', *The Atlantic* (26 November 2018); available at www.theatlantic.com/family/archive/2018/11/arlie-hochschildhousework-isnt-emotional-labor/576637/ (accessed 24 June 2021).

Benería, Lourdes, 'Conceptualising the Labour Force: The Underestimation of Women's Economic Activities', *The Journal of Development Studies*, 17:3 (1981), 10–28.

Bellucci, Stefano, and Andreas Eckert, 'The "Labour Question" in Africanist Historiography', in Stefano Bellucci and Andreas Eckert (eds), *General Labour History of Africa: Workers, Employers and Governments, 20th–21st Centuries* (Woodbridge: James Currey, 2019), pp. 1–13.

Benston, Margaret, 'The Political Economy of Women's Liberation', *Monthly Review*, 21:4 (1969), 13–27.

Berger, Elena L., *Labour, Race, and Colonial Rule: The Copperbelt from 1924 to Independence* (Oxford: Clarendon Press: 1974).

Berger, Iris, 'Sources of Class Consciousness: South African Women in Recent Labor Struggles', in C. Robertson and Iris Berger (eds), *Women and Class in Africa* (New York, NY: Africana Publishing Co., 1986), pp. 216–236.

Berger Gluck, Sherna, and Daphne Patai (eds), *Women's Words: The Feminist Practice of Oral History* (New York, NY: Routledge, 1991).

Bernard, H. Russell, *Research Methods in Anthropology: Qualitative and Quantitative Approaches* (Oxford: AltaMira Press, 2006).

Black, Maggie, *Child Domestic Workers: Finding a Voice. A Handbook on Advocacy* (London: Anti-Slavery International, 2002).

Blackett, Adelle, *Making Domestic Work Visible: The Case for Specific Regulation* (Geneva: International Labour Office, 1998).

Blagbrough, Jonathan, *Child Domestic Work in Indonesia: A Preliminary Situation Analysis* (Geneva: ILO-IPEC, 1995).

Blagbrough, Jonathan, 'Worst Forms of Child Labor: Child Domestic Labor', in Hugh D. Hindman (ed.), *The World of Child Labor: An Historical and Regional Survey* (Abingdon: Routledge, 2015), pp. 86–90.

Blanchet, Thérèse, *Slavery Revisited: Adopting a Child to Secure a Servant: Palok Meye, Palok Chele* (Dhaka: Save the Children, Sweden and Denmark, 2004).

Blanchet, Thérèse, and Anisa Zalman, *Slavery Revisited: Child Domestic Servants* (Dhaka: Save the Children, Sweden and Denmark, 2004).

Blier, Suzanne Preston, 'The Path of the Leopard: Motherhood and Majesty in Early Danhomè', *Journal of African History*, 36:3 (1995), 391–417.

Bond, Virginia, Chipo Chiiya, Mutale Chonta, and Sue Clay with Jean Hunleth, Ligia Kiss, and Cathy Zimmerman, *Sweeping the Bedroom: Children in Domestic Work in Zambia* (Lusaka: UNICEF, 2011).

Boris, Eileen, and Jennifer N. Fish, 'Decent Work for Domestics: Feminist Organizing, Worker Empowerment, and the ILO', in Dirk Hoerder, Elise van Nederveen Meerkerk, and Silke Neunsinger (eds), *Towards a Global History of Domestic and Caregiving Workers* (Leiden: Brill, 2015), pp. 530–552.

Boserup, Ester, *Women's Role in Economic Development* (London: Allen & Unwin, 1970).

Bourdillon, Michael, *Child Domestic Workers in Zimbabwe* (Harare: Weaver Press, 2006).

Bourdillon, Michael, 'Children as Domestic Employees: Problems and Promises', *Journal of Children and Poverty*, 15:1 (2009), 1–18.

Bozzoli, Belinda, 'Marxism, Feminism and South African Studies', *Journal of Southern African Studies*, 9:2 (1983), 139–171.

Bozzoli, Belinda, with the assistance of Mmantho Nkotsoe, *Women of Phokeng: Consciousness, Life Strategy and Migrancy in South Africa, 1900–1983* (Woodbridge: James Currey, 1991).

Bradley, Emily G., *A Household Book for Africa* (Oxford: Oxford University Press, 1939).

Bradley, Emily G., *A Household Book for Tropical Colonies* (Oxford: Oxford University Press, 1948).

Bradley, Emily G., *Dearest Priscilla: Letters to the Wife of a Colonial Civil Servant* (London: Max Parrish, 1950).

Brown, Jill, 'Child Fostering Chains among Ovambo Families in Namibia, Southern Africa', *Journal of Southern African Studies*, 37:1 (2011), 155–176.

Bryceson, Deborah Fahy, 'Domestic Work', in S. Bellucci and A. Eckert (eds), *General Labour History of Africa: Workers, Employers and Governments, 20th–21st Centuries* (Woodbridge: James Currey, 2019), pp. 301–332.

Bryceson, Deborah Fahy (ed.), *Women Wielding the Hoe: Lessons from Rural Africa for Feminist Theory and Development Practice* (Oxford: Berg Publishers, 1995).

Brydon, Lynne, and Sylvia Chant, *Women in the Third World: Gender Issues in Rural and Urban Areas* (New Brunswick, NJ: Rutgers University Press, 1993).

Budlender, Debbie, and Dawie Bosch, *South Africa Child Domestic Workers: A National Report. Investigating the Worst Forms of Child Labour No. 39* (Geneva: ILO-IPEC, 2002).

Bujra, Janet, *Serving Class: Masculinity and the Feminization of Domestic Service in Tanzania* (Edinburgh, Edinburgh University Press, 2000).

Burawoy, Michael, *The Colour of Class on the Copper Mines: from African Advancement to Zambianisation* (Lusaka: University of Zambia, 1972).

Burton, Antoinette, *Dwelling in the Archive: Women Writing House, Home, and History in Late Colonial India* (Oxford: Oxford University Press, 2003).

Camacho, Agnes Zenaida V., 'Family, Child Labour and Migration: Child Domestic Workers in Metro Manila', *Childhood*, 6:1 (1999), 57–73.

Chakaodza, Austin M., *Structural Adjustment in Zambia and Zimbabwe: Reconstructive or Destructive?* (Harare: Third World Publishing House, 1993).

Chaney, Elsa M, and Mary Garcia Castro (eds), *Muchachas No More: Household Workers in Latin America and the Caribbean* (Philadelphia, PA: Temple University Press, 1989).

Chant, Sylvia, *Women-Headed Households: Diversity and Dynamics in the Developing World* (Basingstoke: Palgrave Macmillan, 1997).

Chauncey Jr, George, 'The Locus of Reproduction: Women's Labour in the Zambian Copperbelt, 1927–1953', *Journal of Southern African Studies*, 7:2 (1981), 135–164.

Chen, Martha, 'Recognizing Domestic Workers, Regulating Domestic Work: Conceptual, Measurement, and Regulatory Challenges', *Canadian Journal of Women and the Law*, 23:1 (2011), 167–184.

Cheria, Anita, *Liberation is Not Enough: The Kamaiya Movement in Nepal* (Kathmandu: ActionAid Nepal, 2005).

Chirwa, Wiseman Chijere, 'Child and Youth Labour on the Nyasaland Plantations, 1890–1953', *Journal of Southern African Studies*, 19:4 (1993), 662–680.

Cock, Jacklyn, *Maids and Madams: A Study in the Politics of Exploitation* (Johannesburg: Ravan Press, 1980).

Cock, Jacklyn, '"Guards and Guns": Towards Privatised Militarism in Post-Apartheid South Africa', *Journal of Southern African Studies*, 31:4 (2005), 791–803.

Cock, Jacklyn, and Erica Emdon, '"Let Me Make History Please": The Story of Johanna Masilela, Childminder', in Belinda Bozzoli (ed.), *Class, Community and Conflict: South African Perspectives* (Johannesburg: Ravan Press, 1987), pp. 457–477.

Conroy, Amy A., 'Gender, Power, and Intimate Partner Violence: A Study on Couples from Rural Malawi', *Journal of Interpersonal Violence*, 29:5 (2014), 866–888.

Coquery-Vidrovitch, Catherine, *African Women: A Modern History* (Boulder, CO: Westview Press, 1997).

Cox, Rosie, *The Servant Problem: Domestic Employment in a Global Economy* (London: I. B. Tauris, 2006).

D'Souza, Asha, *Moving Towards Decent Work for Domestic Workers: An Overview of the ILO's Work* (Geneva: International Labour Office, 2010).

Dalla Costa, Mariarosa, and Selma James, *The Power of Women and the Subversion of the Community* (Bristol: Falling Wall, 1972).

Davidoff, Leonora, and Catherine Hall, *Family Fortunes: Men and Women of the English Middle Class, 1780–1850* (Chicago, IL: University of Chicago Press, 1987).

Davies, Natalie Zemon, *Women on the Margins: Three Seventeenth Century Lives* (Cambridge, MA: Harvard University Press, 1997).

De Souza, Juliet Filet-Abreu, 'Paid Domestic Service in Brazil', *Latin American Perspectives*, 7:1 (1980), 35–63.

Delius, Peter, 'Sebatakgomo; Migrant Organisation, the ANC and the Sekhukhuneland Revolt', *Journal of Southern African Studies*, 15:4 (1989), 588–599.

Dimova, Margarita, Carrie Hough, Kerry Kyaa, and Ambreena Manji, 'Intimacy and Inequality: Local Care Chains and Paid Childcare in Kenya', *Feminist Legal Studies*, 23:2 (2015), 168–179.

Ehrenriech, Barbara, 'Maid to Order', in Barbara Ehrenreich and Arlie Russell Hochschild (eds), *Global Woman: Nannies, Maids and Sex Workers in the New Economy* (New York, NY: Henry Holt, 2002), pp. 85–103.

Ellis, Stephen, *External Mission: The ANC in Exile, 1960–1990* (London: Hurst, 2012).

Evans, Alice, 'History Lessons for Gender Equality from the Zambian Copperbelt, 1900–1990', *Gender, Place & Culture: A Journal of Feminist Geography*, 22:3 (2015), 344–362.

Ferber, Marianne A., and Julie A. Nelson (eds), *Feminist Economics Today: Beyond Economic Man* (Chicago, IL: University of Chicago Press, 2020).

Ferguson, James, *Expectations of Modernity: Myths and Meanings of Urban Life on the Zambian Copperbelt* (London and Berkeley, CA: University of California Press, 1999).

Fish, Jennifer N., 'Engendering Democracy: Domestic Labor and Coalition Building in South Africa', *Journal of Southern African Studies*, 32:1 (2006), 107–127.

Fish, Jennifer N., *Domestic Workers of the World Unite!: A Global Movement for Dignity and Human Rights* (New York, NY: New York University Press, 2017).

Fuentes, Marisa J., *Dispossessed Lives: Enslaved Women, Violence and the Archive* (Philadelphia, PA: University of Pennsylvania Press, 2016).

Gaitskell, Deborah, '"Upward All and Play the Game": The Girl Wayfarers' Association in the Transvaal 1925–1975', in Peter Kallaway (ed.), *Apartheid and Education: The Education of Black South Africans* (Johannesburg: Ravan, 1984), pp. 222–264.

Gaitskell, Deborah, Judy Kimble, Moira Maconachie, and Elaine Unterhalter, 'Class, Race and Gender: Domestic Workers in South Africa', *Review of African Political Economy*, 27/28 (1983), 86–108.

Geiger, Susan, *Tanu Women: Gender and Culture in the Making of Tanganyikan Nationalism, 1955–1965* (Portsmouth, NH: Heinemann, 1997).

George, Abosede, *Making Modern Girls: A History of Girlhood, Labour, and Social Development in Colonial Lagos* (Athens, OH: Ohio University Press, 2014).

Gertzel, Cherry, Carolyn Baylies, and Morris Szeftel (eds), *The Dynamics of the One-Party State in Zambia* (Manchester: Manchester University Press, 1984).

Gill, Lesley, *Precarious Dependencies: Gender, Class, and Domestic Service in Bolivia* (New York, NY: Columbia University Press, 1994).

Ginsburg, Rebecca, *At Home with Apartheid: The Hidden Landscapes of Domestic Service in Johannesburg* (Charlottesville, VA: University of Virginia Press, 2011).

Giri, B. R., 'The Bonded Labour Practice in Nepal: "The Promise of Education" as a Magnet of Child Bondedness?', *South Asia Research*, 30:2 (2010), 145–164.

Glenn, Evelyn Nakano, *Issei, Nisei, War Bride: Three Generations of Japanese American Women in Domestic Service* (Philadelphia, PA: Temple University Press, 1986).

Gordon, Suzanne, *A Talent for Tomorrow: Life Stories of South African Servants* (Johannesburg: Ravan Press, 1985).

Gough, Katherine V., '"Moving Around": The Social and Spatial Mobility of Youth in Lusaka', *Geografiska Annaler: Series B, Human Geography*, 90:3 (2008), 243–255.

Gould, Jeremy, *Left Behind: Rural Zambia in the Third Republic* (Lusaka: Lembani Trust, 2010).

Gould, Jeremy, *Postcolonial Legality: Law, Politics, and State Formation in Africa Since the End of the Cold War* (London: Taylor & Francis, 2021).

Grier, Beverly C., 'Child Labour and Africanist Scholarship: A Critical Overview', *African Studies Review*, 47:2 (2004), 1–25.

Grier, Beverly C., *Invisible Hands: Child Labour and the State in Colonial Zimbabwe* (Portsmouth, NH: Heinemann, 2006).

Griffin, Laura, 'When Borders Fail: "Illegal", Invisible Labour Migration and Basotho Domestic Workers in South Africa', in Elspeth Guild and Sandra Mantu (eds), *Constructing and Imagining Labour Migration: Perspectives of Control from Five Continents* (Farnham: Ashgate, 2011), pp. 15–38.

Groves, Leslie, *Good Practice in Working Children's Participation: A Case Study from Brazil* (London: International Save the Children Alliance, 2003).

Guest, Emma, *Children of AIDS: Africa's Orphan Crisis* (London: Pluto, 2003).

Haimbe, Mbozi, 'Madam's Sister', *Granta*, 4 June 2019; available at https://granta.com/madams-sister/ (accessed 10 June 2021).

Hansen, Karen Tranberg, 'Negotiating Sex and Gender in Urban Zambia', *Journal of Southern African Studies*, 10:2 (1984), 219–238.

Hansen, Karen Tranberg, *Distant Companions: Servants and Employers in Zambia, 1900–1989* (Ithaca, NY: Cornell University Press, 1989).

Hansen, Karen Tranberg, 'Body Politics: Sexuality, Gender and Domestic Service in Zambia', *Journal of Women's History*, 2, 1 (1990), 131–135.

Hansen, Karen Tranberg, 'Labor Migration and Urban Child Labor during the Colonial Period in Zambia', in Bruce Fetter (ed.), *Demography from Scanty Evidence: Central Africa in the Colonial Era* (Boulder, CO: Lynne Rienner, 1990), pp. 219–234.

Hansen, Karen Tranberg, 'Introduction: Domesticity in Africa', in K. Tranberg Hansen (ed.), *African Encounters with Domesticity* (New Brunswick, NJ: Rutgers University Press, 1992), pp. 1–33.

Hansen, Karen Tranberg, *Keeping House in Lusaka* (New York NY: Columbia University Press, 1997).

Hansen, Karen Tranberg, *Salaula: the World of Secondhand Clothing and Zambia* (Chicago, IL: University of Chicago Press, 2000).

Hansen, Karen Tranberg, 'Stuck in the Compound: Some Odds Against Social Adulthood in Lusaka, Zambia', *Africa Today*, 51 (2005), 3–16.

Hansen, Karen Tranberg, and Mariken Vaa (eds), *Reconsidering Informality: Perspectives from Urban Africa* (Uppsala: Nordiksa Afrikainstitutet, 2004).

Hartmann, Heidi, 'Capitalism, Patriarchy, and Job Segregation by Sex', *Signs*, 1:3 (1976), 137–169.

Hay, Douglas, and Paul Craven (eds), *Masters, Servants, and Magistrates in Britain and the Empire, 1562–1955* (Chapel Hill, NC: University of North Carolina Press, 2004).

Hepburn, Sacha, '"Bringing a Girl from the Village": Gender, Child Migration and Domestic Service in Post-Colonial Zambia', in Elodie Razy and Marie Rodet (eds), *Children on the Move in Africa: Past and Present Experiences of Migration* (Woodbridge: James Currey, 2016), pp. 69–84.

Hepburn, Sacha, and April Jackson, 'Colonial Exceptions: The International Labour Organization and Child Labour in British Africa, c. 1919–1940', *Journal of Contemporary History* (2021). Online first.

Hertz, Tom, 'The Effect of Minimum Wages on the Employment and Earnings of South Africa's Domestic Service Workers', Working Paper 05/99, University of Cape Town Development Policy Research Unit (2005).

Hirson, Baruch, *Yours for the Union: Class and Community Struggles in South Africa, 1930–1947* (London: Zed Books, 1990).

Hochschild, Arlie Russell, *The Managed Heart: Commercialization of Human Feeling* (Berkeley CA: University of California Press, 1983).

Hochschild, Arlie Russell, 'Global Care Chains and Emotional Surplus Value', in Anthony Giddens and Will Hutton (eds), *On the Edge: Living With Global Capitalism* (London: Jonathan Cape, 2000), pp. 130–146.

Human Rights Watch, *Bottom of the Ladder: Exploitation and Abuse of Girl Domestic Workers in Guinea*, 19:8(A), June 2007; available at www.hrw.org/report/2007/06/15/bottom-ladder/exploitation-and-abuse-girl-domestic-workers-guinea# (accessed 14 August 2020).

Hynd, Stacey, '"Uncircumcised Boys" and "Girl Spartans": Youth, Gender and Generation in Colonial Insurgencies and Counterinsurgency, c. 1954–59', *Gender and History*, 33:2 (2021), 536–556.

Iliffe, John, *The African AIDS Epidemic: A History* (Oxford: James Currey, 2006).

International Labour Organization, *Emerging Good Practices on Action to Combat Child Domestic Labour in Kenya, Tanzania, Uganda and Zambia* (Geneva: International Labour Office, 2006).

International Labour Organization, C189 – Domestic Workers Convention, 2011 (No. 189); available at www.ilo.org/dyn/normlex/en/f?p=NORMLEXPUB:12100:0::NO::P12100_ILO_CODE:C189 (accessed 9 July 2020).

International Labour Organization, R201 – Domestic Workers Recommendation, 2011 (No. 201); available at www.ilo.org/dyn/normlex/en/f?p=1000:12100:::NO:12100:P12100_INSTRUMENT_ID:2551502 (accessed 12 November 2021).

International Labour Organization, 'Decent Work for Domestic Workers', International Labour Conference, 100th Session (Geneva: ILO, 2011).

International Labour Organization, *Guide to Design a Law for Domestic Workers* (Geneva: International Labour Organization, 2012).

International Labour Organization, *Domestic Workers Across the World: Global and Regional Statistics and the Extent of Legal Protection* (Geneva: International Labour Office, 2013).

International Labour Organization, *Ending Child Labour in Domestic Work and Protecting Young Workers from Abusive Working Conditions* (Geneva: International Labour Office, 2013).

International Labour Organization, *Magnitude of Domestic Workers in Zambia: Highlights of Domestic Worker Survey* (Lusaka: International Labour Organization, 2014).

International Labour Organization, *Promoting Decent Work for Domestic Workers: ILO in Action* (Geneva: International Labour Office, 2014).

Jacquemin, Mélanie, 'Children's Domestic Work in Abidjan, Côte d'Ivoire: The Petites Bonnes Have the Floor', *Childhood*, 11:3 (2004), 383–397.

Jacquemin, Mélanie, 'Can the Language of Rights Get Hold of the Complex Realities of Child Domestic Work? The Case of Young Domestic Workers in Abidjan, Ivory Coast', *Childhood*, 13 (2006), 389–406.

Jacquemin, Mélanie, 'Petites Nièces et Petites Bonnes à Abidjan. Les Mutations de la Domesticité Juvénile', *Travail, Genre et Sociétés*, 22:2 (2009), 53–74.

James, Deborah, *Songs of the Women Migrants: Performance and Identity in South Africa* (Edinburgh: Edinburgh University Press, 1999).

Jansen, Ena, *Like Family: Domestic Workers in South African History and Literature* (Johannesburg: Wits University Press, 2019).

Johnson, Chris, *Women on the Frontline: Voices from Southern Africa* (London: Macmillan, 1992).

Johnson-Hanks, Jennifer, *Uncertain Honor: Modern Motherhood in an African Crisis* (Chicago, IL: University of Chicago Press, 2006).

Kaler, Amy, 'Visions of Domesticity in the African Women's Homecraft Movement in Rhodesia', *Social Science History*, 23:3 (1999), 269–309.

Kalula, Evance, 'The Influence of International Labour Standards on Zambian Legislation', *International Labour Review*, 124:5 (1985), 593–609.

Katzman, David M., *Seven Days a Week: Women and Domestic Service in Industrializing America* (New York, NY: Oxford University Press, 1978).

Kilkey, Majella, 'Men and Domestic Labor: A Missing Link in the Global Care Chain', *Men and Masculinities*, 13:1 (2010), 126–149.

King, Alison J., *Domestic Service in Post-Apartheid South Africa: Deference and Disdain* (Aldershot: Ashgate, 2007).

Klomegah, Roger Y., 'Intimate Partner Violence (IPV) in Zambia: An Examination of Risk Factors and Gender Perceptions', *Journal of Comparative Family Studies*, 39:4 (2008), 557–569.

Kongar, Ebru, and Günseli Berik (eds), *The Routledge Handbook of Feminist Economics* (Abingdon: Routledge, 2021).

Larmer, Miles, 'Reaction and Resistance to Neoliberalism in Zambia', *Review of African Political Economy*, 32:103 (2005), 29–45.

Larmer, Miles, *Mineworkers in Zambia: Labour and Political Change in Post-Colonial Africa, 1964–1991* (London: I. B. Tauris, 2007).

Larmer, Miles, *Rethinking African Politics: A History of Opposition in Zambia* (Farnham: Ashgate, 2011).

Larmer, Miles, *Living for the City: Social Change and Knowledge Production in the Central African Copperbelt* (Cambridge: Cambridge University Press, 2021).

Lee, Rebekah, *African Women and Apartheid: Migration and Settlement in Urban South Africa* (London: I. B. Tauris, 2009).

Leow, Rachel, 'Age as a Category of Gender Analysis: Servant Girls, Modern Girls, and Gender in Southeast Asia', *The Journal of Asian Studies*, 71:4 (2012), 976–977.

Lichtenstein, Alex, 'Challenging "Umthetho we Femu" (the Law of the Firm): Gender Relations and Shop-Floor Battles for Union Recognition in Natal's Textile Industry, 1973–85', *Africa*, 8:1 (2017), 100–119.

Lindell, Ilda (ed.), *Africa's Informal Workers: Collective Agency, Alliances and Transnational Organizing in Urban Africa* (London: Zed Books, 2010).

Lord, Jack, 'Child Labour in the Gold Coast: The Economics of Work, Education and the Family in Late-Colonial Africa, c. 1940–57', *Journal of the History of Childhood and Youth*, 4:1 (2011), 88–115.

MacMillan, Hugh, *The Lusaka Years: The ANC in Exile in Zambia, 1963 to 1994* (Auckland Park: Jacana Media, 2013).

Meagher, Gabrielle, 'Is It Wrong to Pay for Housework?', *Hypatia*, 17 (2002), 52–66.

Meebelo, Henry S., *African Proletarians and Colonial Capitalism: The Origins, Growth, and Struggles of the Zambian Labour Movement to 1964* (Lusaka: Kenneth Kaunda Foundation, 1986).

Miles, Miranda, 'Working in the City: The Case of Migrant Women in Swaziland's Domestic Service Sector', in Janet Henshall Momsen (ed.), *Gender, Migration and Domestic Service* (London: Routledge, 1999), pp. 190–212.

Moffett, Helen, '"These Women, They Force Us to Rape Them": Rape as Narrative of Social Control in Post-Apartheid South Africa', *Journal of Southern African Studies*, 32:1 (2006), 129–144.

Morgan, Jennifer, *Laboring Women: Gender and Reproduction in New World Slavery* (Philadelphia, PA: University of Pennsylvania Press, 2004).

Momsen, Janet Henshall (ed.), *Gender, Migration and Domestic Service* (London: Routledge, 1999).

Moore, Henrietta, and Megan Vaughan, *Cutting Down Trees: Gender, Nutrition and Agricultural Change in Zambia* (Portsmouth, NH: Heinemann, 1994).

Muasya, Gladys, 'The Role of House Helps in Work–Family Balance of Women Employed in the Formal Sector in Kenya', in Zitha Mokomane (ed.), *Work–Family Interface in Sub-Saharan Africa* (London: Springer International Publishing, 2014), pp. 149–159.

Mulenga, Friday E., 'Fighting for Democracy of the Pocket: The Labour Movement in the Third Republic', in Jan-Bart Gewald, Marja Hinfelaar, and Giacomo Macola (eds), *One Zambia, Many Histories: Towards a History of Post-Colonial Zambia* (Leiden: Brill, 2008), pp. 243–258.

Murray, Martin J., *Panic City: Crime and the Fear Industries in Johannesburg* (Stanford, CA: Stanford University Press, 2020).

Mususa, Patience, '"Getting By": Life on the Copperbelt after the Privatisation of the Zambia Consolidated Copper Mines', *Social Dynamics: A Journal of African Studies*, 36:2 (2010), 380–394.

Mususa, Patience, 'Topping Up: Life Amidst Hardship and Death on the Copperbelt', *African Studies*, 71:2 (2012), 304–322.

Mutongi, Kenda, *Worries of the Heart: Widows, Family, and Community in Kenya* (Chicago, IL: Chicago University Press, 2007).

Mweemba, Oliver, and Gillian Mann, 'Young Marriage, Parenthood and Divorce in Zambia', Young Lives Research Report (Oxford: Young Lives, 2020).

Myers, Garth Andrew, *Verandahs of Power: Colonialism and Space in Urban Africa* (Syracuse, NY: Syracuse University Press, 2003).

Myers, Garth Andrew, *African Cities: Alternative Visions of Urban Theory and Practice* (London: Zed Books, 2011).

Nadasen, Premilla, 'Citizenship Rights, Domestic Work, and the Fair Labor Standards Act', *The Journal of Policy History*, 24:1 (2012), 74–94.

Nagombe, Magano, 'The Namibia Domestic and Allied Workers Union', in Margaret Hosmer Martens and Swasti Mitter (eds), *Women in Trade Unions: Organizing the Unorganized* (Geneva: International Labour Office, 1994), pp. 45–47.

Namuggala, Victoria Flavia, 'Exploitation or Empowerment? Adolescent Female Domestic Workers in Uganda', *International Journal of Child, Youth and Family Studies*, 6:4 (2015), 561–580.

Njovana, Eunice, and Charlotte Watts, 'Gender Violence in Zimbabwe: A Need for Collaborative Action', *Reproductive Health Matters*, 4:7 (1996), 46–55.

O'Laughlin, Bridget, 'Class and the Customary: The Ambiguous Legacy of the Indigenato in Mozambique', *African Affairs*, 99 (2000), 5–42.

Østreng, Dorte, *Domestic Workers' Daily Lives in Post-Apartheid Namibia*, NEPRU Occasional Paper No.11 (Windhoek: The Namibian Economic Policy Research Unit, 1997).

Pape, John, 'Still Serving the Tea: Domestic Workers in Zimbabwe 1980–90', *Journal of Southern African Studies*, 19:3 (1993), 387–404.

Pariser, Robyn, 'Masculinity and Organized Resistance in Domestic Service in Colonial Dar es Salaam, 1919–1961', *International Labor and Working-Class History*, 88 (2015), 109–129.

Parpart, Jane L., *Labor and Capital on the African Copperbelt* (Philadelphia, PA: Temple University Press, 1983).

Parpart, Jane L., 'Class and Gender on the Copperbelt: Women in Northern Rhodesian Copper Mining Communities, 1926–1964', in Claire C.

Robertson and Iris Berger (eds), *Women and Class in Africa* (New York, NY: Africana Publishing Co., 1986), pp. 141–160.

Parpart, Jane L., 'Sexuality and Power on the Zambian Copperbelt: 1926–1964', in Sharon B. Stichter and Jane L. Parpart (eds), *Patriarchy and Class: African Women in the Home and the Workforce* (Boulder, CO: Westview Press, 1988), pp. 141–160.

Parpart, Jane L., '"Where Is Your Mother?": Gender, Urban Marriage, and Colonial Discourse on the Zambian Copperbelt, 1924–1945', *The International Journal of African Historical Studies*, 27:2 (1994), 241–271.

Parreñas, Rhacel, *Servants of Globalization: Women, Migration and Domestic Work* (Stanford, CA: Stanford University Press, 2001).

Passerini, Luisa, *Fascism in Popular Memory: The Cultural Experience of the Turin Working Class* (Cambridge: Cambridge University Press, 1987).

Penvenne, Jeanne Marie, *African Workers and Colonial Racism: Mozambican Strategies and Struggles in Lourenço Marques, 1877–1962* (Johannesburg: Witwatersrand University Press, 1994).

Penvenne, Jeanne Marie, *Women, Migration and the Cashew Economy in Southern Mozambique: 1945–1975* (Woodbridge: James Currey, 2015).

Phillips, Danielle Taylor, 'Moving with the Women: Tracing Racialization, Migration, and Domestic Workers in the Archive', *Signs*, 38:2 (2013), 379–404.

Phillips, Laura, and Deborah James, 'Labour, Lodging and Linkages: Migrant Women's Experience in South Africa', *African Studies*, 73:3 (2014), 420–424.

Phimister, Ian, 'Workers in Wonderland? White Miners and the Northern Rhodesian Copperbelt, 1946–1962', *South African Historical Journal*, 63:2 (2011), 183–233.

Portelli, Alessandro, *The Death of Luigi Trastulli and Other Stories: Form and Meaning in Oral History* (New York, NY: State University of New York Press, 1991).

Pottier, Johan, *Migrants No More: Settlement and Survival in Mambwe Villages, Zambia* (Manchester: Manchester University Press, 1988).

Potts, Deborah, 'Counter-Urbanisation on the Zambian Copperbelt: Interpretations and Implications', *Urban Studies*, 42:4 (2005), 583–609.

Potts, Deborah, '"All My Hopes and Dreams are Shattered": Urbanisation and Migrancy in an Imploding African Economy – the Case of Zimbabwe', *Geoforum*, 37 (2006), 536–551.

Rakner, Lise, *Political and Economic Liberalisation in Zambia 1991–2001* (Stockholm: Nordic Africa Institute, 2003).

Rakodi, Carole, 'Urban Agriculture: Research Questions and Zambian Evidence', *The Journal of Modern African Studies*, 26:3 (1988), 495–515.

Ray, Manabendranath, and Asha N. Iyer, *Abuse Among Child Domestic Workers: A Research Study in West Bengal* (Kolkata: Save the Children, UK, 2006).

Republic of Botswana, Employment Act 1982 (Cap 47:01) (Act 29, 1982) (Gaborone: Government Printer, 1982); available at www.ilo.org/dyn/natlex/natlex4.detail?p_lang=en&p_isn=842 (accessed 31 July 2021).

Republic of Botswana, Employment (Domestic Employees) Regulations 1984. No. 156 (Gaborone: Government Printer, 1985); available at www.ilo.org/dyn/natlex/natlex4.detail?p_lang=en&p_isn=1249 (accessed 31 July 2021).

Republic of Zambia, *1969 Census of Population and Housing. Final Report Volume 1. Total Zambia* (Lusaka: Central Statistical Office, 1970).

Republic of Zambia, *1980 Census of Population and Housing. Analytical Report Volume 3. Major Findings and Conclusions and Policy Implications* (Lusaka: Central Statistical Office, 1985).

Republic of Zambia, *Monthly Digest of Statistics. January–June 1989* (Lusaka: Central Statistical Office, 1989).

Republic of Zambia, *Monthly Digest of Statistics. July–October 1991* (Lusaka: Central Statistical Office, 1991).

Republic of Zambia, *1990 Census of Population, Housing and Agriculture. Volume 10: Zambia Analytical Report* (Lusaka: Central Statistical Office, 1994).

Republic of Zambia, *National Gender Policy* (Lusaka: Gender in Development Division, 2000).

Republic of Zambia, *2000 Census of Population and Housing. Analytical Report Final* (Lusaka: Central Statistical Office, 2003).

Republic of Zambia, *2000 Census of Population and Housing. Lusaka Province Analytical Report. Volume Five* (Lusaka: Central Statistical Office, 2004).

Republic of Zambia, Statutory Instrument No. 57 of 2006. The Minimum Wages and Conditions of Employment Act (Laws, Vol. 15, Cap. 276). The Minimum Wages and Conditions of Employment (General) Order, 2006 (Lusaka: Government Printer, 2006); available at www.ilo.org/dyn/natlex/natlex4.detail?p_lang=en&p_isn=96082&p_classification=12.02 (accessed 2 March 2022).

Republic of Zambia, Statutory Instrument No. 3 of 2011. The Minimum Wages and Conditions of Employment Act (Laws, Vol. 15, Cap. 276). The Minimum Wages and Conditions of Employment (Domestic Workers) Order, 2011 (Lusaka: Government Printer, 2010); available at www.mlss.gov.zm/?wpfb_dl=38 (accessed 31 July 2021).

Republic of Zambia, *2010 Census of Population and Housing. National Analytical Report* (Lusaka: Central Statistical Office, 2012).

Republic of Zambia, Statutory Instrument No. 45 of 2012. The Minimum Wages and Conditions of Employment Act (Laws, Vol. 15, Cap. 276). The Minimum Wages and Conditions of Employment (Domestic Workers) (Amendment) Order, 2012 (Lusaka: Government Printer, 2012); available at www.mlss.gov.zm/?wpfb_dl=41 (accessed 31 July 2021).

Republic of Zambia, Constitution of Zambia (Amendment). Act No. 2 of 2016 (Lusaka: Government Printer, 2016); available at www.parliament.gov.zm/sites/default/files/documents/amendment_act/Constitution%20of%20Zambia%20%20(Amendment),%202016-Act%20No.%202_0.pdf (accessed 31 July 2021).

Republic of Zambia, Statutory Instrument No. 69 of 2018. The Minimum Wages and Conditions of Employment Act (Laws, Vol. 15, Cap. 276). The Minimum Wages and Conditions of Employment (Domestic Workers) (Amendment) Order, 2018 (Lusaka: Government Printer, 2018); available at www.ilo.org/dyn/natlex/docs/MONOGRAPH/108957/134958/F-1679354362/ZMB108957.pdf (accessed 2 March 2022).

Richards, Audrey, *Chisungu: A Girl's Initiation Ceremony Among the Bemba of Zambia* (London: Routledge, 1956).

Rogers, Barbara, *The Domestication of Women: Discrimination in Developing Societies* (London: Kogan Page, 1980).

Rollins, Judith, *Between Women: Domestics and Their Employers* (Philadelphia, PA: Temple University Press, 1985).

Rude, Darlene, 'Reasonable Men and Provocative Women: An Analysis of Gendered Domestic Homicide in Zambia', *Journal of Southern African Studies*, 25:1 (1999), 7–27.

Rutherford, Blair, *Farm Labor Struggles in Zimbabwe: The Ground of Politics* (Bloomington, IN: Indiana University Press, 2016).

Sangster, Joan, 'Telling Our Stories: Feminist Debates and the Use of Oral History', *Women's History Review*, 3:1 (1994), 5–28.

Schmidt, Elizabeth, *Peasants, Traders, and Wives: Shona Women in the History of Zimbabwe, 1870–1939* (Portsmouth, NH: Heinemann, 1992).

Schmidt, Elizabeth, 'Race, Sex and Domestic Labour: The Question of African Female Servants in Southern Rhodesia, 1900–1939', in K. Tranberg Hansen (ed.), *African Encounters with Domesticity* (New Brunswick, NJ: Rutgers University Press, 1992), pp. 221–241.

Schuster, Ilsa M. Glazer, *New Women of Lusaka* (Palo Alto, CA: Mayfield, 1979).

Schwartz, Laura, *Feminism and the Servant Problem: Class and Domestic Labour in the Women's Suffrage Movement* (Cambridge: Cambridge University Press, 2019).

Seccombe, Wally, 'The Housewife and Her Labour under Capitalism', *New Left Review*, 83 (1974), 3–24.

Sejoe, Mmaskepe, and Linda Magula, *Domestic Workers in Botswana: An Action Research Report* (Gaborone: Ditshwanelo, 1996).

Sheldon, Kathleen, 'Creches, Titias, and Mothers: Working Women and Childcare in Mozambique', in Karen Tranberg Hansen (ed.), *African Encounters with Domesticity* (New Brunswick, NJ: Rutgers University Press, 1992), pp. 290–309.

Sheldon, Kathleen, '"Rats Fell from the Ceiling and Pestered Me": Phrase Books as Sources for Colonial Mozambican History', *History in Africa*, 25 (1998), pp. 341–360.

Sheldon, Kathleen E., *Pounders of Grain: A History of Women, Work and Politics in Mozambique* (Portsmouth, NH: Heinemann, 2002).

Sheldon, Kathleen, 'Markets and Gardens: Placing Women in the History of Urban Mozambique', *Canadian Journal of African Studies/Revue Canadienne des Études Africaines*, 37:2/3 (2003), 358–395.

Shutt, Alison K., *Manners Make a Nation: Racial Etiquette in Southern Rhodesia, 1910–1963* (Rochester NY: University of Rochester Press, 2015).

Simpson, Anthony, and Virginia Bond, 'Narratives of Nationhood and HIV/AIDS: Reflections on Multidisciplinary Research on the HIV/AIDS Epidemic in Zambia Over the Last 30 Years', *Journal of Southern African Studies*, 40:5 (2014), 1065–1089.

Simutanyi, Neo, 'The Politics of Structural Adjustment in Zambia', *Third World Quarterly*, 17:4 (1996), 825–839.

Sommerfelt, Tone, 'Petites Bonnes and Their Parents: Experiences and Motivational Factors', in Tone Sommerfelt (ed.), *Domestic Child Labour in Morocco: An Analysis of the Parties Involved in Relationships to 'Petites Bonnes'* (Oslo: Fafo Institute for Applied Social Science, 2003), pp. 21–69.

Stephens, Rhiannon, *A History of African Motherhood: The Case of Uganda, 700–1900* (Cambridge: Cambridge University Press, 2013).

Stichter, Sharon B., 'Trade Unionism in Kenya, 1947–52: The Militant Phase', in Peter Gutkind, Robin Cohen, and Jean Copans (eds), *African Labour History* (London: Sage, 1975), pp. 155–174.

Stoler, Ann Laura, *Carnal Knowledge and Imperial Power: Race and the Intimate in Colonial Rule* (Berkeley, CA: University of California Press, 2002).

Summerfield, Penny, *Histories of the Self: Personal Narratives and Historical Practice* (Abingdon: Routledge, 2019).

Thompson, Paul, *The Voice of the Past: Oral History* (Oxford: Oxford University Press, 1978).

Thomson, Alistair, *Anzac Memories: Living with the Legend* (Clayton: Monash University Press, 1994).

Thorsen, Dorte, *Child Domestic Workers: Evidence from West and Central Africa* (Dakar: UNICEF, 2012); available at http://sro.sussex.ac.uk/id/eprint/43303/1/Briefing_paper_No_1_-_child_domestic_workers.pdf (accessed 14 August 2020).

Todd, Selina, 'Domestic Service and Class Relations in Britain 1900–1950', *Past and Present*, 203:1 (2009), 181–204.

Tomei, Manuela, 'Decent Work for Domestic Workers: Reflections on Recent Approaches to Tackle Informality', *Canadian Journal of Women and the Law*, 23:1 (2011), 185–211.

Tordoff, William (ed.), *Politics in Zambia* (Manchester: Manchester University Press, 1974).

Tordoff, William (ed.), *Administration in Zambia* (Manchester: Manchester University Press, 1980).

Tostensen, Arne, Inge Tvedten, and Mariken Vaa (eds), *Associational Life in African Cities: Popular Responses to the Urban Crisis* (Uppsala: Nordic Africa Institute, 2001).

Townsend, Camilla, *Malintzin's Choices: An Indian Woman in the Conquest of Mexico* (Albuquerque, NM: University of New Mexico Press, 2006).

Tripp, Aili Mari, 'Deindustrialisation and the Growth of Women's Economic Associations and Networks in Urban Tanzania', in Sheila Rowbotham and Swasti Mitter (eds), *Dignity and Daily Bread* (London: Routledge, 1994), pp. 139–157.

Tripp, Aili Mari, *Changing the Rules: The Politics of Liberalization and the Urban Informal Economy in Tanzania* (London: University of California Press, 1997).

Tripp, Aili Mari, 'Non-Formal Institutions, Informal Economies, and the Politics of Inclusion', Discussion Paper no. 2001/108, UNU/WIDER (2001).

Tronto, Joan C., 'The "Nanny Question" in Feminism', *Hypatia*, 17:2 (2002), 34–51.

UNICEF, *Innocenti Digest. No. 5: Child Domestic Work* (Florence: UN, UNICEF, 1999).

United Nations Development Programme, *Income Inequality Trends in Sub-Saharan Africa. Divergence, Determinants and Consequences: Overview* (New York, NY: United Nations Development Programme, 2017).

United Nations Economic Commission for Africa and United Nations Development Programme, *Economic Growth, Inequality and Poverty in Southern Africa: Issues and Policy Options* (Addis Ababa: Economic Commission for Africa, 2017).

Uzar, Esther, 'Contested Labour and Political Leadership: Three Mineworkers' Unions after the Opposition Victory in Zambia', *Review of African Political Economy*, 44:152 (2017), 292–311.

Van Nederveen Meerkerk, Elise, Silke Neunsinger, and Dirk Hoerder, 'Domestic Workers of the World: Histories of Domestic Work as Global Labour History', in Dirk Hoerder, Elise van Nederveen Meerkerk, and Silke Neunsinger (eds), *Towards a Global History of Domestic and Caregiving Workers* (Leiden: Brill, 2015), pp. 1–24.

Van Onselen, Charles, *Chibaro: African Mine Labour in Colonial Zimbabwe, 1900–1933* (London: Pluto Press, 1976).

Van Onselen, Charles, *Studies in the Social and Economic History of the Witwatersrand, 1886–1914*, Vol. 2 (Johannesburg: Ravan Press, 1982).

Van Walsum, Sarah, 'Regulating Migrant Domestic Work in the Netherlands: Opportunities and Pitfalls', *Canadian Journal of Women and the Law*, 23:1 (2011), 141–165.

Varia, Nisha, '"Sweeping Changes?" A Review of Recent Reforms on Protections for Migrant Domestic Workers in Asia and the Middle East', *Canadian Journal of Women and the Law*, 23:1 (2011), 265–287.

Vogel, Lise, *Marxism and the Oppression of Women: Toward a Unitary Theory* (New Brunswick, NJ: Rutgers University Press, 1983).

Walters, Sarah, '"Child! Now You Are": Identity Registration, Labour, and the Definition of Childhood in Colonial Tanganyika, 1910–1950', *Journal of the History of Childhood and Youth*, 9:1 (2016), 66–86.

White, Fiona, 'Deepening Democracy: A Farm Workers' Movement in the Western Cape', *Journal of Southern African Studies*, 36:3 (2010), 673–691.

White, Luise, *The Comforts of Home: Prostitution in Colonial Nairobi* (Chicago, IL: University of Chicago Press, 1990).

Wilson, Godfrey, *An Essay on the Economics of Detribalization in Northern Rhodesia, Volume 2* (Livingstone: Rhodes-Livingstone Institute, 1941).

Wrigley, Julia, 'Feminists and Domestic Workers', *Feminist Studies*, 17:2 (1991), 317–329.

Yamba, C. Bawa, 'Loveness and Her Brothers: Trajectories of Life for Children Orphaned by HIV/AIDS in Zambia', *African Journal of AIDS Research*, 4:3 (2005), 205–210.

Yow, Valerie, 'Ethics and Interpersonal Relationships in Oral History Research', *Oral History Review*, 22:1 (1995), 51–66.

# Index

EU authorised representative for GPSR:
Easy Access System Europe, Mustamäe tee 50,
10621 Tallinn, Estonia
gpsr.requests@easproject.com

www.ingramcontent.com/pod-product-compliance
Ingram Content Group UK Ltd.
Pitfield, Milton Keynes, MK11 3LW, UK
UKHW021833100926
8556IPUK00004B/326
*9781526162021*